PSYCHOLOGY OF CUSTOMER

ARVIND UPADHYAY

Contents

Preface

Th is book contains a unique collection of chapters written by the world's leading researchers in the dynamic field of Consumer Psychology. Although these researchers are housed in diff erent academic departments (i.e., marketing, psychology, advertising, communications), all have the common goal of attaining a better scientifi c understanding of cognitive, aff ective, and behavioral responses to products and services, the marketing of these products and services, and societal and ethical concerns associated with marketing processes. Consumer Psychology is a discipline at the interface of Marketing, Advertising, and Psychology. Work in Consumer Psychology integrates theories and methods from many diff erent areas and many diff erent approaches to research and practice. Consumer Psychology research focuses on fundamental psychological processes as well as on issues associated with the use of theoretical principles in applied contexts.

Th e chapters present theoretical frameworks that address a broad range of important well-established phenomena in addition to suggestions that will serve as a guide for future research on yet-to-be-discovered phenomena and practices. We were delighted that all of the researchers we contacted agreed that the discipline needed such a resource and that they were willing to write chapters for the book.

1

History of Consumer Psychology

Th e fi eld of consumer psychology is alive and well. A review of recent issues of the Journal of Consumer Research, the Journal of Consumer Psychology, and other major publication outlets reveals continued high levels of interest and research activity on a widening array of basic and applied research topics. Contemporary consumer psychologists can be found in academic departments of advertising, marketing, psychology, human ecology, communications, sociology, anthropology, etc. Consumer psychologists can also be found government agencies, profi t and non-profi t businesses. Training for work in consumer psychology oft en consists of coursework and research in multiple areas (Haugtvedt, 2006). As with most areas of study, the topical focus of contemporary research projects in consumer psychology are not all new. In this chapter, we trace the work of psychologists who can be characterized as pioneers in the fi eld of consumer psychology. Our review is selective and not exhaustive. Our intention is to illustrate how the training, creativity, and motivation of early researchers provided a signifi cant part of the foundation of the fi eld as we know it today and as refl ected by chapters in this volume. Our review focuses on the years between 1895 and 1955. Th e activities in this time frame set the stage for two major events in the 1960s. One major event was the establishment of Consumer Psychology Division (Division 23) of the American Psychological Association in 1960. In the late 1950s, a confl ict over ownership of the discipline took place within the American Psychological Association leading to the establishment of a society of practitioners and academics with sole interest in the psychological response of the consumer. A brief history of this confl ict appears at the end of this chapter. Th e second major event was the publication of three widely recognized textbooks on the topic of consumer behavior. Books by Francesco Nicosia (1966), John Howard and Jagdish Sheth (1965), and James Engel, David Kollat and Roger Blackwell (1968) each contained a comprehensive model of important constructs underlying consumer behavior. Early pioneers of consumer psychology were infl uenced greatly by their training. Prominent perspectives included the mentalist approach (represented by experimental psychologists such as Wundt, James, and Titchener); the behavioral or mechanistic approach (represented by Watson and Th orndike); and the dynamic psychology approach (represented by Freud and McDougall). Early applied psychologists oft en had to hide their interest and research in consumer psychology from some of the leaders of the parent discipline because these leaders felt that the fi eld of psychology had to mature before applications to the business world could be espoused. As will be reviewed, much of the work of these early consumer psychologists focused on responses to advertising. Th is, however, led to other concerns as consumer psychologists of the time were not well accepted by the professional advertising community. Th e practitioners viewed the psychologists as interfering in their work and felt that the scientifi c approaches were irrelevant. All of this changed in the early 1900s. It is important to note that the label "consumer psychology" did not exist during this time period. Rather, work that explored the application of psychological principles to business activity was known simply as "applied psychology" and the proponents were "applied psychologists." Th e fi rst contributions to what would be characterized as "consumer psychology" occurred within what was termed "scientifi c advertising," followed closely by the scientifi c study of personal selling. Th ese early pioneers eventually established a home under the parent applied discipline of industrial psychology which became identifi ed as Division 14 of the American Psychological Association. Use of the term "consumer psychology" did not appear until the late 1950s. THE HISTORICAL CONTEXT LEADING TO THE ADVENT OF COMSUMER PSYCHOLOGY Our 65 year historical review of the study of consumer psychology begins in the last decade of the 19th century. Th e study of consumer psychology emerged from specifi c interest in advertising and how advertising infl uenced people. By the latter half of the 19th century, the advertising industry was well established in the United States. Its growth as an industry paralleled the industrial growth of this country. In the United States the fi rst organized advertising appeared in colonial times and was enhanced through the advent of urban newspapers. As the country expanded, there was an obvious need to extend the reach of advertising. From 1850 to 1900, transportation and technology brought on a "new industrial age." An explosion in manufacturing productivity led to new factories, increased volume, greater diversity in consumer products, and the need for new markets (Oliver, 1956). Advertising became the critical vehicle for achieving growth. As new markets emerged refl ecting new populations centers, so did the concept and practice of national advertising with the advent of large circulation magazines like Atlantic Monthly, Colliers, Cosmopolitan, Harper's Monthly, Ladies Home Journal, McClure's, and the Saturday Evening Post (Kuna, 1976). Th e second half of the 1800s witnessed the advent and growth the advertising agent, the advertising copywriter, and, subsequently, the advertising agency. A new found need for professionalism resulted in numerous ad clubs, associations, trade journals, and codes of ethics (Wiebe, 1967). During this time period, two schools of advertising emerged (refl ecting, but not to be confused with the dominant theoretical perspectives in economics and psychology). Th e fi rst school was based on a rational view of man, the potential consumer who carefully paid attention to promotional messages before making product choices. Th e purpose of advertising was simply to inform the public that the item was available and what it could be used for. Th e public was viewed as skeptical and mostly incapable of being persuaded to act against their better judgment. Th is rational perspective followed classic economic theory that people are self-interested and naturally desire to maximize profi ts while valuing their time. Not surprisingly, the emphasis was therefore on reasonable price and basic selling points. While the rational school was dominant during the 1890s and early 1900s, by 1910 it was supplanted by the non-rational perspective. Followers deemed it likely that the emotions of the public could be manipulated and that people could actually be persuaded to purchase goods. Th is school was much more open and receptive to a psychological approach to understanding audience response to advertising. Also contributing to the non-rational school was psychology's new emphasis on the unconscious and motivational states (e.g. Freud, 1924/1969), as well as on the mechanistic reinforcement of behavior (e.g., Watson, 1913). EARLY ROOTS TO THE STUDY OF CONSUMER PSYCHOLOGY As is the case with most all of experimental psychology, one must go back to Germany in the latter part of the 19th century to understand the roots of what was ultimately to become consumer psychology. Th ese roots began in the laboratory of Wilhelm Wundt (1832–1920) in Leipzig in 1879. Of particular relevance to the study of consumer psychology was Wundt's focus on the topic of attention and his infl uence on a subset of students who would go on to become, much to Wundt's displeasure, the fi rst applied, industrial/organizational psychologists in America. Wundt (as did James and Titchener) believed that psychology needed to fi rst prove its worth and evolve as a pure science before it could adequately respond to problems of the applied world (Kuna, 1976). During this same period of time, William James (1842–1910), trained as a philosopher, was bringing to light the new science of psychology in his laboratory at Harvard University. James promoted a mentalistic perspective for this new science. In his seminal book entitled Th e Principles of Psychology, he defi ned psychology as the "science of mental life, both of its phenomena and their conditions" and, like Wundt, professed that this young science needed to rely on introspective observation (James, 1890/ 1950). Th e focus on this mentalistic approach to attention continued with Wundt's students, Edward Bradford Titchener (1867–1927) at Cornell and Hugo Munsterberg (1863–1916) at Harvard. While Titchener felt applied psychology was premature at best, Munsterberg became the fi rst important voice in the promotion of applied psychology. Indeed, in the 1909 edition of Psychological Bulletin, he promoted founding of the department of applied psychology as part of the Harvard Psychological Laboratory (Munsterberg, 1909). In this announcement he calls for research on "psychotechnical studies, dealing with the psychological conditions in our technical civilization in business and commerce and industry...". (p. 49). He arguably was the fi rst true industrial/organizational psychologist. Although he did little himself to contribute to knowledge regarding consumer related psychological topics, his promotion of applied psychology in business settings, in the face of the purists, provided signifi cant professional support for those psychologists scientifi cally investigating applied business topics. Other students of Wundt's who reinforced the mentalistic focus but turned their interests toward the study of advertising, included Edward Wheeler Scripture at Yale, Harlow Gale at the University of Minnesota, and Walter Dill Scott at Northwestern University. Th e most dominant belief of the mentalists was ideo-motor action. James (1890/1950) defi ned it this way: Th at every representation of a movement awakens in some degree the actual movement which is its object; and awakens it in a maximal degree whenever it is not kept from so doing by an antagonistic representation present simultaneously to the mind. (p. 526)

James viewed ideo-motor action as immediate, that the representations of the movement in the mind remain for a matter of seconds (or less) (James 1890/1950). In the early part of the new century, the mentalistic approach had two challenges: behaviorism and dynamic psychology. Th e two pioneering advocates for behaviorism in America were Edward Lee Th orndike (1874–1949) and John Broadus Watson (1878–1958). Each attempted to discredit the mentalistic approach (as well as the functional approach) by advocating a mechanistic view of behavior. Dynamic psychology, refl ecting the dynamic (changing) nature of human behavior, prescribed that man was better understood through instinctive, unconscious, biologically driven actions (Watson and Evans, 1981). Th e two leading proponents were Sigmund Freud (1856–1939) and William McDougall (1981–1938). Freud was fi rst formally introduced to American psychology in 1909 during his famous visit to Clark University at the invitation of G. Stanley Hall. Because behavior was in constant fl ux, dynamic psychologists viewed the conscious state as less important and less reliable than the unconscious state. McDougall (1912) was the fi rst to propose that rather than being a study of consciousness, psychology was more accurately the study of behavior. He focused on the notion of innate instincts that drive men (and animals) towards goals. Both Freud and McDougall believed that tension reduction was at the root of all motivation and behavior. Th eir perspectives were refl ected in the non-rational school of advertising emerging at the same time (Kuna, 1976). Th eir theories were obviously antithetical to both the mentalistic and the mechanistic perspectives. Th is established interesting confl icts and debates, both among "pure" psychologists as well as those psychologists seeking to focus on applied settings. THE EARLY PIONEERS: 1895?1930 E. W. Scripture and Harlow Gale Although Edward Wheeler Scripture (1864–1943) and Harlow Gale (1862–1945) are not considered by some to be true forefathers of consumer psychology (see Benjamin, 2004), they appear to be the fi rst psychologists interested in consumer related issues, and specifi cally consumer response to advertising (Scripture, 1895; Gale, 1900). As such, their work is part of the history of consumer psychology. In perhaps the fi rst discussion of psychology as it pertains to advertising, Scripture (1895), implicitly employing Wundt's notion of involuntary attention, denoted several psychological "laws" as they relate to advertising. For example, Scripture noted that "bigness" and the intensity of a sensation regulate attention to commercial promotion, noting the eff ectiveness of signage and lighting in stores and theaters. Scripture also considered feeling and expectations, proposing that "the degree of attention paid to an object depends on the intensity of the feeling aroused," and that the level of our expectations would determine the amount of attention paid to an object (Kuna 1976). Here Scripture hints at the notion of incongruity as attracting attention (e.g., putting notices upside down). Although Scripture discussed these psychological issues related to advertising and business, he left it up to others to do the scientifi c investigation. Harlow Gale, an instructor at the University of Minnesota, picked up Scripture's call for greater scientifi c investigation. Gale (1900) conducted what many argue to be the fi rst actual scientifi c studies of advertising and consumer behavior. He began with a qualitative survey mailed to advertising professionals where he posed a series of open-ended questions designed to provide practitioner opinions about the best means to attract attention and induce purchasing through advertising. Th e survey required signifi cant eff ort and resulted in only a 10% response return. Gale then followed the survey with a series of experiments, employing the tachistoscope procedure learned from Wundt. Th e attentional issues he examined included relevant versus irrelevant materials (words and advertising "cuts" or representative images), large versus small style of type, the side of the page fi rst attended to, exposure levels, and colors used in advertising. As he moved from one study to another, he discovered potential confounds and attempted to correct for them in subsequent studies. Perhaps of interest at the time, but not surprising today, he found that gender moderated some of his eff ects. It is interesting to note that Gale may have been the fi rst to use the order-of-merit technique in determining the importance of message arguments. Gale would ask respondents to rank order brands based upon the information provided in advertisements. E. K. Strong Jr. (Strong will be discussed in depth in a subsequent section) fi rst attributed this technique to James McKeen Cattell (Strong, 1911), but later reversed himself, giving credit for the method to Gale (Strong, 1938; see also Kuna, 1979). Th is method was widely used by subsequent researchers in advertising and business studies (but challenged by Adams, 1915, see further discussion later in this chapter). Gale confi ned his work to conducting studies within his classroom and was not willing to establish relationships with members of the advertising industry. He was more interested in giving his students practical experience with psychology. Walter Dill Scott At the turn of the century, the emphasis in psychology was transitioning from a mentalistic perspective, an ideational-cognitive explanation for unconscious phenomena, to the more dynamic notions of instinct and emotion. No more is this transition evidenced than in the long career of Walter Dill Scott (1869–1955). Scott is considered by many as America's fi rst business psychologist and the fi rst true applied psychologist (Jacobson, 1951). Unlike Gale, Scott actively promoted his fi ndings to business and oft en served as a consultant. Aft er his educational studies with both Wundt and Titchener, he began his academic career as a professor at Northwestern University, eventually serving as its president. Aside from studying advertising, he also published in the areas of salesmanship and classifi cation of military personnel. Scott was the fi rst to actively promote the psychological study of advertising. He was very vocal in a series of 12 columns that appeared in Mahin's Magazine and challenged the thinking of those who rejected a scientifi c approach, then represented in Printer's Ink (Kuna, 1976, Watson and Evans, 1981). His fi rst book, Th e Th eory of Advertising (1903), was a compilation of those articles, and was written from a mentalist perspective, purporting that creating involuntary attention was the motive for advertising. Th is book, like his second, was fi lled mostly with advice for practitioners, although it did cite a few select studies. Like Scripture, Scott listed a number of "laws" and principles. Th ese refl ected numerous psychological dimensions and elements inherent in advertising as described in his chapters: apperception/attention, counter infl uences on attention, intensity of sensation, context eff ects, comprehension, repetition and rehearsal, mental imagery, laws of association, suggestion, perceptional illusions, and intensity of feeling (Scott, 1903). By 1905 Scott was deep into solving applied problems for business through various research methods. He was also authoring articles for other magazines including the Atlantic Monthly, Business World, and Advertising World (Kuna, 1976). John Mahin asked Scott for more articles and Scott obliged with 21 more columns. Th is second set of articles formed his second and most famous book. Th e Psychology of Advertising (1908), while still maintaining a mentalist perspective, combined new irrational aspects of consumer behavior to include emotion and instinct, with the old focus on attention and suggestion. More studies were included that incorporated new methods: naturalistic observation, longitudinal study, order-of merit, and memory value of advertising. His thoughts on suggestion in basic psychology became invited articles in the Psychological Bulletin (1910–1916). Scott believed that humans were susceptible to suggestion and that the force of suggestion could lead to action. Eff ective advertising, according to Scott, should suggest a course of action in a manner that ruled out other contrary actions. Th ere are many examples of Scott's infl uence on advertising practitioners including his advice on the association of the advertising with the product (laws included repetition, recency, and vividness), direct commands embedded in advertising, and suggestion as how advertising works with couponing (Scott, 1916). He provided testimony from companies as to the success of his propositions. Of special note is the fact that Scott never published his studies in academic journals nor presented this work at academic conferences, even though he served as APA president. Daniel Starch One could say that Daniel Starch (1883–1979) followed in the footsteps of Walter Dill Scott, carrying on the mentalist tradition. Like Scott, Starch's applied research never appeared in an academic journal. During his time in academia, he chose to reinforce his reputation as an experimental psychologist, publishing on traditional topics including a series of review articles for Psychological Bulletin (1911–1916) on the topic of auditory space. Yet Starch diff ered from Scott in that he attempted to bring an objective scientifi c view to all of his work. Rather than off ering subjective opinions about the psychology of advertising, all of his contentions appear to be empirically supported. Starch reinforced the mentalist approach in his focus on attention, suggestion, and instinct, but he extended it by introducing the concept of consumer "interest," which he later labeled "appeals" (e.g., Starch, 1923). Starch spent most of his relatively short academic life at the University of Wisconsin (1908–1919) and at Harvard (1920–1926). His fi rst book titled Principles of Advertising (1910) consisted of two parts: attracting attention and securing action. While primarily focusing on the attention oriented topics of Scott, Starch did add the notion of primacy and recency of advertisements as attracting more attention in the mind of the consumer. While both Scott and Hollingworth mentioned the importance of optimal length of line in print advertising (as noted in Tinker & Paterson, 1928), Starch was the fi rst to actually conduct studies on this important question (Starch, 1924, 1923). Starch's second book was published in 1914. Th is book addressed not only the psychology of advertising, but also other non-psychological topics like advertising strategy and ethics. Th e book was again organized around attention and securing response. Several laws of attention were presented to include the laws of intensity, counter-attraction, and contrast. In securing a response, Starch focused on argumentation and suggestion. It was under the latter that Starch introduced the strategy of stimulating consumer interest. Interest was an extension of attention, a kind of involuntary prolonged attention to an object. It was assumed that a reader of an ad would be more likely to attend and respond if the stimuli presented in it refl ected the reader's interests. He suggested that illustrations could be used to stimulate interests. Th is book became a standard for the advertising practitioner. It is important to note that for every topic, Starch went to signifi cant lengths to support his contentions with empirical evidence from his own studies or the work of other psychologists or practitioners. In 1924 while still at Harvard, Starch became heavily involved in supervising research for the American Association of Advertising Agencies. In 1932 Starch left academia altogether and started Daniel Starch & Staff , a marketing research company providing subscribing companies with data on the eff ectiveness of their ads. Starch became well known for his methodological innovations, including the Starch Recognition Procedure in 1922, which measured consumer reading habits, and the Buyometer in 1948, which isolated the infl uence of magazine advertising on sales (Kuna, 1976). He retired in 1968 at the age of 85. BEHAVIORISM IN ADVERTISING RESEARCH While the mentalistic approach was prevalent at the turn of the century, it was not without challenges. One of those challenges came from the faculty at Columbia University. James McKeen Cattell (1860–1944) had established multiple university laboratories for the study of psychology aft er returning from the tutelage of Wundt in Leipzig. He welcomed new faculty and students to Columbia in the early 1900s, especially those who had interests in applied psychology. Indeed, over time he recruited a remarkable group of faculty to include Robert Sessions Woodworth (1869–1962), Edward Lee Th orndike (1874–1949), Harry Levi Hollingworth (1880–1956), Edward Kellogg Strong Jr. (1884–1963), and Albert T. Poff enberger (1885–1977). Th orndike (1911) had introduced laws of eff ect (i.e., the role of "satisfi ers" and "annoyers" as reinforcing and inhibiting behavior) and exercise (i.e., connection of a response to a situation). In applying these laws to advertising, Hollingworth felt that, rather than focusing on whether an ad attracted someone's attention, the true measure of the eff ectiveness of an ad is ultimately refl ected with the actual purchase behavior. Hollingworth held that research conducted by advertisers was by its very nature, fl awed, as it didn't control for numerous extraneous variables (seasonal sales, competitor actions, amount of media, etc.). Hollingworth had advertisers send him ads to test in his lab. Interestingly, his lab tests were highly correlated with the actual sales fi gures related to each ad. In several studies, Hollingworth (e.g., 1911) examined the same variables considered by Gale and Scott, (e.g., images, wording, size, color, position, and type style) but considered the variance of the response rather than introspection. As his studies progressed, he considered individual diff erences such as gender and socioeconomic diff erences. In some cases his results contradicted the results of Gale and Scott. Hollingworth even constructed a panel of New York City residents, the fi rst systematic eff ort to track consumption behavior (Kuna, 1976). In 1913, Advertising and Selling: Principles of Appeal and Responses was published. Building on his earlier work but appearing to move away from behaviorism, his next book on the topic, Advertising: Its Principles and Practice (1915) captured four principle functions of advertising: securing attention, holding attention, establishing associations, and infl uencing conduct by making associations dynamic. Hollingworth's objectivity in his empirical methods clearly infl uenced other younger applied psychologists. One of these was Edward K. Strong Jr. Th orndike's (1913) classic paper rejected ideo-motor action and promoted new laws of habit, eff ect, and exercise, Watson released his treatise on behaviorism (1913), and Hollingworth's (1913) book refl ected aspects of this new wave of thought. Cattell had earlier challenged the claim that introspection was the most valid methodology for the study of psychology. His focus was on reducing qualitative responses into quantitative data. As an example, his version of the order-of-merit method was strictly objective, requiring subjects to order stimuli on some criterion (Kuna, 1976; 1979). Strong and Hollingworth took a more "molar" view of behaviorism, with a focus on complex stimuli as opposed to discrete stimuli. Rather than being preoccupied with people's thoughts, they measured what they felt were surrogates for behavioral response to advertising stimuli. Th ey employed the order-of-merit method as well as a refi ned recognition test that Strong (1914) developed in a reaction to the traditional mentalist recall measures. Strong believed that recognition was the best surrogate for actual purchase behavior and tested the infl uence of several presentation variables to include size and frequency, and repetition intervals One other behaviorist from this time period is worth considerable note. It is important to refl ect on the contribution to consumer psychology of John Broadus Watson. His treatise on behaviorism in 1913 earned him great acclaim as a psychologist, as he informed the world that eff orts based on psychology principles should lead to greater control and prediction of behavior. Watson's studies provided demonstrations of the infl uence of association and conditioning on behavioral responses (e.g., Watson and Raynor, 1920).

He loudly and passionately disclaimed any reason for a mentalist perspective. He became the chair of the psychology department at Johns Hopkins University, editor of the Psychological Review, and served as a president of the American Psychological Association in 1915. However, a scandal led to his termination and exit from academic life, and a transition into a career in advertising. Stanley Resor, the "dean of American advertising," hired Watson to work for him at J. Walter Th ompson in New York. Watson quickly found leverage for success in his psychological expertise. Th e business world embraced him and his leadership and philosophy resulted in numerous successful advertising campaigns. Resor showcased Watson in such a way that it legitimized the role of psychologists working in advertising. ADVANCING AND APPLYING THE PSYCHOLOGICAL SCHOOLS OF THOUGHT To understand how dynamicism eventually evolved from mentalistic and behavioralistic approaches, one needs to consider the infl uence that Freud had at the time. His infl uence was subtle. Although Gale, Scott, and Starch all brought forth such notions of the unconscious as instincts, emotions, and interests, they continued to off er explanations consistent with a mentalistic outlook. Th orndike (1911) explained instinct and motivation as an inherited response tendency, adhering to a behavioral explanation where the catalyst for the response was a stimulus, not a condition of the being. It was McDougall who took direct aim in diff erentiating his purposive psychology from Watsonian behavioral psychology as refl ected in the following passage: Th e two principal alternative routes are (1) that of mechanistic science, which interprets all its processes as mechanical sequences of cause and eff ect, and (2) that of the sciences of mind, for which purposive striving is a fundamental category, which regard the process of purposive striving as radically diff erent form mechanical sequence. (1923, p. vii) Enter Robert S. Woodworth, a colleague of Th orndike and Hollingworth at Columbia. Woodworth is credited with putting the organism in the stimulus-organism-response (S-O-R) model and thus fi nding a home for the contribution of motivation and instinct to human behavior. In his book Dynamic Psychology (1918), he attempted to bring together (and even expand) the work of Freud and McDougall with mainstream psychology. It is important to note that the term "psychodynamic" as oft en describes Freud and his adherents' theories, is not viewed as the same as "dynamic psychology." While both referred to notions of the unconscious mind, the former term typically includes identifi cation of certain emotional confl icts and the resolution of these confl icts with specifi c defense mechanisms. Dynamic psychology was focused upon the infl uence of basic motivational drives on behavior. McDougall spoke of "drives" as strong and persistent stimulation, as initiating goal-directed actions through selective excitation of response mechanisms related to particular goals (e.g., consumption behaviors). Hollingworth and Strong, as colleagues of Woodworth, were naturally exposed to his thinking and his ideas regarding drives and organism responses, even his early ideas on psychoanalysis. Indeed, Hollingworth earlier had occasion to meet Jung and be exposed to Freud's ideas. Although Hollingworth and Strong were reticent to adopt the dynamic approach, Hollingworth challenged business leaders to better understand the role of motives, interests, and instincts (Kuna,1976). Finally, in Hollingworth's multiple-authored book, Advertising: Its Principles and Practice (Tipper, Hollingworth, Hotchkiss, & Parsons, 1915), he provided a listing of a hierarchy of human needs (e.g., comfort, play, sociability, competition, shyness, revenge, and pride) as representative of the individual, not a specifi c stimulus. He also revised his functions of advertising from his previous book to now include tabulation of the fundamental needs of men and women, analysis of the satisfying power of the commodity in terms of the consumer's needs, establishing the association between need and commodity, and making the association dynamic. Th is was a remarkable transference. Strong too experienced this transference and by 1925 his thinking culminated in his book, Th e Psychology of Selling and Advertising. While Strong provided leadership in the adoption of the dynamic approach to applied psychology, his eventual fame came from a diff erent applied focus. Although he continued to conduct research in advertising, he also served on the committee on Classifi cation of Personnel during World War I. In 1923, he published the Strong Vocational Interest Blank (SVIB) which became the most widely used career interest inventory in publication, a revision of which is still employed today in helping individuals understand their natural work propensities. Th e infl uence of the work of Hollingworth and Strong on other psychologists was considerable. Another Columbia colleague, Joseph V. Breitwieser, made extensive reference to the work of both Hollingworth and Strong in his textbook Psychological Advertising (1915). Th eir work to adopt the order-of-merit method resulted in subsequent usage by many investigators. By 1923, Starch had conducted at least 34 studies using the method. Henry Foster Adams and Dexter Kitson In his book entitled Advertising and Its Mental Laws (1916a), Adams appears to be carrying on the mentalist tradition by specifi cally citing the work of those we've previously discussed: Gale, Scott, Hollingworth, Strong, and Starch. However, Adams himself conducted numerous empirical studies. Adams believed in testing factors in isolation applying a "mathematical exactness" in examining various elements found in advertising. Although he respected their contributions, Adams was especially critical of Hollingworth and Strong's use of the order-of-merit method (Adams, 1915). In Advertising and Mental Laws he repeats his criticism but also devotes one chapter on the use of statistical tools to examine response to advertising (correlation and variance), and another on experimentation in advertising. One important contribution from Adams' book was his ordering of certain advertising stimulus factors, as he perceived them related to key response variables: attention, association, memory, perception, and aesthetics. Adams also considered the eff ectiveness of diff erent media. He concluded the book with chapters on fusion (a nod to behaviorism) and action. Th e book, for the most part, was still a tribute to the mentalistic approach. His concluding chapter dealt with the empirical fi ndings related to gender diff erences. He noted that women paid attention more to size, personal appeals and observed events while men attended more to successive presentations, pictures, industrial-job related, and recommendations of authorities. Of peculiar interest, he found that memory tests contradicted the attention eff ects. For example, women had better memory with successive presentations and pictures, while men had better memory based on size of ad and for trade names. Th e comprehensive books by Adams and Starch, each promoting the importance of the empirical results to date, set the tone for much work to follow. In a short period of time following these books, numerous studies were reported. For example, Adams (1916b), still maintaining the mentalist approach, went on to study the relative memory for duplication and variation, and sizes of ads (Adams 1917), as well as the eff ect of order of presentation (Adams, 1920).

Henry Dexter Kitson helped set the stage for this focus on other aspects of the consumer in his book titled Th e Mind of the Buyer, published in 1921. His fi rst chapter examines the "stream of thought" in a sale, prescribing six stages in a sale: attention, interest, desire, confi dence, decision and action, and satisfaction. Th e book clearly takes an eclectic approach, citing researchers and theorists from all three schools of psychology: mentalist, behaviorist, and dynamic. Kitson contributed to the study of advertising as well, especially with his studies regarding illustrations within advertising

(Kitson, 1921), and more specifi cally the use of color (Kitson, 1922a), various art forms (Kitson, 1922b), package illustrations (Kitson & Campbell, 1924), and illustrations containing people (Kitson & Allen, 1925). Indeed, in 1921, Kitson presented his "historical method of investigating problems in advertising." Th is appears to be the fi rst documented use of content analysis methodology in advertising studies. In 1925, Kitson and Allen reported a trend in the usage of illustrations containing people in advertising, aft er analyzing 20 years of ads from Saturday Evening Post, Literary Digest, and Women's Home Companion. Th is continued focus on illustration is one of the fi rst examples of programmatic research in consumer psychology. Albert T. Poff enberger Albert T. Poff enberger (1885–1977) studied at Columbia under Cattell and Woodworth. Th e infl uence of these associations are refl ected in his lifelong interest in physiological psychology and objective response. His dissertation was titled Reaction Time to Retinal Stimulation (Wenzel, 1979). He never lost this interest and continued in this vane through much of his career. However, his strongest interest was in the area of applied psychology (see 1921 edition of American Men in Science). Aft er conducting a number of studies, he published the book entitled Psychology in Advertising in 1925. Th is imposing tome is a remarkable recapitulation of all the conceptual and empirical work up to that time. Aside from a through review of traditional subjects like memory and attention, and some focus on methodology, statistics, measurement, and appeal, Poff enberger provided new reviews in comprehension, "feeling tone," attitude, human desires, and individual and group diff erences, among others. Poff enberger followed this book with Applied Psychology: Its Principles and Methods (1927, 1932). Here he defi ned applied psychology as "every situation in which human behavior is involved and where economy of human energy is of practical importance." In the section on Advertising and Selling, he explores the desires, habits, and logic of the consumer, and reviews the state of psychology as it has been applied to advertising and selling strategies to date. Poff enberger contributed heavily to the service of the discipline culminating in his election to the presidency of the APA in 1934. OTHER CONTRIBUTORS DURING THIS TIME PERIOD Others, notably Heller and Brown (1916) in their study on memory for street-car signage, Laslett (1918) in a study of relevance of illustrations, Hotchkiss and Franken (1920) in their study of attention factors, and Turner (1922) in his examination of testimonials used in advertising, continued the mentalist tradition. However, a number of applied researchers were beginning to employ more objective measures refl ecting a clear leaning toward the behavioral approach. Poff enberger was arguably the most prolifi c examining face types (Poff enberger & Franken, 1923), return of coupon resulting from advertising (Poff enberger, 1923a), belief consistency with advertisement (1923b) and the value of lines used in advertising (Poff enberger & Barrows, 1924). In what was to become a signifi cant subject of study, as we shall see in the next section of this chapter, Nixon (1924, 1926) examined attention and interest in advertising and concluded that differences in attention between color ads and black and white ads lasted only briefl y. He voiced concern over he reliability of diff erences in memory tests between the two types of ads, and designed and employed a method whereby researchers could observe where visual attention was focused. Up to this point, researchers from Gale forward suggested that more attention would be paid to relevant messages about products as opposed to irrelevant messages. Likewise Laslett (1918) found that relevant illustrations led to better recall. However, using Nixon's method of "visual fi xation," irrelevant pictures paired with products garnered more attention than did relevant pictures. As was noted above (and will be discussed in depth below), at this time psychologists began to consider other aspects of consumer behavior. For example, Geissler (1917) pointed out that consumers needed to be approached in more ways than just advertising and began to study processing that occurred in consideration of purchase. Heller (1919) studied the impact of package labels on purchasing, while Kitson (1923) authored a conceptual article examining the consumer's role in market strategy. Laird (1923) compared demographic and socioeconomic diff erences in the selection of toothpaste, and Hotchkiss and Franken (1923) considered the importance of brand familiarity. James McKeen Cattell was eventually dismissed from Columbia because of his opposition to the draft . In 1921 he, along with Columbia colleagues Woodworth and Th orndike, formed the Th e Psychological Corporation in New York. Th ey began by developing psychological tests and related materials that could be used in education, business, and government. In the following years, the company hired academics to run sponsored studies. As we shall see, a number of these research studies were eventually published in academic journals. It is interesting to note that through mergers and acquisitions, the corporate entity evolved and still exists today although under a diff erent name (Harcourt Assessment). THE POST?DEPRESSION ERA THROUGH WORLD WAR II: 1935?1945 Th e end of the Depression triggered signifi cant research by economists studying product demand and usage. Th e Journal of Marketing, initiated in 1935, devoted a signifi cant amount of journal space to articles authored by individuals trained in economics and measuring product demand and use. During this same period, applied psychologists were attempting to better understand consumer response to commercial product promotion. Th e decade following the depression was marked by the advent of a new media form—radio—that quickly found signifi cant application for commercial advertising. As we shall address next in this section, there were numerous areas of consumer research that appeared to be focused on print and radio eff ectiveness (including comparative eff ectiveness); salesperson eff ectiveness; consumer preference, consumer motivation, and concern over research methods. We shall take each in turn and discuss how these applied psychologists addressed these various consumer related interests and issues. It is interesting to note that unlike the prolifi c work from key pioneers during the previous time period, this time period is marked with contributions from authors who published but a few articles refl ecting consumer psychological topics. However, this work, in bulk, does demonstrate a signifi cant level of progression forward in the discipline. FOCUS ON MEDIA DIFFERENCES Several applied psychologists approached the issue of comparing the eff ectiveness of visual versus spoken ads by mimicking the diff erences between print, posters, and radio media. Th is eff ort was initially refl ected in a signifi cant number of memory studies. Burtt and Dobell (1925) reported a series of studies that sought to replicate Ebbinghaus' (1885) notion of a forgetting curve, one that begins with a sharp decline fl attening out over time. Th ese researchers provided respondents with a long paired list of products and fi ctional brand names, two studies projected onto a screen, (over diff erent time frames) and one provided by audio means. Th e results of all three studies reinforced the same type of forgetting curve, but the initial audio memory test yielded better results in both recall and recognition than did the projected pairs on a screen. Noting that advertising posters seen on streets are also an important type of advertising, Brutt and Crockett (1928) studied memory for diff erent types of posters. Th eir results refl ected signifi - cant primacy and recency eff ects and that distance from the viewer makes a diff erence in memory for the add (refl ecting the best visual angle). Stanton (1934) and Dewick (1935) conducted similar experiments where they provided a series of print advertisements and spoken advertisements in a counterbalanced study using common products. Th e brand names were mentioned three times in the script which lasted about 35 seconds. Th ey then recorded recall scores for the product class and the brand name, employing both immediate and delayed recall tests. Th e fi ndings of both studies revealed that there were no consistent diff erences upon immediate recall. Aft er 5 to 7 days, there was the beginning of a favored auditory response, and in the Stanton study signifi cant diff erences favoring auditory response were found for 21-day recall. In the Dewick study, recall of "ideas" mentioned in the advertisements were elicited, and while both visual and auditory memory decayed aft er 6 days, the visual decay in memory was signifi cantly greater than the auditory. In hindsight, it would be interesting to know, in the delayed conditions, if individuals during their everyday normal experience, heard or read more ads for the products used in the study. If the former, that might explain the greater recall scores for auditory messages due to greater exposure to the brand name, product class, and advertising message. It is interesting to note that in the early 1930s William Stanton, while a PhD student at Ohio State, developed a forerunner of the radio and television rating audimeters, later developed for A.C. Nielsen by MIT. Stanton went on to become an executive with Columbia Broadcasting Company and an important pioneer in subsequent radio audience studies (Maloney, 1987, as cited in Kassarjian, 1994). In perhaps what was a precursor to television and was refl ected in the speaking movies of the time, Elliot (1936, 1937a, 1937b, 1937c) reviewed the literature on memory of visual and auditory stimuli dating back to Ebbinghaus and developed a series of studies comparing visual, auditory, and the combination of visual and auditory (termed "television" in one of his studies). In all cases, he found an advantage for the combination of the two as regards memory for an advertising message as well as a trade name. His studies also revealed certain gender eff ects but these eff ects were somewhat inconsistent across studies. In general, the diff erence of eff ectiveness of television over other modes was stronger for women than men. A number of studies attempted to understand people's attitudes toward radio advertising in general (Cantril & Allport, 1935; Kornhauser & Lazarsfeld 1937; Sayre, 1939). Cantril and Allport, and Kornhauser and Lazarsfeld employed two measures (estimated time that commercials were heard, and amount of money willing to pay annually to remove advertisements) that they deemed refl ective of possible positive or negative attitudes towards radio advertising. However, employing a Likert scale, Sayre found no correlation between a direct measure of attitude and the other two scales. William Stanton, mentioned above, conducted radio studies under the guidance of Cantril and Allport at Princeton. Th e three were instrumental in bringing Paul Lazersfeld to the United States. Lazersfeld, a mathematics PhD from the University of Vienna, had established a radio research organization in Europe and conducted the fi rst major study on radio audience listening. Lazersfeld soon left Princeton and founded what was to become the Bureau of Applied Social Research at Columbia University. Lazersfeld, in turn, was instrumental in bringing his Viennese students, Ernest Dichter and Herta Herzog to the U.S. Dichter's contribution to consumer psychology will be discussed in a subsequent section (Maloney, 1987 as cited by Kassarjian, 1994). Guest and Brown (1939) tested recall for radio advertising based on a number of variable diff erences. In a controlled study employing both ads and music programming for an hour, they found no diff erences for temporal position, whole versus part methods of presentation, nor for repetition. Th ey did fi nd an inverse relationship between recall and amount of material, less material presented led to better recall. In all cases, the average number of thought passages retained was small. Wolfe (1941) found a high correlation, .78, between women who could associate a product with a program. Th ese strong results for early radio recall are intuitive given that each program was typically sponsored by only one product. Th us the repetition of the program with one sponsor likely led to a high level of rehearsal and retention. Fay and Middleton (1941) examined the gender of commercial announcers and found no diff erences in gender preference for announcers, but found that women tended to have a higher preference for announcers across both male and female products, then did males. FOCUS ON MECHANICAL FEATURES OF PRINT AND POSTER ADVERTISEMENTS Several important mechanical factors in print advertising were considered during this time period as they infl uenced reader response. Th e impact of color in advertising took center stage in the early 1930s along with an examination of positioning, type style, and amount of copy. In the latter half of the 1920s and early 1930s, several studies pertaining to color, size and position in print advertising appeared. Nixon (1926, 1927) reported the fi rst of several perceptual studies. Th ese two studies compared color and black and white ads, using a measure of attention to the ad. He found no signifi cant diff erences between color and black and white ads but did fi nd that females tended to pay more attention to the ads than did males. Sumner (1932) studied the infl uence of color on legibility (blue print on a gray or white background scored highest however there were only 5 subjects. Dorcus (1932) examined people's habitual word associations with colors as they might be a factor in advertising (for a comprehensive review of studies on response to color going back 30 years, see Dorcus 1926). As noted in a 1932 edition of Printer's Ink, Starch, in an analysis of 5 million inquiries, studied 4 million returns from 3,349 advertisements. He found that "color ads brought 53% more returns per 100,000 than did black and white advertisements of similar size and character" (p. 65). While still considering the eff ects of color, researchers also began to consider size and placement issues. In 1930, Cutler reported no recall diff erences for the same ad that appeared in magazines of diff erent size. Ferguson (1934) supported Starch's fi ndings by comparing position of magazine advertisements in the Saturday Evening Post (e.g., inside front cover, page opposite the table of contents, outside back cover), and found some diff erences for position, but also found that color typically out- performed black and white ads. Ferguson made an additional interesting contribution by noting potential diff erences in target readership: "those who buy SEP in order to read the articles and stories, 2) those who buy SEP for humor, and 3) those who buy SEP to mainly look at the ads." Ferguson (1934, 1935) concluded that contrary to belief, his fi ndings revealed no relationship between the size of an advertisement and its attention value, no preferred positions, and no preference for right versus left hand pages, nor position on the page. Lucas (1937) employed a more sophisticated study as a follow up to Ferguson and found contradictory results. Specifi cally he found that the diff erential changes for the advertising by placement and size correlated strongly with recall and recognition, that women respond better to color than men, and that right- and left - hand page locations are of equal value for full-page ads, but right-hand position is better recalled for smaller ads. Guilford and Ewart (1940) examined the diff erence in reaction time resulting from the potential distraction of print ads that appeared in color or black and white. Listening and responding to the noise of the timer motor which was about the same decibel as the projector of the ads, they found that both types of ads served as signifi cant distractors, but did not diff er in reaction time. McNamara (1941) voiced the criticisms regarding previous attention and memory studies in the lab (see subsection on methodology below for these criticisms), and reported a study employing eye movement photography. He found no diff erences in attention to the prime positions (inside front, back, etc.), nor for right- versus left -hand pages, but did fi nd diff erences favoring two-column ads found on the outside left page and ads that were found in the upper corners. Th e continued investigation into typeface response was another mechanical feature of the early 1930's. In 1933, Davis and Smith, building on the earlier work of Poff enberger and Barrows (1924), considered emotional response to diff erent forms of typeface. Respondents were asked to match typefaces with advertised products as well as emotions, revealing some diff erences based on such typeface characteristics as size, condensation, boldness, use of italics, etc. In a similar study, Schiller (1935) replicated the earlier study of Poff enberger and Franken (1923) examining the eff ectiveness of certain types of typefaces as representing certain products. However, in her study she also considered color of the typefaces. In a follow up to Kitson's earlier content analysis on the use of illustrations, Klapp (1941) found that not only did advertisements without pictures decrease signifi cantly over 4 decades (1900– 1940), as did ads with pictures but not including people, but that ads with people, especially refl ecting relevancy with the product, increased dramatically (1900—16.2%; 1915—34.7%; 1930—49%; 1940—67.1%). One popular question of advertising eff ectiveness that still evokes research today is the issue of relative eff ectiveness of negative versus positive message appeals. Investigation of this question can be traced back to the historical content analysis work of Harry Kitson (reported in Lucas & Benson, 1929a). Kitson conclusion as well as Scott's was that in general, it was best to use positive appeals. Kitson based his opinion on the usage rate diff erences found in his content analysis favoring positive appeals. However, it is interesting to note that some practitioners of the day disagreed (Lucas & Benson, 1929b). Lucas and Benson undertook a program of research on this topic with a series of experiments. Reinforcing the practitioner opinion, across varied message appeals (negative versus positive) refl ecting ads for several diff erent product classes, these researchers found no diff erences in the amount of coupons returned based on the valance of appeal type (Lucas & Benson, 1929b), and no diff erences in recall among adults (Lucas & Benson, 1930a). However, they did fi nd that among children, positive ads were recalled better than negative ads, especially among boys. Th ey noted that as children age, diff erences between appeals and gender disappear. Lucas and Benson (1930b) also published Psychology for Advertisers, an extensive book that summarized advertising eff ectiveness research to date, and focused on the mechanics of print appeals and how these appeals could facilitate the eff ort of salespeople. Focus on the amount and proximity of ads: In 1935, Fred

McKinney designed a study to examine "retroactive inhibition." In earlier basic psychology studies, numerous results refl ected "retroactive inhibition, distraction due to similar material that appears immediately subsequent to the targeted stimulus presentation. In his fi rst study to apply retroactive inhibition to advertising, McKinney sought to discern how memory for parts of an ad (i.e., product name, slogan, headline, reading and picture content), are susceptible to subsequent reviewing of ads. McKinney found slight retroactive inhibition with slogans being the most aff ected and name of product the least aff ected. He does draw the obvious conclusion that placement of ads in relative isolation is the most eff ective for memory of the ad. Blankenship and Whitely (1941) focused on the eff ects of proactive inhibition to memory by providing both normal and similar preceding stimulus ads (containing a list of products and associated prices and comparing them to conditions containing a similar list of nonsense names and associated numbers. Aft er subjects were asked to recall the inhibitory stimulus lists, they were then exposed to a regular ad with listed products and associated prices, and recall scores were taken. Th e results consistently demonstrated a proactive inhibition eff ect on memory. In a similar application, McNamara and Tiff en (1941), using the Purdue Eye Camera, found that ads adjacent to cartoons inhibited the time spent on the advertising. Franzen (1940), in perhaps the fi rst look at fatigue resulting from clutter, examined ad visibility reported in interviews comparing two magazines, one with 33% more advertising than the other. More fatigue was clearly present in the interview assessing memory for ads in the larger magazine. FOCUS ON THE EFFECTIVENESS OF SALESPEOPLE Salesperson eff ectiveness was viewed strictly as a "personnel" issue in the early part of the 20th century. Many applied psychologists developed theories as to what comprised a good salesperson (e.g., Link, 1932, 1938; Nixon, 1931, 1942; Snow, 1926; 1929). Indeed, Nixon's bibliography in his second edition of his Principles of Selling (1942) lists over a hundred books on the topic. Applied industrial psychologists had reported numerous studies correlating traits, interests, intelligence, and demographic factors with objective measures of performance like total sales (e.g., Freyd, 1922; Craig, 1933; Dodge 1938a, 1938b). An example of this type of study was conducted by the Psychological Corporation and reported by Schultz (1934). Schultz described results from a study in which sale personnel were measured on the traits of ascendance/ submission (measured by Beckman's revision of the Allport Ascendance-Submission Test), and introversion/extroversion (measured by the Root

Introversion-Extroversion Test). Intelligence, interests, and general demographic factors were also assessed. Level of ascendance and extroversion correlated with performance. Intelligence screened out "poor" performance but was not related to best or average performance. Age, education, experience, race, and length of service did not reveal any appreciable diff erences. Interestingly, the employment of E. K. Strong's Vocational Interest survey generated mixed performance results, identifying individuals that were among the best as well as the poorest performers. In 1937, McKinney developed a strategy for rating sales messages. Developing two scripts of the sales "interview" partialed into message segments, student evaluators rated each segment as to their perceived value on a 10-point scale from "poor" to "excellent". Mitchell and Burtt (1938) extended McKinney's work by comparing four pairs of contrasting appeals: 1) demonstration versus oral elaboration; 2) presentation of facts versus short appeals; 3) a "breezy" versus a dignifi ed approach; and 4) a domineering versus a friendly approach. Results favored the demonstration, presentation of facts, and a friendly approach. Th ere was no diff erence between "breezy" and dignifi ed approaches. Arthur Dodge (1938a, 1938b) conducted studies testing multiple facets of personality against salesperson performance. Compared to poor salespeople, better salespeople tended to report themselves as less moody, more self-suffi cient and self-confi dent, more aggressive and more willing to assume responsibility, less self-conscious, more social, less desirous of talking about self, less resentful of criticism or discipline, and more radical and unconventional. Hampton (1940) found similar results for small grocer retailers. While these studies suggested these personality variables refl ected tendencies of salespeople, none boasted what would be termed "strong" diff erences.

FOCUS ON RESEARCH METHODS Although by the mid 1920s there existed several methods in the study of response to advertising, two appeared to be most popular: recall and tests of association (recognition). Indeed, Poffenberger stated "as there are numerous brands of the commonly used articles that really diff er little in quality, it is largely a matter of obeying the laws of recall that determines which particular brand shall be bought" (quoted in Lucas & Benson, 1930a, p. 219). Hotchkiss and Franken (1927), in their book entitled Th e Measurement of Advertising Eff ects, used tests of association and usage to demonstrate the public's familiarity with diff erent brands of commodities. Th is work replicated the earlier work of Donovan (1924) by also examining the association of commodities with brands, and the subsequent work of Asher (1928) that revealed a correlation between newspaper advertising expenditures and recall of certain types of retail stores (e.g., drug stores, ladies' stores, real estate companies, automobile agencies) but not other stores (shoe stores, restaurants, music stores, jewelry stores). One of the benefi ts to practitioners derived from this method is the ability to focus on competitor infl uences. Signifi cant criticism of research methods arose during this period. Using a method of triple associates (as reported by Link, 1934), experiments were conducted by the Psychological Corporation employing 14,000 consumers and conducted by 60 examiners. Hathaway and Welch (1934) questioned the amount of guessing that occurred during this procedure. Link (1932 article cited in McNamara 1941) questioned whether advertisements tested under artifi cial conditions or with subjects who were arguably not the target of the product promotion provided a valid test. Earlier Poff enberger (1925) questioned whether studies were holding other factors constant like form of layout, quality, and such. Lucas (1937) questioned the inability to control for infl uence of past ads in present copy testing, suggesting that it was likely impossible to rule out the cumulative eff ects of similar copy. Gaudet & Zients (1932) suggested that content analyses conducted at certain intervals could not rule out cycling eff ects that might not be detected with a linear increase. During this time period, treatises began to appear on the types and combinations of questions to ask to ascertain psychological insights into marketing related behaviors (i.e., purchase rationale, advertising eff ectiveness, post-purchase evaluation) (Lazarsfeld 1934; Kornhauser & Lazarsfeld, 1935). Several individuals suggested improved methods for understanding the impact of radio advertising (Likert, 1936; Gaskill & Holcomb, 1936). With these criticisms came other new methods of inquiry. Ruckmick (1939) found that respondents' arousal levels as a refl ection of varied advertising, could be measured through detecting sweat gland activity. He found that 3-second exposures to print ads across a repeated series, revealed a relatively consistent pattern. Karslake (1940) presented a study employing a new technique called the Purdue Eye Camera. He compared results employing objective attention measures from the camera against reported results in surveys and found minimal correlation, contending that attention scores resulting from a camera are more accurate than self-reported attention scores. D. B. Lucas (1940) voiced concern regarding the validity of examining recognition of specifi c advertisements apart from the context in which the advertising appears. Indeed, he noted the potential for false recognition rates based on a person's familiarity with other similar ads for the same product. Teaching at New York University, Lucas developed a continuing study of magazine readership of four weekly magazines and created a corrected recognition formula that accounted for false recognition scores. His method was based on exposing respondents to pre- and post-publication exposure advertising. As noted in this chapter, Lucas published multiple studies over the course of 2 decades and his research contributed signifi cantly to knowledge of advertising response at that time. He became the fi rst technical director for the Advertising Research Foundation (ARF).

Welch (1941) recommended that ad copy testing employ four known scales as a system of measurement rather than rely on any one scale. Th ese four measures consisted of brand familiarity (Geissler 1917; Hotchkiss & Franken 1923, 1927), brand preference (Link 1932; Laird cited in Poffenberger 1932; Market Research Corporation of America 1935), theme familiarity (from Link's triple associates test (Link 1932, 1934), and theme credence (Link 1932; Market Research Corporation of America, 1937). In 1941 and 1942 the New York Times ran split-run copy tests providing an opportunity to reply and obtain a free sample. Employing similar ads advertising "False Teeth" or "Dental Plate," in both cases "False Teeth" was slightly stronger in number of replies. Zubin and Peatman (1945), citing these studies, developed and tested a more statistically valid method for using split run copy testing data. Th ey concluded by off ering a number of important assumptions to include the randomness of the samples drawn from the population, equal numbers of potential buyers of the product, the availability and inclusion of the maximum size of the sample of potential buyers, and that clipping the coupon is a direct result of the advertisement and not some other factor. FOCUS ON PREFERENCE Several researchers during this period addressed how consumers were reacting to various packaging types, primarily as viewed in the size and shape of glass containers. In an earlier book published in 1928, Franken and Larrabee reviewed initial thoughts about packaging and a procedure to consider packaging preference. Employing an accepted method from Franken and Larrabee (1928), Hovde (1931) conducted a controlled fi eld study to fi nd the "best all-around" glass container. He employed multiple examples of caviar and herring containers representing two sizes, 4 oz. and 10 oz. Th e study was conducted in grocery stores in Philadelphia, beginning with 70 women and 30 men. It is interesting to note that Hovde kept adding groups of respondents to the initial sample until the results became consistent. Hovde began by instructing potential respondents as to the necessity of fi nding a container that allowed for complete extraction of what was contained inside. His fi rst question sought to address attention value by inquiring as to "which container your attention is most forcibly drawn." Ranking every container employing an order of preference method, respondents were also asked for their reasons for their selection. A second question sought to uncover degree of identifi cation by measuring which container could best be remembered if one forgot the trade name. In one of the fi rst studies on consumption and children, Guest (1942, 1944) surveyed over 800 school children from 3rd grade through the senior year in high school to assess degree of loyalty to brands versus product class. His results revealed that 1) brand loyalty was stronger than product class loyalty, 2) children form loyalty to brands at an early age, and 3) loyalty evolves and strengthens over time. FOCUS ON MOTIVATION Th e focus on consumer motives began to take hold in the United States with the hiring of Viennese psychologist Ernest Dichter by the Getchell agency in 1940 (see Allen 1941). Dichter sought clues into human motivation by questioning selected "indicator groups," individuals who would be proactive in providing insights into product usage. Dichter used this information to provide a "psychological inventory" of basic motives for specifi c product purchases. Th is information in turn, would help advertising creatives develop messages that would directly address the customer motives (a fuller description of Dichter's contribution appears in the next section).

In 1941, Allen authored an article that applied Allport's (1937) notion of functional autonomy to better understanding consumer motives. In this paper, Allen presents a list of "primary wants" that are more direct (e.g., appetizing food, comfortable surroundings, welfare of loved ones, social approval, play) and "secondary wants" that are more removed (e.g., health, convenience, cleanliness, style/beauty, dependability/quality). Allen provides examples of typical product/service appeals that would provide the linkage between product/service and motive. In the years leading up to World War II, numerous European scholars like Lazersfeld, Dichter, and Politz (the European pollster) fl ed from their home countries to the United States and to American universities or industry. Th e nature of consumer research was also changing as former academics like George Gallup and Daniel Starch pioneered the profi table marketing research industry. THE EARLY YEARS AFTER WORLD WAR II During the fi nal phase of this review (post-World War II–1960), we return to two major contributors to the discipline of consumer psychology and a number of smaller, but nonetheless, important players. Ernest Dichter Considered by many a founding father of motivational research, Ernest Dichter was born in Vienna in 1907 and lived across the street from Sigmund Freud's famous offi ce. Dichter discovered early he had a strong interest in psychology. Aft er completing his doctoral studies, he began his career as a practicing psychoanalyst. Indeed his dissertation topic was a "self-appraisal of one's own abilities." He soon found his way to work under Paul Lazarfeld's Vienna centre for industrial research. Dichter immigrated to New York in 1937 where he quickly found he was invited to consult with major companies about his insights into the psychology of the consumer. Dichter was quite controversial. Denouncing all marketing research except his own as "nosecounting and "census-taking" (Fullerton & Stern, 1990, cited in Kassarjian, 1994), he became a highly vocal proponent of his own methodology which relied heavily on Freudian psychology (Stern, 2004). Indeed, his own mentor, Paul Lazersfeld became one of his harshest critics, along with researchers Gallup, Politz, and the Marketing discipline's Wroe Alderson (Ferber & Wales, 1958; Kassarjian, 1994) To better understand human motivation, Dichter employed in-depth interviews and projective techniques to tap both conscious and subconscious states thought to guide the behavior of the consumer. He felt that his background in psychoanalysis provided him with insights into hidden motives behind purchasing behavior. From this understanding, he was able to work with advertisers to create impactful brand slogans— "Wash your troubles away" for Procter & Gamble's Ivory Soap. From 1943 to 1946 Dichter was employed by the Columbia Broadcasting System (CBS). In 1946, Dichter founded his Institute for Motivational Research on the Hudson River just north of New York City. A Harvard Business Review article (Dichter 1947) refl ected his belief that past methods only scratch the surface and that advertising and personal selling have dynamic eff ects on the consumer. He also pointed out the importance of multiple motives and refl ects that Freud's multiple levels of consciousness provide reason for the importance of "modern" (qualitative) psychological methods. Dichter (1948) also employed multiple techniques (i.e., depth interviewing, role playing, sociometric maps) to discover what he termed the "real" reasons are behind brand purchasing.

Vance Packard's Th e Hidden Persuaders (1957) made Dichter a household name, suggesting that Dichter was the master manipulator of the consumer mind. Packard brought Dichter a signifi cant amount of fame and fortune, creating a signifi cant corporate demand for his consulting services. He published several books, with the Handbook of Consumer Motivation (1964) perhaps the most popular and most widely cited. It is important to note that Dichter's research went far beyond just the study of the consumer. His work also refl ected the study of human motives behind topics like voter participation, religious tolerance, and racial prejudice. Dichter, always the business man, founded multiple research institutes in Europe as well the Hudson River Institute. Many of these are still active today. George Katona George Katona is considered to be the dean of behavioral economics. Aft er an receiving a degree in law from the University of Budapest, he received his PhD in Germany under Georg Elias Nathanael Muller at Gottingen in 1921 following in the tradition of Wundt and Titchner. He came to the United States in 1933 and started employment as an investment counselor. In 1936, he began lecturing at the New School for Social Research and was heavily infl uenced by his colleague, the Gestalt psychologist Max Wertheimer. Wertheimer (and other gestalt psychologists), along with Watson's behaviorism and Freud's dynamic approach, had begun to successfully turn psychology away from the experimental work that followed the tradition of Wundt and Titchner (Boring, 1950). In 1945, Katona joined the faculty at the University of Michigan. Katona, along with Likert, Campbell and others, founded Michigan's Business Survey Research Bureau, and he became the director of the economic behavioral program. His pioneering achievement was in the application of consumer psychology to economic forecasting. In contrast to existing economic theory that relied chiefl y on factual demographic driven input (e.g., income, ability to buy), Katona believed that a consumer's willingness to buy, as denoted by the consumer's attitudes and expectations (his view of consumer psychology), was a critical economic indicator. Katona authored numerous articles during his lifetime and published more than a dozen books including Th e Powerful Consumer (1960) and Th e Mass Consumption Psychology (1964).Th ese books contained his caution to other economists as well as practitioners against stereotyping consumers as having simplistic motives and being easily manipulated. Perhaps Katona's most enduring legacy was his initiation of the Survey of Consumer Attitudes for the University of Michigan Institute for Social Research, today employed as a major indicator of economic stability of markets. THE CONTRIBUTION OF OTHERS DURING THIS PERIOD Immediately following the war came an emphasis on consumption by U.S. citizens who had just experienced several lean years of sacrifi ce. An explosion of manufacturing and new products led to new applied questions; for example, could the consumer discriminate in taste for food and drink. Pronko and Bowles reported three studies investigating whether drinkers of colas could discriminate between brands (Pronko & Bowles, 1948, 1949; Bowles & Pronko, 1948). It is not clear whether they gave respondents varied strategies for taste testing, but the results consistently refl ected that there was no consistency in consumer discrimination of brands of cola. Another important question that emerged during this time was based on the need to determine why consumers patronized certain retail stores. Heidingsfi eld (1949) surveyed patrons of downtown Philadelphia department stores to ascertain the motives for store selection. In rank order the factors included the nature of merchandise, prices, physical factors, and service. Blankertz (1949) reports a similar study by a group at his own university, but challenges both of these studies on issues of methodology. He provides several examples such as the notion that attitudes are relatively weak refl ections of other important contributing factors like distance. He also argued against the wisdom of depending on attitude scores given their lack of ability to predict store expenditures, and the belief that reports of attitudes may refl ect rationalization rather than other internal states (e.g., aff ect). In 1950, Mason Haire published his famous article in the Journal of Marketing that called into question people's willingness to share their real responses. With the advent of instant coff ee and consumers' reluctance to adopt it, studies suggested that taste was the reason. However, Haire was skeptical of this fi nding and designed a projective test to see if there were other underlying reasons. He employed two groups of homemakers, both of whom were provided with a shopping list. All the products on the list were held constant except that one list contained Nescafe Instant Coff ee while the other contained "1 lb. Maxwell House Coff ee (Drip Ground)." He then asked his two sample segments to describe a person who would be shopping for these products. Th e respondents with the Maxwell House Coff ee on their list consistently described the person in more positive terms (e.g., housewife, concerned about what she served her family) than did those who received the list with Nescafe Instant Coff ee (e.g., single woman living from one day to the next). Th ere was no indication that taste was a factor. Th e real reason had much more to do with how a person using instant coff ee would be perceived. In 1952, Dik Twedt from Northwestern University conducted a survey study of 34 variables believed to be related to magazine readership scores. Prior to this, there were a number of individuals, including James D. Woolf, formerly the vice-president of the J. Walter Th ompson advertising agency, claiming that content, rather than mechanical factors, were what pulled individuals to read ads (Woolf, 1951, see also earlier study by Ferguson, 1935). Using a popular trade magazine, Twedt's study actually revealed that a signifi cant portion of explained variance for readership was due to three mechanical factors, size of advertisement, number of colors, and square inches of illustration. It is also of interest that Dik Twedt (1965) authored .

2

CONSUMER INFORMATION PROCESSING

People's judgments and decisions are typically based on only a small subset of the knowledge they could potentially apply. Furthermore, when they receive new judgment-relevant information, they construe its implications without considering all of the alternative interpretations it might have. Th e concepts and knowledge they employ in each case are not necessarily either the most relevant or the most reliable, but rather, are the cognitions that come most easily to mind. Th is general tendency, which has been documented at all stages of information processing from the initial acquisition and comprehension of information to the generation of an overt response, is one of the most widely accepted phenomena to emerge in the past three decades of psychological research (Bargh, 1997; Higgins, 1996; Wyer, 2004). Nowhere is its importance greater than in the domain of consumer judgment and decision making. Th at is, purchase decisions, like judgments and behavior more generally, are oft en based on whatever criteria happen to be salient at the time. Because of its pervasiveness, the role of knowledge accessibility is a central component of almost every theoretical formulation of social information processing to appear in the past three decades, ranging from general formulations of judgment and behavior (Bargh, 1997; Carlston, 1994; Smith, 1990; Wyer, 2004; Wyer & Srull, 1989) to more specifi c formulations of attitude formation and change (Chaiken, 1987; Petty & Cacioppo, 1986), attitude-behavior relations (Fazio,

1990), impression formation (Higgins, Rholes, & Jones, 1977; Srull & Wyer, 1979), stereotype activation and suppression (Bodenhausen & Macrae, 1998), the eff ects of the media on perceptions of social reality (Shrum, 2002), the impact of aff ect and subjective experience on judgments and decisions (Schwarz, 2004; Schwarz & Clore, 1996; Strack & Deutsch, 2004), goal-directed behavior (Chartrand & Bargh, 2002), cultural infl uences on behavioral decisions (Briley & Wyer, 2002; Hong, Morris, Chiu, & Benet-Martinez, 2000), and perspective eff ects in judgment (Adaval & Monroe, 2002). In the area of consumer research, the role of knowledge accessibility is implicit if not explicit in research on subliminal advertising (Moore, 1982, 1988; Trappey, 1996; see also Vargas, this volume), brand awareness (Kardes, Gurumurthy, Chandrashekaran, & Dronoff , 1993), pricing (Adaval & Monroe, 2002), and product evaluation more generally. Extensive reviews of theory and research on knowledge accessibility are available elsewhere (Higgins, 1996; see also Bargh, 1994, 1997; Förster & Liberman, in press; Wyer, 2004), and we will not repeat this material unnecessarily. Th e fi rst section of this chapter reviews alternative conceptualizations of knowledge accessibility phenomena, drawing largely from research and theory in cognitive and social psychology. Later sections provide examples of the role of knowledge accessibility at several diff erent stages of information processing, including the attention to and comprehension of information, the representation of the information in memory, the computation of inferences on the basis of previously acquired knowledge, and behavior decisions. In the course of this discussion, we review representative research and theory in consumer judgment and decision-making in which diff erences in knowledge accessibility come into play. GENERAL CONSIDERATIONS Stages of Information Processing Th e processing of information for the purpose of making a judgment or decision can occur in several stages. For example: 1. Attention—people pay diff ering amounts of attention to the various aspects of the information they receive. 2. Encoding and comprehension—people interpret individual pieces of information in terms of previously formed concepts that they exemplify, and may organize clusters of features with reference to a more general knowledge structure or "schema." Th us, they might interpret a $70 pair of jeans as expensive, or comprehend a temporally related sequence of events that occur at a restaurant in terms of a prototypic "restaurant script" (Schank & Abelson, 1977). 3. Inference—people oft en infer the likelihood that a statement or assertion is true, or the frequency with which a particular event has occurred. At the same time, they estimate the likelihood that an event will occur in the future, or that a certain state of aff airs did or does exist. Th ey sometimes infer that an object has a particular attribute, or might evaluate it as either favorable or unfavorable. In other cases, they make a comparative judgment of several objects or events along a given dimension, or might compute a preference for one alternative over another. 4. Response processes—people transform the implications of their subjective judgment into an overt response or behavioral decision. Processing at each of these stages typically requires the activation and use of previously acquired concepts and knowledge. Th erefore, it may depend in part on which of several potentially relevant subsets of this knowledge happens to be most accessible. TYPES OF KNOWLEDGE REPRESENTATIONS Th e knowledge that comes into play at these stages of processing can be of two general types. Declarative knowledge concerns the referents of everyday life experiences (persons, objects, events, attitudes and values, oneself, etc.). In contrast, procedural knowledge refers to the sequence of actions that one performs in pursuit of a particular goal (driving a car, using a word processor, etc.) Whereas declarative knowledge is refl ected in the information we can recall about an entity or that we implicitly draw upon in the course of attaining a particular objective, procedural knowledge is refl ected in the sequence of cognitive or motor acts that are performed in the pursuit of this objective. People can, of course, have declarative knowledge about how to attain a particular objective, and might sometimes consult this knowledge for use as a behavioral guide. Once the procedure is well learned, however, it may oft en be applied automatically, with little if any conscious cognitive mediation. Th ese automated procedures can be conceptualized as "productions" of the sort suggested by J. R. Anderson (1982, 1983; see also Smith, 1990, 1994). Th us, they may be metaphorically have the form of "If [X], then [Y]" rules in which [X] is a confi guration of perceptual or cognitive stimulus features and [Y] is a sequence of cognitive or motor acts that are elicited automatically when the eliciting conditions are met. Th ese productions, which are acquired through learning, are strengthened by repetition, and can ultimately be activated and applied with minimal cognitive mediation. Th e routines involved in driving a car (e.g., putting in the clutch, turning on the ignition, putting the car in gear, gradually releasing the clutch while stepping on the gas, etc.) initially require conscious thought. However, they ultimately come to be performed without consulting declarative knowledge about the sequence of steps involved, and require few if any cognitive resources (Schneider & Shiff rin, 1977). As Bargh (1997) argues, a very large amount of our social behavior is likely to involve the use of these automatically activated productions. Th e infl uence of both declarative knowledge and procedural knowledge is apparent at all of the aforementioned stages of processing. Many eff ects that are attributed to the accessibility of declarative could be due to the accessibility of procedural knowledge instead. In this chapter, we focus primarily on the accessibility of declarative knowledge (Smith, 1990). Nevertheless, the accessibility of procedural knowledge is likely to have a particularly important impact on overt behavior as will be seen. Declarative knowledge can consist of general semantic concepts (honest, woolen, etc.) or categories (lawyer, Irishman, high-tech, designer jeans, etc.) Alternatively, it could comprise a confi guration of features that are organized temporally, spatially or causally and are stored in memory and later retrieved as a unit. Th ese knowledge representations could pertain to a specifi c person or experience (e.g., George W. Bush, the 2004 Super Bowl game, my trip to Bermuda in 1985, last night's dinner at Jaspa's Restaurant) or a more general characterization that applies to several individuals or events (reactionary politicians, football games, vacation trips, restaurant visits). Representations of a situation-specifi c sequence of events may constitute a story (Schank & Abelson, 1995). However, more generalized sequences of events can function as implicit theories that convey the antecedents and consequences of diff erent types of experiences involving oneself or others (Dweck, 1991; Dweck, Chiu, & Hong, 1995; Ross, 1989; Wyer, 2004). Th ese representations come into play in not only comprehending new experiences but also reconstructing past events and predicting future ones. Other generalized event sequences can constitute plans or procedures that are used as behavioral guides in attaining a particular goal. Th e knowledge representations that people construct can be coded in diff erent modalities. Although much of our knowledge is coded verbally, a very large portion of it (particularly the knowledge we acquire through direct experience) is nonverbal, consisting of mental images that have both visual and acoustic components (Wyer & Radvansky, 1998). Finally, the knowledge we acquire can elicit subjective reactions (e.g., positive or negative aff ect) that, once experienced, can exert an infl uence on the processing of information at each of the stages listed earlier. Th ese reactions, once elicited, can be a major source of the information people use as a basis for judgments and decisions (Schwarz & Clore, 1996; Strack & Deutsch, 2004). On the other hand, they can infl uence the interpretation of information (Adaval, 2003; Isbell & Wyer, 1999), and the weight that people attach to it when making a judgment (Adaval, 2001). Although aff ect, or subjective experience more generally, is not itself a part of the knowledge one stores in memory, it can be elicited by this knowledge (Wyer, Clore, & Isbell, 1998). Its infl uence can nevertheless be conceptualized in terms very similar to that of other aspects of knowledge that people have accessible at the time they receive information and make a judgment or decision. Despite these diff erences in the content and structure of knowledge, the processes that govern its accessibility in memory are similar. In the next section, we propose a set of principles that describe these processes. Th ese principles potentially apply at all stages of processing. BASIC PRINCIPLES Several theories of information processing purport to account for the determinants and eff ects of knowledge accessibility (e.g., Higgins, Bargh, & Lombardi, 1985; Smith, 1990; Wyer & Carlston, 1979; Wyer & Srull, 1989; Wyer, 2004). Although these theories oft en make diff erent specifi c assumptions about the mechanisms that underlie memory storage and retrieval, they agree that the knowledge one retrieves and brings to bear on the processing of information is a function of its association with the thoughts and concepts that happen to be activated at the time the knowledge is sought. Th e cognitions that cue its retrieval can include aspects of the information to be processed and the situational context in which it is presented. Th ey can also be internally generated. For example, people who wish to purchase a car may intentionally retrieve a set of attributes that characterize a high quality automobile and use the attributes as guides in construing the implications of information about a particular car they are considering. In many cases, however, thoughts that one has recently had for another, objectively irrelevant purpose can also cue the retrieval of knowledge from memory. A fairly large number of concepts and knowledge representations can oft en be associated with a given set of retrieval cues, and people are usually neither able nor motivated to consider all of them. Th is observation leads to the most fundamental principle on which theory and research on knowledge accessibility is based: Principle 1. People rarely retrieve and use more knowledge than is necessary to attain the objective they are pursuing. When each of several knowledge representations is suffi cient to attain this objective, the fi rst representation that comes to mind is most likely to be applied. Th is means that if two or more diff erent concepts or knowledge representations can be used to attain a particular goal, the one that is identifi ed and applied most quickly and easily will be employed. For example, suppose to attribute concepts, "tasty" and "unhealthy" are equally applicable for interpreting information that a drink has artifi cial sweeteners. In this case, the one that comes to mind fi rst is most likely to be applied. Similarly, if several criteria (e.g., brand name, specifi c attributes) are potentially available for evaluating a product, the criteria that can be applied most easily are most likely to be considered. Principle 1 does not necessarily imply that the fi rst knowledge that comes to mind is the only knowledge to be employed. Th is is true only if it is deemed suffi cient to attain the objective one is pursuing. Chaiken (1987; Chaiken, Liberman, & Eagly, 1989) assumed that people who process information for a particular purpose fi rst invoke the criterion that they can apply most quickly and easily and evaluate their confi dence that the results of applying it is suffi cient to attain the objective they are pursuing. If their confi dence is above a minimum threshold, they use it without further ado. If their confi dence is below threshold, however, they apply the next most accessible criterion, and continue in this manner until their threshold is reached. Th e threshold that individuals apply in any given situation can increase with the importance of the goal to which the processing is relevant. It can also depend on the time and eff ort the person is able to devote to this activity. Th erefore, the less motivated people are to engage in extensive cognitive processing, or the less time they have available, the more likely they are to use the fi rst criterion they consider to the exclusion of others. Th e suffi ciency principle has broad applicability, and versions of it can be found in diverse theories of judgment, including the conception of satisfi cing (Simon, 1955) and the impact of aff ect on judgment (Schwarz & Clore, 1996). Its importance is apparent throughout this chapter. DETERMINANTS OF KNOWLEDGE ACCESSIBILITY Most theories agree on four determinants of knowledge accessibility: (1) the strength of association between the knowledge to be accessed and concepts that have already been activated in the situation at hand, (2) the recency with which knowledge has been acquired and used, (3) the frequency with which it has been employed, and (4) the amount of processing in which it has been directly or indirectly involved. Strength of Association As noted earlier, the accessibility of knowledge in memory at any given moment is determined in part by the strength of its association with situational, informational, or internally generated features that exist at the moment and, therefore, serve as implicit or explicit retrieval cues. Th ese associations may be either semantic or experience-based. Th us, for example, the word "bread" might cue the retrieval of "butter," and a picture of a yellow double arch is likely to stimulate a concept of McDonald's. Th e retrieval of such associated cognitions may be a conditioned cognitive response to the stimulus concept or cognition that is acquired through learning in much the same way as other, noncognitive responses. In many instances, however, the features of a stimulus are associated to a similar extent with more than one concept or unit of knowledge. In this case, other factors come into play. Recency and Frequency When two concepts or knowledge units are equally useful in attaining a particular processing objective, the one that has been used more recently in the past is likely to be applied again. Th is eff ect was fi rst identifi ed in social psychology by Higgins, Rholes, and Jones (1977). Th ey showed that unobtrusively exposing participants to a trait concept while they performed an ostensibly unrelated "priming" task* increased their use of this concept to interpret the information they later received about a fi ctitious target person and, consequently, infl uenced their liking for this person. Th ese eff ects have been identifi ed even when the concepts are primed subliminally (Bargh & Pietromonaco, 1982). Th e accessibility of knowledge can also be determined by the frequency with which a unit of knowledge has been activated and used in the past (Higgins et al., 1985; Srull &Wyer, 1979). Frequently encountered concepts and knowledge can become chronically accessible in memory (Higgins, King, & Mavin, 1982) and, therefore, can have eff ects independently of situational factors that might activate them (Bargh, Bond, Lombardi, & Tota, 1986). Th e cognitive processes that theoretically underlie the eff ects of frequency of use and the eff ects of recency of use may diff er (cf. Higgins et al., 1985; Wyer, 2004; Wyer & Srull, 1989). Consequently, these factors may contribute independently to their overall accessibility in memory (Bargh et al., 1986). However, THE INFLUENCE OF AWARENESS ON THE IMPACT OF ACCESSIBLE KNOWLEDGE People can be infl uenced by information that they do not know they have received. Bargh and his colleagues (for reviews, see Bargh, 1994, 1997) have identifi ed these eff ects at several diff erent stages of processing. For example, subliminally presented trait concepts can infl uence people's interpretation of information about a target person's behavior and, consequently, judgments of this person (Bargh & Pietromonaco, 1982); subliminally primed evaluative-toned concepts can aff ect the ease with which participants identify other words that are evaluative similar or dissimilar (Bargh, Chaiken, Raymond, & Hymens, 1996; Bargh, Chaiken, Govender, & Pratt, 1992). Subliminally priming high or low numbers can infl uence people's judgments of the expensiveness of a product they are later asked to evaluate (Adaval & Monroe, 2002), and subliminally exposing people to faces of a stereotyped group can infl uence the likelihood of behaving in ways that are characteristic of that group (Bargh, Chen, & Burrows, 1996). Corrections for Bias Even when people are exposed to information overtly, they may not be aware of its possible eff ect on their judgments in other, ostensibly unrelated situations. People are likely to assume that concepts and knowledge that come to mind when they think about a stimulus are activated by this stimulus alone. Consequently, they are likely to consider the implications of these cognitions to be representative of the knowledge they have available about the stimulus and, therefore, to be an appropriate basis for judgments and decisions they might make concerning it. Only if they are aware that the knowledge that comes to mind might be biased, will they try to correct for this infl uence. In such cases, they might discount implications of the knowledge entirely and search for alternative criteria to use. Lombardi, Higgins, and Bargh (1987), for example, found that when participants were able to recall the priming words to which they had been exposed (suggesting that they were aware of their possible infl uence), they were actually less likely to use the primed concepts to interpret the stimulus information than they otherwise would have been. In some instances, however, participants may believe that their interpretation of information might be biased but are either unmotivated or unable to correct for it. In a series of studies by Martin, Seta, and Celia (1990), for example, participants were clearly aware that the concepts they had employed in an ostensibly irrelevant task could infl uence their interpretation of the information they received subsequently. In these conditions, the primed concepts only had a positive infl uence on their judgments when participants were either unable to devote the cognitive eff ort required to identify and use a diff erent concept (e.g., under high situational distraction) or, alternatively, were unmotivated to expend this eff ort (e.g., they were low in need for cognition, or felt little personal responsibility for the judgments to be made). In a particularly intriguing demonstration of these contingencies, Martin (1986) primed trait concepts using procedures similar to those employed by Martin et al. (1990). However, some participants were ostensibly interrupted before they completed the priming task, whereas others were led to believe they had fi nished it. (In fact, all participants were exposed to the same number of primes, regardless of whether they were interrupted or not.) Participants who were interrupted apparently continued to ruminate about the task (Zeigarnik, 1938), and this cognitive activity prevented them from searching for alternative concepts to use in interpreting the target information they received subsequently. Th us, the primed concepts had a positive impact on the judgments they made on the basis of this information. When participants believed they had completed the priming task, however, they did not ruminate about it and devoted their cognitive resources to arrive at an unbiased interpretation of the target information. Consequently, the priming eff ects observed under interrupted-task conditions were not evident. Rather than searching for alternative judgmental criteria to use, people who believe their judgments may be biased may sometimes fi nd it easier to make a tentative judgment and then to adjust this judgment to compensate for the eff ects that the judgment-irrelevant knowledge is likely to have had. In this case, however, they may not know how much to adjust. If they do not adjust enough, the knowledge will continue to exert an infl uence. If they adjust too much, it could have a negative, contrast eff ect (Ottati & Isbell, 1986). Which eff ect occurs is likely to depend in part on individuals' implicit theories of the amount of bias produced by the external situational factors in question (Wegener & Petty, 1997; see also Strack, 1992). Adjustment processes of particular relevance for consumer research were identifi ed by Schwarz and Bless (1992; see also Strack et al., 1993). When people are exposed to items in an opinion survey, questions that occur at one point in the survey may activate concepts that are used as a basis for responses to later questions. However, if respondents are aware of this infl uence, they may try to correct for it. Indeed, they may believe that the questioner does not intend to ask the same question twice. In this case, they may use diff erent criteria in responding to the questions even if the questions appear related.

Several other studies provide evidence of this eff ect. Strack, Martin, and Schwarz (1988; Strack & Martin, 1987), for example, asked participants to report their satisfaction with their marriage and also their satisfaction with life as a whole. When the questions appeared on separate pages of the questionnaire, responses to the questions were correlated .55. When the second question immediately followed the fi rst, however, the correlation was reduced to .26. Respondents in the latter case apparently assumed they should use diff erent criteria for evaluating their life as a whole than they used in responding to the fi rst item, and consequently excluded their marriage from consideration. Similarly, Ottati, Riggle, Wyer, Schwarz, and Kuklinski (1989) found that asking participants their opinions about the rights of a positive or negative social group (e.g., whether the American Civil Liberties Union or the American Nazi Party should be allowed to speak on campus) had a positive infl uence on their responses to a general question (whether people should be allowed to express their views in public) when the items were separated by six other, unrelated ones. When the group-specifi c item immediately preceded the general one, however, participants appeared to exclude the group from consideration in responding to the general question. As a result, the groupspecifi c item had a negative, contrast eff ect on their responses. Th e methodological implications of these fi ndings are obvious. In much research on consumer behavior, multiple items are used to assess the same construct (e.g., liking for a product). Th is is done under the assumption that the use of several related provides a more reliable estimate of the construct of concern. In fact, however, by stimulating participants to use diff erent criteria for responding to the items than they otherwise might, the procedure could oft en have precisely the opposite eff ect. To summarize: Principle 4. Knowledge that becomes accessible in memory for reasons that are unrelated to a judgment or decision will infl uence this judgment or decision if participants either are unaware of the conditions that activated the knowledge or, alternatively, are unaware of the relation between these conditions and the judgment or decision to be made. Even if people are aware of the biasing infl uence of judgment-irrelevant knowledge, they may not be motivated or able to correct for its infl uence or, alternatively, may not know how much they should adjust their response to compensate for its eff ect. Th e contingencies implied by Principle 4 should not be overemphasized. As we noted earlier, people are unlikely to pay much attention to the extraneous situational factors that infl uence the knowledge they bring to bear on their judgments and decisions. Rather, they attribute the accessibility of this knowledge to the person or object they are judging. Consequently, the infl uence of extraneous determinants of knowledge accessibility may be quite pervasive. Th e Eff ects of Th ought Suppression on Knowledge Accessibility People who consciously try to avoid the use of a concept or body of knowledge in interpreting information or making a judgment are oft en successful. However, active attempts to avoid using a judgmental criterion oft en require thinking about the criterion to be avoided. Th e eff ort expended in an attempt to suppress its use can actually increase its accessibility in memory relative to conditions in which this eff ort is not made. Consequently, once the restrictions on its use are lift ed, the suppressed concept or knowledge may be more likely to be used than it otherwise would. Th is possibility, which was identifi ed empirically by Wegner (1994), was applied in an innovative series of studies by Macrae, Bodenhausen, and their colleagues (for a review, see Bodenhausen & Macrae, 1998). In one set of studies (Macrae, Bodenhausen, Milne, & Jetten, 1994), participants received a picture of a skinhead along with other verbal information and were told to form an impression of the person. However, some participants were told explicitly not to rely on a stereotype in arriving at their impression. Th eir judgments of the target indicated that the instructions were successful. Nevertheless, they responded more quickly than control participants to stereotype-related words in a subsequent word-identifi cation task. Furthermore, they described a second skinhead more stereotypically once the restriction on the use of this stereotype was lift ed, and avoided sitting close to a skinhead while waiting for a later part of the experiment. In short, the active suppression of a stereotype-related knowledge actually increased its accessibility in memory, and this knowledge infl uenced both later judgments and behavioral decisions once the sanctions against using it were removed. Th e four principles summarized in this section typically apply independently of the type of knowledge involved and the type of judgment or decision to which this knowledge is applied. In the following sections, we review representative studies in both psychology and consumer research that bear on the eff ects of knowledge accessibility at diff erent stages of processing. In this context, we note some additional considerations that arise in conceptualizing the eff ects at these stages. ATTENTIONAL PROCESSES Selective Information Seeking Individual pieces of information are more likely to be identifi ed and thought about if they can be interpreted in terms of concepts and knowledge that are easily accessible in memory. Th is may be true even if the other information available is equally relevant to the goal one is pursuing. Th e concepts that exert this bias could be activated either by the particular goal one is pursuing and by goal-irrelevant situational factors that happen to make these concepts come to mind. Th e Eff ect of Goals on Selective Attention Th e bias produced by goal-directed information seeking was demonstrated by Snyder, Swann, and their colleagues (Snyder, 1981; Snyder & Swann, 1978; Swann & Giuliano, 1987). Suppose people wish to decide if a person or object belongs to a certain category (e.g., extrovert, good secretary, high quality DVD player, etc.). To make this assessment, they are likely to activate a set of attributes that characterize members of this category and to search for information that can be encoded in terms of these attributes. At the same time, they may be disposed to ignore information that is not interpretable in terms of category-consistent features. Th us, for example, people who want to determine if someone is an extravert may activate attribute concepts such as "talks a lot," "likes parties," "says hello to strangers on the street," etc.) and may search for information that can be interpreted in terms of these concepts. In doing so, they may ignore information that is interpretable in terms of attributes that might disconfi rm the target's membership (e.g., "goes for long walks alone," "avoids large crowds," etc.) Th is selective search could produce a bias in the conclusions that are drawn. Snyder and Swann (1978; see also Swann & Giuliano, 1987) gave some participants the opportunity to select questions to ask a person for the purpose of deciding if the person was an extravert, and gave others the opportunity to select questions to decide if (s)he was an introvert. Participants selected questions that presupposed the attribute they were attempting to evaluate (e.g., "What do you like about parties?") and, therefore, were likely to elicit answers that confi rmed the person's membership in the category they were considering (Snyder & Swann, 1978). Alternatively, they selected questions, affi rmative answers to which provided this confi rmation (e.g., "Do you like parties?") (Swann & Giuliano, 1987). In another study (Snyder & Cantor, 1979), participants read a paragraph about a person that contained equal amounts of extraverted and introverted behavioral descriptions with instructions either to decide if the person was an extravert or to decide if she was an introvert. Th ey paid more attention to descriptions that confi rmed the person's membership in the specifi c category they were considering, as inferred from both their judgments and the information they later identifi ed as relevant to these judgments. Initial preferences can operate in much the same way as hypotheses. Chernev (2001), for example, found that participants with an initial preference for a product tended to pay greater attention to information that confi rmed their preference than to information that disconfi rmed it, thus biasing the eff ects of the information in the direction of their initial attitude. Similarly, Yeung and Wyer (2004) found that consumers who had formed an initial impression of a product on the basis of a picture later recalled information about the product's specifi c attributes that was consistent with this impression rather than inconsistent with it. A quite diff erent demonstration of the impact of goal-directed processing on selective attention to information was provided by Ross, Lepper, Strack, and Steinmetz (1971). Participants read a clinical case study with instructions to explain either why the protagonist might have committed suicide aft er leaving therapy or, alternatively, why he might have donated a large sum of money to the Peace Corps. Later, they were asked to predict the likelihood that the protagonist engaged in a number of activities, including the one they had considered earlier. Participants were given convincing evidence that neither the experimenter nor anyone else actually knew what had happened to the protagonist aft er leaving therapy. Nevertheless, they predicted the outcome they had explained to be more likely than the outcomes they had not explained. Participants in generating their explanation selectively attended to features that were consistent with this explanation. Later, they used this selective subset of features as a basis for their prediction to the exclusion of other information that had been presented. Th e Impact of Aff ect on Selective Attention When people's processing objectives do not bias the information to which they attend, goal-irrelevant factors may have an impact. One such factor may be the aff ective reactions that people happen to be experiencing at the time the information is received. A study by Bower, Gilligan, and Monteiro (1981) is illustrative. Participants under hypnosis were instructed to recall a past experience that made them feel either happy or sad and then to maintain these feelings aft er they were brought out of their hypnotic state. Th en they read a passage about two persons that described both happy events and unhappy events that occurred to them. Finally, they recalled the information they had read. Participants who had been induced to feel happy recalled a greater proportion of positivelyvalenced events, and a lower proportion of negatively-valenced events, than did participants who were induced to feel sad. It is unclear whether these eff ects were due to the aff ect that participants were experiencing per se or to the semantic concepts that were activated in the course of inducing these feelings (e.g., Niedenthal & Setterlund, 1994; Niedenthal, Halberstadt, & Setterlund, 1997; Wyer, Clore, & Isbell, 1999). Be that as it may, the study provides strong evidence that concepts activated by experiences of which participants were not consciously aware can bias the information they later identify and encode into memory.

In a study of greater relevance to consumer judgment (Adaval, 2001), participants who had been induced to feel happy or unhappy were later asked to judge an article of clothing that was described by an attribute that was either likely to be evaluated on the basis of subjective criteria (e.g., how it felt to wear it) or not. Participants weighted attributes more heavily in making their judgments if the aff ect they elicited was similar to the aff ect they were experiencing than if it was not. Th us, as in Bower et al.'s (1978) study, participants appeared to give more attention to information that was aff ectively congruent with the feelings they were experiencing for other, unrelated reasons, and so this information had more impact on the judgments they reported later. Th e aforementioned studies converge on the conclusion that people with a specifi c subset of concepts accessible in memory (either because of a goal they are pursuing or for other, unrelated reasons) oft en give greater attention to aspects of information that can be easily encoded in terms of these concepts, and so the information has greater impact on judgments and decisions than it otherwise would. Selective attention to information that can be interpreted along an accessible dimension could occur as well. Evidence that persons interpret individual product attributes along dimensions that happen to be accessible in memory was obtained by Park, Yoon, Kim, and Wyer (2001) in a study to be described in more detail presently. Categorical vs. Piecemeal Information Processing Th e impact of aff ect on selective attention can result from other processes as well. Bless (2001)suggests that people who experience positive aff ect tend to use broader, categorical criteria for judgment than others do. Th is could result from a more general disposition to perceive the world as unproblematic and, therefore, to believe it is unnecessary to consider information in detail in order to make a judgment (Schwarz & Clore, 1990). In the consumer domain, this suggests a tendency for persons who experience positive aff ect to give more weight to global judgmental criteria (e.g., brand name, country of origin, etc.) than to specifi c attribute information. However, although this appears to be true, it is not for the reason that Schwarz and Clore's (1990) conceptualization suggests. Tesser (1978) suggests that people tend to evaluate a stimulus more extremely aft er thinking about it more extensively. If this is so, and if positive aff ect increases the attention to categorical bases for judgment, people may think about this information more extensively at the time it is presented and, therefore, may perceive its implications to be more extreme. Th is shift in the interpretation of the information could lead it to have greater impact independently of the weight attached to it at the time of judgment. Adaval (2003) confi rmed this possibility. She employed procedures developed by Anderson (1971, 1981) to distinguish between the scale values assigned to individual pieces of information (an indication of their evaluative implications) and the weight attached to them at the time of judgment.

Inducing participants to experience positive aff ect at the time they received product information increased the extremity of the evaluative implications they attached to brand name without aff ecting the weight they attached to it. (Th at is, they evaluated favorable brands more favorably, and unfavorable brands more unfavorably, than control subjects did.) Moreover, once this interpretation was made, its impact persisted over time, as implied by Principle 3. Th us, participants who had received information about a product's brand name were asked 24 hours later to indicate their preference for this product and another that was normatively similar to it favorableness. Participants who had been happy at the time they considered the fi rst product preferred it to the second product if the products' brand names were both normatively favorable. However, they preferred the second product to the fi rst if the products' brand names were both unfavorable.THE INTERPRETATION OF AMBIGUOUS INFORMATION Several examples of the eff ect of attribute concept accessibility on the interpretation of ambiguous information were provided in our general discussion of knowledge accessibility earlier in this chapter (cf. Bargh & Pietromonaco, 1982; Higgins et al., 1977; Srull & Wyer, 1979) and do not need to be reiterated. However, some additional considerations warrant further consideration. DIMENSIONAL VS. CATEGORY ACCESSIBILITY Information can be ambiguous in terms of both the attribute dimension to which it pertains and the value it implies along this dimension (Higgins & Brendl, 1995). Th e attribute information "50% more banana fl avoring," for example, has implications for both taste and healthfulness. Along a dimension of taste, however, it could be interpreted either favorably (as sweet) or unfavorably (as too sweet). Th e dimension along which the attribute description is interpreted may depend on whether health-related or taste-related concepts are more accessible in memory at the time. An additional consideration arises, however. People are likely to interpret the aforementioned product description more favorably if concepts associated with good taste have been primed than if concepts associated with bad taste have been primed. However, the attribute's implications along a dimension of healthfulness are unambiguously negative. In this case, what eff ect does priming "healthy" have, as opposed to priming "unhealthy?" Many bipolar attribute concepts ("bad" vs. "good,", "hot" vs. "cold, etc.) may be strongly associated in memory (Colombo & Williams, 1990). To this extent, priming one of these concepts may activate the second as well. In the present example, "healthy" and "unhealthy" might be strongly associated. If this is so, priming both concepts might increase the tendency to interpret the attribute described by "50% more banana fl avoring" as unhealthy. Park et al. (2001, Experiment 2) showed this to be true. Participants received materials that activated concepts associated with good taste, bad taste, good health, or bad health. Th en, as part of an ostensibly unrelated experiment, they received an ad that contained a description of a milk product similar to that in the preceding example. Th at is, it had ambiguous implication for taste but clearly implied that the product was unhealthy. Aft er seeing the ad, participants fi rst generated an openended description of the product and then evaluated it. Participants who had been primed with a taste-related concept were more likely to describe the product in terms of this concept rather than its bipolar opposite. In contrast, participants who had been primed with a health-related concept were likely to describe the product as unhealthy regardless of whether good health or bad health was primed. Furthermore, their overall evaluations of the product were aff ected in the manner suggested by their open-ended attribute descriptions. ASSIMILATION AND CONTRAST Park et al's (2001) study provides an example of conditions in which activating a concept can have a contrast eff ect on the interpretation of information. (Th at is, priming "healthy" led participants to judge the product as more unhealthy, and to evaluate it more unfavorably, than they otherwise would.) However, contrast eff ects can also occur for other reasons. Herr (1986), for example, exposed participants to names of either moderately hostile individuals (e.g., Mohammed Ali) or extremely hostile persons (e.g., Adolf Hitler) before they evaluated a person whose behaviors were ambiguous with respect to hostility. Although priming moderately hostile exemplars had a positive impact on participants' judgments of the target's hostility, priming extremely hostile exemplars had a contrast eff ect. Th ere are two interpretations of these fi ndings. First, when the implications of a concept are so extreme that the concept cannot be applied to stimulus information, it may be used as a standard of comparison. As a result, the stimulus might be assigned a lower value along the dimension of judgment than it would if the standard were more moderate. Second, standards of comparison are more likely to be used when the priming stimuli are people or objects of the same type as the target rather than general attribute concepts of the sort that were primed in the studies by Higgins and others (Moskowitz & Skurnik, 1999; Stapel & Koomen, 1997). In Herr's study, participants may have interpreted the target's behavior in terms of the attribute concepts activated by the priming stimuli in all conditions, regardless of the extremity of these stimuli. Once this interpretation was made, however, they may have spontaneously compared the target to the type of persons described in the priming task, and this eff ect may have overridden the eff ect of the primed concepts on the interpretation of the information at an earlier stage of processing. DESCRIPTIVE VS. EVALUATIVE ENCODING Th e criteria that people bring to bear on the interpretation of information can be either descriptive or evaluative. Th us, "stole a magazine from the newsstand" could be interpreted either as "dishonest" or, more generally, as "bad." Similarly, "60 miles per gallon," could be interpreted as either "fuel effi cient" or "desirable." Normally, the concepts that are accessible at the time information is fi rst interpreted are likely to infl uence evaluations only if they are descriptively applicable. In the aforementioned study by Higgins et al. (1977), for example, priming trait concepts such as adventurous or reckless aff ected the interpretation of information that a person wanted to cross the Atlantic in a sailboat, but priming evaluatively toned but descriptively inapplicable concepts ("kind," "hostile," etc.) did not. Th ere are two qualifi cations on this conclusion, however. 1. Once information about a stimulus is interpreted in terms of concepts that are accessible at the time, the stimulus may be attributed the characteristic implied by the interpretation. Once this occurs, the stimulus may be inferred to have other characteristics that are descriptively irrelevant to the primed concept but have become associated with this type of stimulus through learning. Th us, for example, priming a concept of hostility could aff ect the interpretation of a target person's behaviors that were ambiguous with respect to this particular attribute. If the target is inferred to be a "hostile person" on the basis of this interpretation, he may then be attributed other characteristics that have nothing to do with hostility per se but are stereotypically associated with individuals who possess this attribute (Srull & Wyer, 1979, 1980). 2. Traits with extreme evaluative implications may be spontaneously associated with a concept that summarizes these implications through learning. In these circumstances, priming the trait concept may spontaneously activate the evaluative concept that is associated with it as well. Th us, for example, "malevolent" may activate a negative evaluative concept ("bad"). Th e latter concept, once activated, could then infl uence the interpretation of information that is ambiguous with respect to other attributes that have evaluative implications (Stapel & Koomen, 2000). GOAL?ACTIVATED PRIMING EFFECTS To reiterate, people's goals at the time they receive information can activate concepts that are relevant to these goals. Th ese concepts may infl uence not only which information they encode into memory, as noted in the preceding section (Snyder & Cantor, 1979) but also the interpretation of information to which the concepts apply. A study by Higgins and Rholes (1978) exemplifi es these eff ects. Participants who had read a passage about a target person that was ambiguous with respect to the traits it implied were told to describe the person to another who either liked or disliked him. Th ey communicated their description in terms that were evaluatively consistent with the attitude of the individual to whom they were communicating. As a consequence, both their own liking for the person and their memory for the original information were biased toward the implications of the communication they had prepared. Th is bias was not evident when participants anticipated writing a communication about the person but did not actually do so. Th us, their interpretation of the information in terms of goal-activated concepts was not spontaneous, but occurred only in the course of generating a goal-relevant message. Once this interpretation was made, however, it aff ected participants' own impression and evaluation of the target person, as implied by Principle 3. It is interesting to speculate about the implications of these results for consumer judgments and decisions. For example, word-of-mouth communications about a product are oft en tailored to fi t the expectations of the person to whom one is communicating (Grice, 1975; see also Higgins, 1981; Schwarz, 1994; Strack, 1994). As a result, they are likely to infl uence communicators' own interpretation of the information being transmitted and, perhaps, their evaluations of the product they are describing. For similar reasons, sales persons' own evaluations of the products may be infl uenced in a direction that is consistent with the communication they generate when extolling the product's virtues to their customers. (Th e tendency for people to change their attitudes to conform to implications of the communications they have generated is also predicted by cognitive dissonance theory, of course; see Festinger, 1957.) At the same time, the objective of selling the product is not suffi cient to induce this change; the sales persons must actually deliver the communication for their underlying evaluations to be aff ected. HIGHER ORDER COMPREHENSION PROCESSES Th e preceding research focused on the eff ect of single concepts on the interpretation of single pieces of information. However, more complex bodies of knowledge can oft en infl uence the interpretation of new information. Th is knowledge might be chronically accessible as a result of its frequent use in the social environment in which one participates on a daily basis. On the other hand, situationspecifi c features that are contained in this knowledge could also activate it. Research in many areas exemplifi es this possibility. Chronic Accessibility of Knowledge In an early study by Anderson, Reynolds, Schallert, and Goetz (1977), music education majors and physical education majors read a passage about a social interaction that could be interpreted as either a card game or the rehearsal of a woodwind ensemble (e.g., "...they couldn't decide exactly what to play. Jerry eventually took a stand and set things up...Karen's recorder fi lled the room with soft and pleasant music...fi nally, Mike said, 'Let's hear the score'...Th ey listened carefully and commented on their performance.") Aft er reading the passage, participants were asked what the protagonists had commented on. Responses indicated that music majors were signifi cantly more likely to interpret the interaction as a music rehearsal than physical education majors were. Correspondingly, physical education majors were more likely than music education majors to interpret a second ambiguous passage as the description of a wrestling match rather than a jail break. Apparently, concepts that were chronically accessible as a result of their vocational and educational goals aff ected their interpretation of the story and, therefore, their responses to questions about it. Th e knowledge that is necessary to comprehend information can oft en be called to mind by a single word or phrase. In a study by Bransford, Barclay, and Franks (1972), participants were asked to learn sentences such as "Th e haystack was important because the cloth would rip," "Th e notes were sour because the seam was split," etc. Th eir memory for these ostensibly anomalous sentences was typically very poor. However, participants' memory improved substantially when the sentences were preceded by with a single word ("parachute" and "bagpipes," in the preceding examples). Th e word apparently stimulated the activation of a complex body of knowledge that permitted participants to construct a mental representation of the situation described by the sentence that followed it, thus giving the sentence meaning and facilitating memory for it. In other research (Bransford & Johnson, 1972; Bransford & Stein, 1984), paragraphs containing a series of ostensibly unrelated sentences were given meaning, and therefore remembered better, by providing a title that allowed the sentences to be conceptually integrated. Framing Eff ects Th e importance of Bransford's work lies in its implication that simple words and phrases can prime quite diverse bodies of knowledge for use in interpreting information and construing its implications. Th ese eff ects can be refl ected in not only memory but also judgments. Th is is evidenced by Tversky and

Kahneman's (1982; Kahneman & Tversky, 1982) research on decisions under uncertainty. To give a well-known example, imagine that 1,000 people are in danger of being infected with a deadly virus, that one serum, A, is defi nitely eff ective but in short supply, and that a second, B, is available to all but of uncertain eff ectiveness. Consider two possibilities: 1. If serum A is administered, 350 people will be saved. If serum B is administered, there is a 65% chance that everyone will be saved but a 35% chance that no one will be saved. 2. If serum A is administered, 650 people will die. If serum B is administered, there is a 35% chance that everyone will die but a 65% chance that no one will die. Although the choice alternatives are identical, people are more likely to choose serum A in the fi rst case, but serum B in the second. Presumably the fi rst set of alternatives stimulates people to think about living, and so people choose the alternative that guarantees this positive outcome. However, the second set stimulates people to think about dying, and so they choose the alternative that has a chance of avoiding this negative fate. MEMORY PROCESSES Th e factors that infl uence the eff ect of knowledge accessibility on comprehension and judgment obviously exert this infl uence through their mediating eff ect on the concepts and cognitions that people retrieve from memory. In this section, we will restrict our discussion to research in which memory is the primary concern, independently of the eff ects that the remembered information has on judgments or decisions. In doing so, we focus on two memory phenomena: (1) the role of implicit theories on constructive and reconstructive memory, and (2) the interference of accessible knowledge representations on memory for the information on which these representations were based. THE ROLE OF IMPLICIT THEORIES ON RECONSTRUCTIVE MEMORY People may not pay equal attention to all details of an experience at the time it occurs. Moreover, unless the experience is particularly noteworthy, it may get "buried" among the large number of other experiences that people have in their daily lives. Th is is particularly true when the events that compose the experiences are rather commonplace. In many cases, people may interpret these experiences in terms of an implicit theory they have acquired about the type of events that occurred. If such a theory is frequently used, it may become more accessible in memory than the experiences that it is used to interpret (Principle 2). Consequently, if people are called upon to remember the experience, they may reconstruct it on the basis of this theory without searching memory for a representation of the experience itself. Studies by Michael Ross (1989) support this contention. For example, women's recall of their mood swings during their most recent menstrual cycle were more highly correlated with their implicit theories of how they typically felt during their menstrual period than with the feelings they had actually reported at the time. In a second study (Conway & Ross, 1984), participants who received feedback about the results of a study skills training program recalled their pre-training ability to be lower if they believed that the training was eff ective than if they did not, independently of their actual improvement over the training period. Th e role of implicit theories in memory is also suggested in a study by Bem and McConnell (1972). Participants whose attitudes toward a position had been assessed in an earlier experimental session were either asked to generate a counter-attitudinal communication voluntarily or told to do it without being given a choice. Aft er generating their message, they were asked to recall the attitude they had reported in the earlier session. Participants recalled having more favorable attitudes toward the position advocated when they had generated the communication voluntarily than when they had not been given a choice. Participants apparently used their most recent behavior as a basis for inferring what their attitude must have been, based on an implicit theory that people who advocate a position voluntarily are likely to advocate it personally, without consulting their memory for the actual attitude they had reported. INTERFERENCE OF ACCESSIBLE KNOWLEDGE ON MEMORY According to Principle 3, mental representations that have been formed from information are typically more accessible in memory than the information on which they are based. Th erefore, they tend to be used as a basis for reconstructing this information without recourse to the original material. In some cases, this can lead to memory errors. Schooler and Engstler-Schooler (1990) showed that people are less able to identify a face they have seen if they had described the face verbally at the time they fi rst encountered it than if they had not. Adaval and Wyer (2004) obtained analogous eff ects in a situation more closely approximating those that occur outside the laboratory. Specifi cally, participants who had seen a movie about an interaction between a married couple were asked either to describe the sequence of events they had seen or to describe their impressions of the protagonists. Both writing tasks decreased participants' later recognition of things the protagonists had said during the interaction. Furthermore, describing the events that occurred decreased recognition of nonverbal behaviors as well. In this research, as in Schooler's, the mental representations that participants constructed in the course of writing the description, which were more abstract than the visual representation that they formed of the stimulus information at the time they encountered it, were later used as a basis for their recognition responses instead of this representation. Consequently, recognition accuracy decreased. Th e representations that people construct as a result of post-information processing can not only interfere with the events they actually observe but also can produce intrusions. A classic study by Loft us and Palmer (1974) showed that asking participants questions about a traffi c accident they had seen in a picture (e.g., "How fast was the car going when it smashed into the tree?") led them to reconstruct a memory of the accident in the course of generating an answer that contained features that they had not actually seen but were consistent with the implications of the question. Consequently, their later use of this reconstructed representation as a basis for recalling the picture's content produces intrusion errors. Other studies demonstrate the implications of reconstructive processes for the reliability of both "eye-witness" testimony (Loft us, 1975) and early childhood memories (Loft us, 2000). Although the preceding examples pertain to the interference eff ects of recently constructed representations, recently used representations can have similar eff ects. Perhaps the best known examples of this infl uence are the part-list cueing eff ects identifi ed by Slamecka (1968; Rundus, 1973). Th at is, when participants who have learned a series of stimulus items are given a subset of these items to use as retrieval cues, their memory for the remaining items in the list decreases. In a quite diff erent paradigm, Macrae et al. (1995) found that when participants have been exposed to an Asian woman, they are subliminally primed with concepts pertaining to one of the two stereotypes that could be used to describe the person, the accessibility of concepts related to the other, unprimed stereotype (as inferred from response times in a lexical decision task) decreased. Although the specifi c phenomena summarized in this section are somewhat remote from consumer behavior, their potential implications are nonetheless fairly clear. For example, people who have communicated about a product to others may not only choose to evaluate the product in a manner that is consistent with the communication they have generated as suggested in the previous section, but their memory for their actual experience with the product may be infl uenced correspondingly. Furthermore, their implicit theories about the quality of a product or service provider, if easily accessible in memory, could also bias their memory for their past experience independently of their actual reactions to the product or service at the time the experience occurred (Ross, 1989). INFERENCE AND EVALUATION PROCESSES Inferences are of many types. For example, people oft en infer the likelihood that a product has a certain attribute, that a statement is true, that an event will or did occur, or that a decision will have certain consequences. Second, they may estimate the magnitude of an attribute (the age of a bottle of wine, the price of a cashmere sweater). Th ird, they may evaluate a product as good or bad, or may have a preference for one alternative over another. In each case, however, the inference is unlikely to be based on an extensive analysis of all of the knowledge one has acquired that might be relevant, or a exhaustive construal of its implications (Principle 1). Rather, it is based on only a subset of relevant knowledge that happens to come to mind most easily. A complete discussion of these possibilities would far exceed the scope of this chapter. We therefore restrict our discussion to a few representative examples.

Probability estimates can usually be viewed as beliefs. Th ey can pertain to the occurrence of a past or future event (e.g., that Saddam Hussein had a stockpile of nuclear weapons, the United States will go to war with China before the end of the decade), or to the existence of a present state of aff airs (e.g., Texas is bigger than Alaska, George W. Bush will receive the Nobel Peace Prize). Or, they could concern the causal relation between two events or states. More generally, beliefs are estimates of the likelihood that a proposition about an event, state or relation is true. People who are asked their belief in a proposition may oft en search memory for previously acquired knowledge that bears on it. In some cases, this knowledge could itself be a semanticallycoded proposition whose features are very similar to those of the proposition being evaluated. Alternatively, people may identify a second proposition that, if true, has implications for its validity. Finally, it could be an implicit theory that has implications for the validity of the proposition being judged. A theory of comprehension by Wyer and Radvansky (1998; see Wyer, 2004) formalizes the fi rst possibility. Th ey assumed that to comprehend a piece of information, people form a mental representation of its features and search memory for a previously formed representation that contains these features. If similarity of the features of the new representation to those of an existing memorial representation is very high, people not only comprehend it but spontaneously identify it as true. One implication of this conceptualization is that past experiences that lead a statement to be represented and stored in memory will increase the likelihood that people consider the statement to be true if they encounter it at a later point in time (Begg, Anus, & Farinacci, 1992). In a study by Hasher, Goldstein, and Toppin (1977; see also Hawkins & Hoch, 1992; Kelley & Lindsey, 1993), people completed a belief questionnaire in two diff erent experimental sessions. Some items in the fi rst questionnaire, which concerned obscure facts that few if any participants were likely to know, were repeated in the second. Participants typically judged these propositions as more likely to be true in the second session than they had initially. Exposure to the items in the fi rst session apparently led them to seem more familiar in the second session, and so participants' belief in their validity increased. In a conceptually similar study, Jacoby, Kelley, Brown, and Jasechko (1989) found that exposing participants to fi ctitious names during an initial experimental session increased participants' beliefs that the names referred to well-known persons when they encountered the names 24 hours later. Th ese eff ects occur in part because the information to which people are exposed becomes dissociated from its source. If this is so, the information could have an eff ect on beliefs even when it is identifi ed as invalid at the time it is fi rst received. Th is possibility was demonstrated by Skurnik, Yoon, Park, and Schwarz (in press). Participants were exposed to statements about commercial products either one, two, or three times, in each case accompanied by an indication that the statement was not true. Participants, a short time aft er exposure to the statements, were less likely to believe the statements were true if they had been exposed to them three times than if they had been exposed to them only once. Aft er a 3-day delay, however, older participants were more likely to believe the statements in the former case. (Th is was not true of college-age participants, suggesting that these subjects were less likely to dissociate the statements from their initial context than older subjects were.)

particular objective in mind may simply store the information in memory without attending to the context in which they encountered it. Th is information may later be retrieved out of context and used as a basis for judgment. Shrum (2000) and his colleagues provide abundant evidence of this in research on the eff ects of watching television on perceptions of social reality. Th at is, people typically overestimate the incidence of objects and events in the real world when these entities occur frequently on television. Furthermore, the amount of this overestimation increases with the amount of television that people watch. Th us, heavy television viewers are more likely than light viewers to overestimate the incidence of crime, the numbers of lawyers and doctors, and the number of people who have swimming pools in their back yard (O'Guinn & Shrum, 1997). Th is "cultivation eff ect" (Gerbner, Gross, Morgan, & Signorielli, 1994) occurs independently of the educational and socioeconomic level of respondents. Rather, heavy television viewers are more likely to have instances of these stimuli easily accessible in memory and, therefore, estimate them to occur more frequently in the real world than light viewers do (O'Guinn & Shrum, 1997; Shrum, Wyer, & O'Guinn, 1998). Additional Considerations Th e ease of retrieving instances of an object or event should be distinguished from the actual number of instances that are retrieved. In fact, the eff ects of these variables can be opposite in direction. Th is possibility has been demonstrated in a number of innovative studies by Schwarz and his colleagues (for a review, see Schwarz, 1998, 2004). In one study, for example (Schwarz et al., 1991), people were asked to recall either 6 instances of assertive behavior or 12 such instances. Although 12 behaviors are likely to imply greater assertiveness than only six, participants judged themselves to be less assertive in the former condition than the latter. Th at is, participants who were asked to recall 12 assertive behaviors found it very diffi cult to do so. Consequently, they inferred that they actually did not have the attribute in question. Similar eff ects have been identifi ed in other domains. For example, people who were asked to generate seven arguments in support of a position tended to report less favorable attitudes toward the position than those who were asked to generate only three (Wänke, Bless, & Biller, 1996), and individuals who generate many reasons why an event might not occur are more likely to believe that it did occur than are individuals who generate few such reasons (Sanna & Schwarz, 2003; Sanna, Schwarz, & Stocker, 2002). Similar eff ects have been found in the consumer domain. For example, people report less favorable attitudes toward commercial products (e.g., a BMW) if they have listed many reasons for using the products than if they have listed only one (Wänke, Bohner, & Jurkowitsch, 1997). In a similar study, participants judged a computer they had seen advertised more favorably aft er being asked to recall two favorable features of the computer than aft er being asked to recall eight (Menon & Raghubir, 2003). Interestingly, this diff erence was reversed under conditions in which subjects were likely to attribute the ease of recalling these features to other, extraneous situational factors (i.e., distracting music).

MAGNITUDE ESTIMATES People are oft en called upon to make judgments of magnitude. Th ey might estimate the height of a mountain, the age of an antique, or the price of a product. Th ese estimates are likely to be made with reference to a previously acquired body of knowledge about the type of stimulus being judged. Th e way in which this knowledge is used can depend on whether the estimate is in physical units (feet, years, dollars, etc.) or subjective ones (high or low, old or young, expensive or cheap, etc.). In each case, however, the estimate can depend on the particular subset of judgment-relevant knowledge that happens to be accessible at the time. Estimates in Physical Stimulus Units Consumers who consider the purchase of a particular product are likely to compare its features to those of other products they have encountered in the past. For example, they may evaluate a car's fuel effi ciency in relation to the average miles per gallon of other automobiles they have seen. Or, the price they are willing to pay for the car could require an estimate of the price at which the product is typically available elsewhere. However, people may rarely have these quantities stored in memory, and consequently may consider a range of values to be plausible. Th is range may depend on the particular subset of past experiences that they use to compute it. Strack and Mussweiler (1997) formalize this process and provide compelling evidence of its occurrence (Mussweiler & Strack, 1999, 2000a, 2000b; for a review, see Mussweiler, 2003). In their research, participants are typically asked to decide if a stimulus attribute is greater or less than either a high value (e.g., is the price of the average BMW greater or less than $100,000) or a very low one ($3,000). Having done so, they then make their own estimate of its value. In making their comparative judgment, participants theoretically activate concepts about a subset of stimuli whose values are close to the "anchor" value they are asked to consider. Th en, they use these concepts to estimate the actual value when they are asked to report it later. Th us, in our example, participants estimate the average price of a BMW to be higher if they have been asked to compare this price to a higher value than if they have been asked to compare it to a lower value. Th is is true even when this value is implausible. In fact, it even occurs when participants believe that the "anchor" value was chosen at random and was objectively irrelevant to the stimulus being judged (Strack & Mussweiler, 1997). Adaval and Wyer (2005) found that exposing participants to a high or low anchor price can aff ect their estimates of not only the average price of a product in the marketplace but also the price they are personally willing to pay for it. Nunes and Boatwright (2004) reported conceptually similar eff ects in fi eld research and sowed that the eff ects can generalize over product domains. For example, passersby at a beachfront stand were willing to pay more money for a CD if the sweaters displayed at a nearby stand were on sale for a high price than if they were on sale for a low price. Th is result should not be overgeneralized, however. Adaval and Wyer (2005) found that the impact of context prices on estimates of prices of products in other categories depends on the relevance of the thoughts activated by the comparative judgment task. Th us, making comparative judgments of clothing articles stimulated participants to think about the subjective reactions they might have to the use of these articles and to the shopping experience itself. Consequently, it infl uenced the price they were willing to pay for electronic products to which the (e.g., aff ect-related) concepts activated by these thoughts were also relevant. However, making comparative judgments of an electronic product stimulated participants to think about features that were specifi c to the type of product being judged. Consequently, it had little impact on the price they were willing to pay for clothing articles. Subjective Magnitude Estimates As the preceding considerations suggest, people frequently fail to remember the specifi c physical characteristics of a stimulus. (Consumers, for example, are unable to remember the price of a product they have purchased only seconds aft er they put in their shopping cart; see Dickson & Sawyer, 1990.) Rather, they encode an object's physical units into subjective units at the time they encounter them and this encoding, once stored in memory, is later retrieved and used as a basis for later judgments and decisions. Th e rules for transforming physical stimulus values into subjective values were described by Ostrom and Upshaw (1968; see also Parducci, 1965), and have been explicated in consumer research by Janiszewski and Lichtenstein (1999) and Lynch, Chakravarti, and Mitra (1991). According to Ostrom and Upshaw, people subjectively position the range of subjective values they have available to correspond to the range of physical stimulus values they consider to be relevant. Th us, the higher the range of physical stimulus values they consider, the lower the subjective value they assign to any given stimulus within this range. In some instances, the range of physical values they consider is determined by the type of stimuli being judged. For example, people might judge a baby as "big" but an apartment as "small" although few babies are as large as apartments. When the range of values that are relevant to a judgment are less clear, however, it may depend on the subset of physical stimulus values that happen to be accessible in memory at the time. Consequently, it may be infl uenced by factors of which they are unaware, and that are objectively irrelevant to the judgment to be made. Adaval and Monroe (2002) confi rmed this possibility.

Participants were subliminally exposed to either high or low numbers in the course of performing an ostensibly unrelated perceptual task, and then were asked to judge a particular product on the basis of price and attribute information. Participants judged the product to be less expensive if they had been exposed to high numbers than if they had been exposed to low ones. Interestingly, they judged the product to be lower along other dimensions as well. Apparently, exposure to the numbers during the priming task aff ected the perspective that participants adopted in transforming objective stimulus values into subjective values regardless of the dimension to which the judgments pertained. In summary, both physical stimulus estimates and subjective judgments can be infl uenced by the particular subset of knowledge that happens to be accessible at the time the judgments are made. However, the eff ects of this knowledge on the two types of judgments may be opposite in direction. For example, activating knowledge about high-priced products can increase participants' estimates of the average price of these products in the marketplace and the price they are willing to pay for them. On the other hand, this activated knowledge may also increase the range of values that compose the perspective that participants bring to bear on their subjective estimates to the product's cost. Th us, it may decrease their judgments of the product as expensive. EVALUATIONS AND AFFECT?BASED JUDGMENTS Evaluations that are reported along a good-bad dimension are essentially estimates of magnitude. However, they are distinguished from other magnitude estimates in two ways. First, they typically apply to a stimulus as a whole, and may refl ect the combined implications of inferences about a number of more specifi c attributes (for discussions of these integration processes, see Anderson, 1971, 1981; Fishbein & Ajzen, 1975). Second, evaluations of a stimulus are oft en based on not only its descriptive features but also the aff ect that people happen to experience and attribute to their feelings about the stimulus. Th e possible use of aff ective reactions as bases for judgment, which was initially demonstrated by Schwarz and Clore (1983), is very well established both in consumer research (Pham, 1998, 2004; Yeung & Wyer, 2004, 2005) and more generally (Schwarz & Clore, 1996; Wyer, Clore, & Isbell, 1999). Not all evaluations are based on aff ect, of course (Zanna & Rempel, 1988). Some products are typically evaluated on the basis of purely functional or utilitarian criteria. Consumers may consider their feelings to be irrelevant to their evaluation of these products and so the aff ect they are experiencing has little informational infl uence (Adaval, 2001; Pham, 1998, 2004; Yeung & Wyer, 2004). In other instances, both aff ective and nonaff ective criteria may be employed. Th en, because aff ective reactions to a stimulus typically occur spontaneously, without a detailed analysis of its specifi c features (Lazarus, 1982, 1991; Zajonc, 1980), they are likely to be highly accessible and, therefore, likely to be applied (for an exception, see Levine, Wyer, & Schwarz, 1994). Indeed, they may oft en be used to the exclusion of other information when people are unable or unmotivated to search for additional judgmental criteria (Schwarz & Clore, 1988; see also Forgas, 1995). Th is contingency was demonstrated by Shiv and Fedorikhin (1999). Participants in the study were given a choice of eating either chocolate cake or fruit salad. In the absence of distraction, a large proportion of participants chose the fruit salad. When participants were required to keep a multiple-digit number in mind while making their decision, however, their preferences for the chocolate cake signifi cantly increased. Apparently participants who were able to think about the implications of their decision based their choice on health-related criteria. In the presence of distraction, however, the cognitive deliberation required to make this choice was aborted, and preferences were based on hedonic (i.e., aff ective) criteria. Further evidence that aff ect is more likely to come into play when participants are unable to think critically about their judgments was obtained by Albarracin and Wyer (2001). Participants in this study were fi rst induced to feel either happy or unhappy by writing about a past experience. Th en, they were exposed to a persuasive message containing either strong or weak arguments in favor of comprehensive examinations. When participants received the message in the absence of distraction, they based their attitudes toward the exams on the content of the message they received. When they were distracted, however, they based their attitudes on the aff ect that they were experiencing as a result of the past experience they had recalled, and the eff ect of the message content signifi cantly decreased. Th us, as in Shiv and Fedorikhin's (1999) research, participants' aff ective reactions had a greater impact on judgments when other criteria could not easily be applied. Eff ects of Extraneous Aff ect on Evaluations Albaraccin and Wyer's (2001) results exemplify a more general phenomenon. Th at is, people oft en cannot easily distinguish between their aff ective reactions to a stimulus and the feelings they may be experiencing for other, unrelated reasons. Consequently, aff ect from sources that have nothing to do with the object being judged can have an impact on their evaluation of it. Th us, for example, people who have been thinking about a personal experience shortly before they are called upon to evaluate a product may evaluate the product more favorably if they feel happy as a result of these ruminations than if they feel sad. Numerous situational factors can obviously infl uence the accessibility and use of aff ect as a basis for judgment, including the weather (Schwarz & Clore, 1983), a small gift (Isen, Shalker, Clark, & Karp, 1978), performance on an achievement test (Ottati & Isbell, 1996), and proprioceptive feedback (Strack, Martin, & Stepper, 1988). Th is research typically assumes that judgments are based on an integration of judgment-relevant criteria at the time the judgment is made. In many instances, however, people are likely to form an initial impression of an object before they receive information about its specifi c features. Once this initial impression is formed, it can later be recalled and used as a basis for judgment without construing the implications of information received subsequently (Principle 5). In this case, the feelings that people happen to be experiencing at the time their initial impression is formed may infl uence their impression and, as a result, may aff ect the judgments and decisions they report later. Furthermore, the impact of their feelings may be evident even aft er the feelings themselves have dissipated. Th ese considerations are particularly important in purchasing situations. Consumers oft en form a general impression of a product from seeing it in a store window or magazine. In such conditions, the aff ect they happen to be experiencing at the time they form this impression could infl uence their later evaluation of the product independently of any information about its specifi c features that they acquire later. Yeung and Wyer (2004) confi rmed this possibility experimentally. Participants who saw an aff ect-eliciting picture of a product before they received information about its specifi c features formed an initial impression on the basis of this picture, and this impression infl uenced their later product evaluations independently of the specifi c attribute information they received later. Furthermore, the aff ect they were experiencing for unrelated reasons at the time the picture was presented had an impact on judgments through its mediating impact on this initial impression. For aff ective reactions to have an impact, however, they must not only be accessible but also be relevant to the judgmental goal one is pursuing. Aff ective reactions infl uence product evaluations at the time of judgment only if the product is one that is typically based on hedonic rather than utilitarian criteria (Pham, 1998). Similarly, they infl uence people's initial impressions only if they are relevant to these impressions. Th us, in Yeung and Wyer's (2004) study, the feelings that participants were experiencing for extraneous reasons infl uenced their initial impressions only if the picture on which they based these impressions elicited aff ect; they had no infl uence when the picture conveyed functional characteristics of the product that were not themselves aff ect eliciting. Responses to Aff ect-Congruent Information A by-product of the use of aff ect as information may be its infl uence on the attention that is paid to the information that elicits this aff ect and, therefore, the weight that is attached to it in making a judgment. A formal statement of this possibility is provided by Adaval's (2001) aff ect-confi rmation theory. She proposed that when information about a product's specifi c attributes elicits positive or negative aff ective reactions, the feelings that consumers are experiencing for other reasons can appear either to confi rm or to disconfi rm the implications of these reactions, making consumers more or less confi dent that they have assessed these implications correctly. Consequently, these feelings infl uence the weight they attach to the attribute information in making a judgment. Consistent with conclusions drawn by Pham (1998), however, this diff erential weighting only occurs when people consider their aff ective reactions to be a relevant basis for construing the information's evaluative implications. When the attribute information describes functional rather than hedonic qualities, the aff ect that people experience has no infl uence on the weight they attach to it. A recent study by Förster (2004) is also worth noting in this context. He found that proprioceptive feedback (e.g., nodding or shaking the head) infl uenced participants' evaluations of a product, but only when the implications of the feedback were congruent with the intrinsic favorableness of the product being judged. Th at is, head nodding infl uenced evaluations of favorable products but not unfavorable ones, whereas head shaking aff ected evaluations of unfavorable products but not favorable ones. To the extent proprioceptive feedback elicits aff ect that is used as a basis for judgment (e.g., Strack, Martin, & Stepper, 1988), these results are consistent with Adaval's (2001) aff ect-confi rmation theory. Other interpretations of these fi ndings are possible, however, as noted later in this chapter. Eff ects of Brand-Elicited Aff ect Th e use of aff ect as a source of information plays a particularly important role in evaluations of brand extensions. It seems reasonable to suppose that the eff ect of a favorable brand name on evaluations of its extension is greater when the extension is physically or functionally similar to the parent brand category than when it is not (Aaker & Keller, 1990; Bottomley & Holden, 2001). However, Barone, Miniard, and Romeo (2000) found that stimulating participants to experience positive aff ect at the time they made similarity judgments led them to judge moderately similar extensions as more similar to the parent brand than they otherwise would and, therefore, more similar to the parent brand in favorableness. However, this eff ect occurs only when (a) participants estimate similarity before they evaluate the extension (Yeung & Wyer, 2005) and (b) are suffi ciently motivated to take parent-extension similarity into account (Barone, 2005). When participants evaluate extensions without judging similarity, the aff ect they are experiencing has a direct, informational impact on judgments that is not mediated by its infl uence on similarity perceptions. PREFERENCE JUDGMENTS Purchase decisions are oft en comparative. Th at is, consumers decide which of several alternative products they prefer. In some cases, these decisions are likely to be determined by computing an overall evaluation of each choice alternative independently and comparing the magnitude of these separate evaluations. Th is process, however, requires cognitive eff ort. Consequently, if purchasers have not previously made overall evaluations of the products they are considering, they may resort to diff erent strategies that are easier to apply. For example, people may oft en perform a dimension-by-dimension comparison, choosing the product that is superior on the greatest number of dimensions. Or, when this procedure does not lead to a clear solution, they may resort to other, heuristic criteria. For example, suppose a product A is superior to B along one attribute dimension but is inferior to B along a second. Nevertheless, suppose consumers believe that A is superior to a third alternative but B is not. Th en, they may consider this to be suffi cient justifi cation for choosing A despite the fact that a direct comparison of the products is not diagnostic (Shafi r, Simonson, & Tversky, 1993; Simonson, 1989; but see Huber, Payne, & Puto, 1982, for a diff erent interpretation). Th is criterion may only be applied, however, if independent evaluations of the products have not already been computed. If these evaluations have already been made and are easily accessible in memory at the time the products are compared, participants may base their preferences on these evaluations instead (Park & Kim, 2005). Research on preference judgments has typically been based on the implicit assumption that these judgments are based primarily on the information that is provided in the experiment about the stimuli being judged. Consequently, the role of knowledge accessibility in these judgments has not been directly examined. Nevertheless, several phenomena identifi ed in research in this area provide examples of its infl uence. 1. If the products described are encountered successively, people may focus their attention on the last alternative, which they have encountered more recently and is presumably more accessible in memory (Principle 2). Th us, they focus their attention on features of this product that the fi rst does not have, and base their preference on the evaluative implications of these features while ignoring features of the fi rst alternative that the second does not possess. Th erefore, suppose both alternatives have unique positive features that are similar in favorableness. Th en, people are likely to choose the second product they consider, as it has positive features that the fi rst does not possess. In contrast, suppose the alternatives have unique negative features. In this case, people are likely to choose the fi rst product they encountered, as the second has negative features that the fi rst does not (Houston, Sherman, & Baker, 1989).

2. If two choice alternatives have common features and, therefore, are not diagnostic, consumers may ignore them and concentrate their attention on only those features that are unique to each option. Consequently, these latter features, which are processed more extensively, become more accessible in memory than others (Craik & Lockhart, 1972). Th erefore, if consumers are later called upon to evaluate each alternative separately, the unique features are likely to be given relatively more weight than the shared features. Th us, for example, consumers who have compared two options that have unique favorable attributes and common unfavorable ones may mentally cancel the unfavorable attributes and consider only the favorable ones in making their choice. As a result, they should later evaluate both products more favorably than they would if the comparative judgment had not been made. Similarly, persons who compare products with common favorable and unique unfavorable features should later evaluate the products more unfavorably than they would otherwise (Houston & Sherman, 1995). Th is can even occur when persons are not explicitly asked to make these comparisons (Brunner & Wänke, 2006; but see Wang & Wyer, 2002, for contingencies in the occurrence of these eff ects). BEHAVIORAL DECISIONS Some of the most important demonstrations of the infl uence of knowledge accessibility have emerged in research on its impact on overt behavior. Persons who have unobtrusively been exposed to stimuli that are associated with aggressiveness (e.g., by waiting for the experiment in an offi ce that contains ROTC equipment) are more likely to administer shocks to a confederate in a learning experiment (Berkowitz & LePage, 1967). Priming hostility-related concepts in a sentence-construction task (Srull & Wyer, 1979) can have similar eff ects (Carver, Ganellen, Froming, & Chambers,

1983). A particularly compelling series of studies by Bargh, Chen, and Burrows (1996) provide more direct evidence that semantic concepts can have a direct impact on behavior that is not mediated by their infl uence on how the object of the behavior is interpreted. In one study, for example, participants were primed with concepts associated with rudeness in the course of performing a sentence construction task. Th ese participants were more likely than control participants to interrupt an experimenter's conversation with a graduate student in order to return the questionnaire they had completed. However, their behavior was apparently not mediated by their interpretation of the experimenter's behavior as impolite; judgments of him were unaff ected by the priming task. In a second study, college-age participants completed a sentence construction task that required the use of concepts associated with the elderly. Aft er leaving the experiment, these participants walked more slowly to the elevator than control subjects did. Finally, Caucasian participants who were subliminally exposed to faces of African Americans in the course of performing a boring perceptual task displayed more nonverbal indications of irritation than control participants upon being asked to perform the task a second time. Using similar priming techniques, Colcombe (reported in Wyer, 2004) found that subliminally priming African American faces decreased performance on a test of mathematics ability while increasing performance in tests of rhythm memory and basketball shooting. Numerous other examples are reviewed by Dijksterhuis, Smith, van Baaren, and Wigboldus (2005). Th ese eff ects could refl ect the impact of "If [X], then [Y]" productions of the sort mentioned earlier in this chapter. Th at is, a confi guration of stimulus features could, in combination, activate a sequence of behaviors that are performed spontaneously, with little if any cognitive deliberation. Th e confi guration could include not only concepts activated by the situation in which the behavior occurs but also cognitions that happen to be accessible for other reasons. However, people need not be aware of all of the features of this confi guration in order for the production to be activated. Th is possibility was demonstrated by Chartrand and Bargh (1996). Th ey found that subliminally priming concepts associated with a goal-directed production can activate the production without conscious awareness of the goal to which it was relevant. Although the evidence that behaviors can be infl uenced by subliminally primed concepts and cognitions is very clear, the cognitive mechanisms underlying these eff ects are less so (cf. Dijksterhuis et al., 2005; Janiszewski & van Osselaer, 2005; Strack & Deutsch,

2004). Why does priming a stereotype of the elderly, or of African American faces, infl uence the behavior of persons who are not themselves members of the stereotyped category? One possible answer is suggested by Prinz (1990), who postulated that in order to comprehend another's behavior, one must mentally simulate the performance of the behavior oneself. Th is process could establish a direct link between the representation of another's behavior and a representation of one's own, and the product activated by the latter representation, along with features of the situation itself, could elicit this behavior under conditions in which it is appropriate. Another possibility is that priming a stereotype activates a general value (e.g., that people should not to taken advantage of, that academic achievement is unimportant, etc.) and that these values, once activated, have a mediating infl uence on people's behavior un the situation at hand. Th us, stimulating people to think about Nobel Prize winners leads them to perform better in a game of Trivial Pursuit (Dijksterhuis & van Knippenburg, 1998), and priming concepts associated with the elderly decreases college students' performance on a memory test (Dijksterhuis, Bargh, & Miedema, 2000). Colcombe's fi nding that subliminally priming faces of African Americans led Caucasian participants to perform more poorly than control participants on a mathematics test, but better than controls in tests of rhythm memory and basketball shooting, is also consistent with this interpretation. Th at is, African Americans are stereotypically disinterested in intellectual achievement while valuing musical and athletic ability. Th erefore, priming the stereotype activated these values, and the accessibility of these values aff ected the eff ort that participants expended on the task they were given to perform. Other fi ndings confi rm this view. For example, subliminally priming faces of Asians, who stereotypically attach high value to intellectual achievement, led participants to perform better on a mathematics test than control subjects (see Wyer, 2004). Furthermore, priming the stereotypes of a punk decreased performance on an analytical task but increased performance on a creativity task, whereas priming the stereotype of an engineer had the opposite eff ects (Förster, Friedman, Butterbach, & Sassenberg, 2005). Th ese fi ndings clearly have implications for the eff ects of movies and television on both consumption and other behavior. Th ey could also account for the eff ects of unobtrusively placing brands in the context of television shows to which they are objectively irrelevant. However, it is important to keep in mind that priming concepts in themselves are oft en not suffi cient to activate behavior unless the behavior is appropriate in the situation at hand. Th us, activating concepts of African Americans doesn't lead people to express hostility unless the situation with which they are confronted is frustrating or in other ways conducive to the behavior. As Colcombe's research shows, priming the same concepts in other situations can have quite diff erent eff ects. Th e situational cues that determine the activation of prime-related behavior may be internally generated. Strahan, Spencer, and Zanna (2002), for example, showed that subliminally priming thirst-related words led participants to drink more of a beverage they were provided during the course of a simulated taste test. However, this was only true when participants had gone without drinking for several hours prior to the experiment and, therefore, were thirsty at the time the priming occurred. A contingency in these eff ects may be the extent to which persons are generally sensitive to internal cues; DeMarree, Wheeler, and Petty (2005), for example, found that priming eff ects on behavior were less evident among high self-monitors, who typically focus their attention on external cues, than among low self-monitors. Be that as it may, both Colcombe's and Strahan et al.'s studies both indicate that behavior is determined by both activated knowledge and situational features in combination. In considering the implications of this work for consumer behavior, therefore, it would be a mistake to assume that activating concepts and knowledge will stimulate purchase or consumption behavior in the absence of a stimulus situation in which these behaviors are appropriate. EFFECTS OF BODILY FEEDBACK ON INFORMATION PROCESSING One of the more interesting areas of research to emerge in recent years has concerned the impact of bodily feedback on judgments and behavior. Bodily movements (e.g., fl exing or extending the arm, or shaking or nodding the head) can elicit proprioceptive feedback. Th is internally generated stimulation can serve as features of a cognitive production that, in combination with other stimulus features, spontaneously elicit a sequence of behavior. Furthermore, this can occur without conscious awareness. Förster and Strack (1996), for example, showed that when participants were unobtrusively induced to nod or shake their heads while learning a list of positively-and negatively-valenced words, they had better memory for the words that were compatible with the implications of their head movements. Similarly, people were better able to generate names of liked celebrities when they were fl exing their arms (a behavior associated with approach) than when they were extending them (a behavior associated with avoidance), but were better able to generate disliked celebrities in the latter condition than in the former (Förster & Strack, 1997, 1998). Analogous eff ects have been identifi ed in research on consumption behavior. For example, people drink a larger amount of a positively fl avored drink if their arms are fl exed than if they are extended (Förster, 2003). Th e approach tendency that was associated with the bodily feedback was apparently restricted to positively valenced stimuli, however. Arm fl exion or extension had no impact on drinking behavior when the drink was neutral in taste. Th e infl uence of proprioceptive feedback is not restricted to the activation of cognitive productions, of course. It can also exert an infl uence behavior through its informational properties. For example, people who nod their head while engaging in cognitive activity may perceive themselves to approve of the activity and, as a result, may be more infl uenced by its implications. Brinol and Petty (2003) unobtrusively induced participants to nod or to shake their head while listening to a persuasive message that contained either strong or weak arguments. Participants were more inclined to agree with the position advocated in strong-argument messages if they nodded their head while listening to them. However, they were less inclined to agree with the position advocated in weak-argument messages in these conditions. Apparently, participants were disposed to elaborate the positive implications of strong arguments but to counterargue the implications of the weak arguments. Th e proprioceptive feedback associated with head nodding increased their confi dence in the implications of these cognitive responses and, therefore, increased the use of these implications as a basis for judgments. CHAMELEON EFFECTS According to Prinz's (1990) conceptualization of observational learning, a direct link can oft en be established between others' motor behavior and one's own. Th is could occur even if the behavior in question is incidental. Th is possibility is suggested by the "chameleon eff ect," that is, a tendency to unconsciously imitate the nonverbal behavior and mannerisms of other persons in the situation with whom one interacts (Chartrand & Bargh, 1999; for a review, see Chartrand, Lakin, & Maddux, 1995). Th us, for example, participants in a group discussion are more likely to cross their legs or stroke their chin if others in the discussion are doing so. Similar eff ects have been investigated in consumer behavior research. Johnston (2002), for example, found that people ate more ice cream in the presence of a confederate who did likewise. Ferraro, Bettman, and Chartrand (cited in Chartrand, 2005) found that participants' choice of snacks was unconsciously infl uenced by another's choices in the same situation. Th ere are undoubtedly analogous eff ects outside the laboratory. People at a party, for example, are more likely to eat or drink if others are doing so than if they are not. Similarly, people are more apt to make purchases if they are accompanied by other individuals who are on a shopping spree. Although there are obviously other explanations of these phenomena (e.g., bowing to social pressure), the role of nonconscious imitative behavior in a consumer context is worth examining. IMPULSIVENESS Th e role of accessible concepts and knowledge on the spontaneous activation of behavior is particularly important in conceptualizing the antecedents of impulsive consumption (Rook & Fisher, 1995). Several conceptualizations of impulsiveness have been proposed (Baumeister, 2002; Baumeister & Vohs, 2004; Carver, 2004; Strack & Deutsch, 2004). Th ese conceptualizations have typically focused on the antecedents of behavioral self-regulation. In many instances, the behavior can be conceptualized in terms of individual and situational diff erences in the types of cognitive productions that are activated in the situations at hand. In a conceptualization of impulsive eating behavior, Schachter (1968; Schachter & Rodin, 1974) identifi ed individual diff erences obesity that were traceable to diff erences in the sensitivity to internal vs. external stimuli. Specifi cally, obese individuals' behavior is generally infl uenced by external stimulus features, whereas nonobese persons' behavior is more infl uenced by internal cues. Th us, for example, obese persons eating behavior is relatively more infl uenced by the physical attractiveness of the food, and by the time of day (as indicated by a clock on the wall), whereas nonobese individuals' eating is more infl uenced by knowledge of the food's nutritional value, or by how hungry they feel. Th ese diff erences could be conceptualized in terms of individual diff erences in the sorts of cognitive productions that guide behavior in the situations in question. Although an analysis of impulsive purchase behavior is beyond the scope of this chapter, it may be conceptualized in similar terms. Th at is, purchasing, like eating, may be governed by cognitive productions that are activated by a confi guration of both external and internally generated stimulus features. Diff erent confi gurations of situational features may activate diff erent productions and, therefore, infl uence the occurrence of the behavior. Luo (2005), for example, found evidence in a scenario study that persons report a greater tendency to engage in impulsive buying in the presence of peers, but less tendency to do so in the presence of family members, than in other conditions. Moreover, this was particularly true when the purchasers were generally susceptible to social infl uence and the individuals they imagined accompanying them were cohesive. If participants' selfreported behavior in imagined purchasing situations refl ects their actual purchasing dispositions, Luo's fi ndings would be consistent with the possibility that diff erent cognitive productions are spontaneously activated, and generate diff erent sequences of behavior, depending on the specifi c individuals who happen to be present in the purchase situation.

GOALS AND MOTIVES Th e infl uence of accessible knowledge on goal-directed behavior can be of two types. First, as noted in the previous section, goal-directed sequences of behavior may exist in memory in the form of cognitive productions that are activated spontaneously by a confi guration of both situational features and other concepts and knowledge that happen to be accessible at the time. Th e latter concepts can be activated in any number of ways. Fitzsimons and Bargh (2003), for example, found that stimulating participants to think about their mother led them to try harder to succeed in a later achievement situation. Bargh et al. (2001) showed that goal-directed consumption activity could also be activated without awareness. In a particularly interesting study, Fitzsimons, Chartrand, and Fitzsimons (2005, cited in Chartrand, 2005), subliminally priming logos of Apple (a company associated with innovativeness), led individuals to generate more unusual uses of an object in a subsequent creativity test. Th e assumption that these eff ects are mediated by cognitive productions should be qualifi ed. As Bargh et al. (2001) note, a distinction may need to be made between the activation of a goal per se and the activation of other types of mental representation. As implied by Principle 2, the eff ects of activating most representations of knowledge decrease over time. In contrast, the salience of a goal may have increasing eff ects over time as long as the goal is not satisfi ed. Results reported by Bargh et al. (2001) and Chartrand, Huber, and Shiv (2005) suggest such increases. Th erefore, the interpretation of such eff ects in terms of cognitive productions is not completely clear. However, goals, and the sequence of steps required to attain them, are also part of declarative knowledge, and can exist as mental representations in memory. Th is possibility is implicit in Schank and Abelson's (1977) conception of a cognitive script and its relation to plans, goals and behavior. Th at is, prototypic sequences of events (e.g., the actions that occur when visiting a restaurant) could exist in memory and be used not only to predict and explain others' behavior but as guides to one's own goal-directed activity. Evidence of the existence of these representations has been obtained by Kruglanski et al. (2002). Th ey found that subliminally priming concepts associated with a goal increases the accessibility of concepts associated with the means of attaining it. In addition, priming concepts associated with means increases the accessibility of concepts that are associated with goals to which they are relevant. A goal can be viewed as a concept of a desirable state, along with a series of behavioral events that, if they occur, lead to the occurrence of this state (Shah, Kruglanski, & Friedman, 2003; Wyer & Srull, 1989). To this extent, concepts associated with the end state may activate a sequence of behaviors that could potentially attain it (Chartrand & Bargh, 2001). Furthermore, thoughts about the means of attaining a goal may activate concepts associated with the goal itself (Kruglanski et al., 2002), and these concepts, once activated, not only can facilitate goal-directed behavior to which they are relevant but also can interfere with goal-directed activity to which they are not relevant (Shah & Kruglanski, 2002, 2003). Goals, and the behavior that facilitates their attainment, can be represented in memory at several levels of specifi city (Vallacher & Wegner, 1987). Moreover, they may vary in their immediacy. In many instances, a plan-goal hierarchy may exist with more specifi c and immediate goals serving as means to the attainment of more general, long-range goals (Srull & Wyer, 1986). Th us, studying may be a means of attaining a good grade in calculus, which is a means of attaining the goal of getting into graduate school, which is a means of getting a well paying job, etc. CULTURAL AND SOCIAL INFLUENCES ON REGULATORY FOCUS At the most general level, behavior is likely to be governed by a desire to maximize pleasure and minimize pain. However, many behaviors have both costs and benefi ts, and so the behavior that potentially has the most desirable consequences can have undesirable consequences as well. Under these circumstances, a person's choice can depend on which set of consequences is more important. Th e relative emphasis placed on positive vs. negative outcomes of a decision has been conceptualized in some detail by Higgins (1997, 1998). Specifi cally, people who are confronted with a decision may be promotion focused. Th at is, they may be motivated by the positive consequence of a decision while ignoring the negative consequences that might result. Others, however, may be prevention focused, or motivated by the desire to avoid negative consequences of a decision while giving relatively little weight to the positive eff ects it might have. Chronic individual diff erences in these motivational orientations may exist (Higgins et al., 2000). On the other hand, the motivational orientations can also be infl uenced by situational factors that make one or another set of criteria accessible in memory (for example, whether alternative outcomes are framed in terms of gains vs. nongains or losses vs. nonlosses; Idson, Liberman, & Higgins, 2000; Lee & Aaker, 2004; Monga & Zhu, 2005). Furthermore, once these orientations are activated, their eff ects may generalize over domains, aff ecting decisions in situations that are quite unrelated to the one that stimulated them (Briley & Wyer, 2002). A specifi cation of these dispositions and the factors that activate them has obvious implications for an understanding of consumer decision making. Many products have both positive and negative features, and a decision to choose one product over another can oft en depend on which set of features is weighted more heavily.

3

Consumer Memory, Fluency, and Familiarity

Memory is the record of our personal past. As such, it is useful for remembering. But memory is also much more than that: it also involves the capacity to learn, to be infl uenced by prior experience, and to behave diff erently in the future as a consequence of an experience. Memory is the controller of all acquired human behavior, including speech, conceptual knowledge, skilled activities, social interactions, and consumer preferences. To achieve a true understanding of any aspect of human behavior, it is therefore essential to have an eff ective theory of memory. During the 1970s, the notion of associative memory was introduced (Anderson & Bower, 1973). Following the assumption that elaboration is related to the creation of associative pathways in memory; the notion that elaboration could impact attitudes became an important research question. Elaborative processing became a heavily studied determinant of information accessibility (e.g., Kardes, 1994) and attitude formation (Kisielius & Sternthal, 1986; McGill & Anand, 1989). Such eff ects have been explained by a multiple-pathway explanation (cf. Anderson, 1983), although more recently explanations have favored the reconstruction hypothesis (e.g., Walker, 1986). Despite the popularity of thinking about memory in terms of "construction" (e.g., Loft us & Palmer, 1974; Loft us, 1979), during the 1980s, "separate systems" approaches to memory became popular, and continue to be popular today. We will focus on these approaches: fi rst outlining them in detail, and then contrasting them with the SCAPE framework. SEPARATE SYSTEMS THEORIES Th ree major dichotomies were proposed as the basic organization of memory, each pointing to some clear contrast in behavior.

Each dichotomy is based on observations of various dissociations in performance on some tasks. For example, recognition performance has been found to be aff ected by varying levels of processing (Jacoby & Dallas, 1981) or delay of test (Tulving, Schacter, & Stark, 1982) while leaving identifi cation performance unaff ected. Amnesic patients demonstrate implicit learning (Knowlton & Squire, 1994) and respond to repetition priming (Warrington & Weiskrantz, 1970), despite poor recognition performance. Th ese dissociations are taken as evidence of Nature's seams, the lines along which mind can be split and compartmentalized into convenient and independent sub-units, each of which can be studied without consideration of the other. Th e episodic/semantic dichotomy of memory is arguably the most dominant of the three dichotomies. It distinguishes the preservation of detail and context of prior experiences from the preservation of context-free, abstract, summary properties of those experiences (e.g., Tulving, 1983, 1985). Th e former supports tasks such as recall and recognition; the latter supports tasks requiring perception, identifi cation, and conceptual and categorical knowledge. Also common is the procedural/declarative dichotomy which is based on the distinction between a declarative system, supporting tasks requiring conscious deliberation about the content and source of current knowledge, and a procedural system, supporting tasks requiring specifi c skills, or motoric ability (Cohen & Squire, 1980). Th e distinction is between intentional acquisition, storage, and retrieval of information versus non-refl ective acquisition and application of prior experience, as evidenced by perceptual, cognitive, and sensorimotor performance on tasks demonstrating skill or involving repetition priming. Skill is considered to be a product of multiple prior experiences; priming is considered to be a product of a single prior experience. Evidence of either is measured by the observed savings or facilitation in performance, in the absence of conscious awareness, control, or volition. Th e third dichotomy entails an implicit/explicit distinction that emphasizes the diff erential role of consciousness in performance, contrasting tasks such as recall and recognition, in which awareness of prior experience is important, versus tasks which measure repetition priming (Graf & Schacter, 1985). An implicit form of memory exists to account for eff ects of prior experience on current behavior in the absence of conscious awareness (e.g., eff ects observed in a priming task); an explicit form of memory exists to account for behavior accompanied by conscious awareness (e.g., eff ects observed in a remembering task). Th ese separate systems theories of memory are based on the assumption that the fundamental functions of mind are obvious: they consist of the capacity to perform each of the various activities that humans are faced with in the social world, such as recognition, knowing, and responding appropriately but unconsciously in skilled activities such as speech and dance. Th e important research question is thus not what the functions of mind are, but how they are performed. It has further been assumed that diff erent functions of mind are served by separate dedicated mechanisms, and that the dissociated patterns of performance observed in performing various tasks is a consequence of the diff erent principles by which the separate mechanisms work. Finally, because of this correspondence of mechanism with function, it has been assumed that each mechanism serves each function directly. Th us, for example, because recognition of a particular face or event requires diff erentiation among many others, that function is served by a specifi c retrieval mechanism; whereas classifi cation of an object such as a dog in the street could benefi t from experience of many similar beasts, and so instead relies on abstraction of knowledge across events and activation of a general concept node. Applied to consumer memory, the separate systems distinctions have been useful for compartmentalizing consumer knowledge. For example, a "retrieval set" is distinguished from a "knowledge set" (e.g., Alba & Chattopadhyay, 1985), or a "consideration set" is distinguished from an "awareness set" (see Shapiro, MacInnis, & Heckler, 1997). In each example, the former is episodic in nature, the latter semantic. As such, the assumptions of the distinction are oft en used for hypothesis testing, and taken for granted. For example, many consumer researchers assume that activation of nodes in semantic memory is a necessary by-product of cueing to a brand category or feature (e.g., Cowley & Mitchell, 2003; Nedungadi, 1990; Shapiro, 1999), and oft en discuss "activation" as a causal mechanism, rather than a proposed theoretical construct. Th is chapter argues that current major theories of memory are problematic, and instead favors an account of memory called SCAPE, which is an acronym for "Selective Construction And Preservation of Experiences" (Whittlesea, 1997). Th is account is a synthesis of ideas from the attribution theory of remembering (e.g., Jacoby & Dallas, 1981; Jacoby, Kelley, & Dywan, 1989; Whittlesea, 1993), the episodic-processing account of concept acquisition (e.g., Whittlesea & Dorken, 1993), instance theory (e.g., Brooks, 1978; Medin & Schaff er, 1978; Jacoby & Brooks, 1984), skill transfer (e.g., Kolers & Smythe, 1984), and transfer-appropriate processing (TAP; e.g., Morris, Bransford, & Franks, 1977;

Roediger & Challis, 1992; Masson & MacLeod, 1992). In accordance with the SCAPE framework, we suggest that the functions of mind identifi ed by separate systems (and most contemporary) theories are misleading: they are categories of mental performance that make sense from the point of view of the user of memory (one's conscious self), but do not correspond in any direct way with the fundamental principles of memory. We further argue that the real underlying mechanisms of memory are unitary and serve all of these user-defi ned functions; and moreover that they do so indirectly, such that the mechanism responsible for a certain behavior in no way resembles the behavior. Among other claims, we deny that remembering consists of retrieval; that spreading activation and inhibition are valid mental operations; that conscious and unconscious performance have diff erent causal agents; and that controlled and automatic behavior diff er in any meaningful way. A FUNCTIONAL ANALYSIS However obvious the contrasts between explicit and implicit performance, or between remembering and knowing, it will be argued in this chapter that none of those are fundamental functions of mind. Instead, they are emergent categories of behavior, useful in describing diff erences in a person's behavior from the outside, and perhaps in describing their current intentions, but not diagnostic of the underlying principles by which mind is organized. Th e problem, we assert, stems from a levels-of-analysis problem, confusing what a system achieves in operating on the world with the means by which that operation is attained. To take a simple example of the problem, in attempting a functional analysis of an automobile, one might perform an examination of the variety of things that cars are used for. Following such an examination, one might be tempted to say that a car's chief functions are transportation, ego projection, sport, and courtship. Certainly these are valid and separate categories of interaction with the world that cars enable us to achieve. However, they do not reveal anything about the underlying aff ordances that support these achievements (capacities such as steering, propulsion, shock absorption, and containment), and even less about the mechanisms that support these aff ordances (rack and pinion steering, disk brakes, Otto-cycle engine, and so on). Th at is, the functions of a system that are evident to and of value to the user of the system may not in any way resemble the basic principles by which the system operates. In consequence, arguing basic mechanism from dissociations among classes of activity that are important to the user is fraught with danger. More important, we believe that Nature, in her subtlety, oft en arranges for behaviors that are of advantage to her off spring to come about in ways that are startlingly indirect. As an example, consider a well-known phenomenon: that of a sunfl ower's tendency to follow the path of the sun over the course of a day, known as heliotropism. A direct mechanism to bring about this correspondence would require, in addition to some mechanical means of twisting, (a) that the plant knows, at a given moment, where the sun is, (b) that it also knows the direction in which it is currently pointed, and (c) that it has some means of calculating the diff erence. Clearly, such a direct mechanism is wrong. In fact, the mechanism is indirect, having the eff ect of bringing about alignment with the sun without any computation of that alignment. Th e actual, more subtle, explanation of this behavior is that red and blue wavelengths of light respectively increase and reduce photosynthesis and the resulting uptake of water into the stem's cells. Th e gradient of blue light across the plant stem in full sunlight causes cells on the shady side of the stem to increase photosynthesis and water uptake, expanding their size, whereas photosynthesis in cells on the sunny side is reduced, leading these cells to shrink. Th is combination of eff ects causes the head of the plant to twist, bending toward the sun. Th at the plant faces the sun accurately is in some sense an accident, resulting from the ratio of swelling in cells on opposite sides of the stem; the real cause of that eff ect is that ancestral sunfl owers that had better ratios of swelling, so that they followed the sun more precisely, out-competed those that did so less eff ectively. Th us, the success in sun-following, although vital to the plant, is better thought of as an incidental benefi t or by-product of its fundamental architecture, rather than as an inherent function of that architecture. Th ese two examples illustrate the diffi culty of functional analysis aimed at understanding the fundamental principles of a system that control that system's interactions with the world. We will propose a diff erent dichotomy of functions of mind, of production versus evaluation, that is fundamental to the SCAPE framework of memory (Whittlesea, 1997). Th is dichotomy is much more abstract than any of those recounted earlier, and much less easily tied to any specifi c behavior that a person performs. However, we will argue that it provides a more thorough explanation of the variety of human performance than do any of the other so far mentioned accounts. THE SCAPE FRAMEWORK According to the SCAPE account, there is only one memory system, which contains only representations of the experience of processing the stimuli in various tasks and contexts. In any processing event, this memory system interacts with the environment; the environment constrains some activities and aff ords others (e.g., you can use a pencil as a weapon or to stir coff ee, but cannot fl y on it). Th e central function of memory is construction: memory never simply registers or records the environment, but instead imposes selection, organization, and meaning on it. It is this experience of construction that will be encoded in memory, and that will control performance on subsequent interactions involving stimuli, tasks, and contexts that are similar on relevant dimensions. Th e construction function has two aspects: (1) the production of psychological events, controlled by the interaction of the stimulus, task, and context, with representations of previous processing experiences in memory; and (2) the evaluation of the signifi cance of that production, given the stimulus, task, and context. Th e former leads to performance: the occurrence of all manner of perceptual, cognitive, and motoric events. Th e latter results in phenomenology: the subjective reaction to current processing that causes people to adopt the attitude that they are remembering, understanding, or identifying an object, either correctly or committing an error. Th e production function begins by selecting some aspect of the current situation as a stimulus, or focus of attention, the rest as context. Th is selection depends on a variety of factors, including the prior history of memory with various aspects of the environment, each aspect's salience or apparent signifi cance (threat, novelty, interest), and the preparedness of the system to perform some activity given how and what it has just been processing. Th is process continues on to construct a mental model of the event: of a percept of the stimulus, of its identity, class or covert properties, or of the detail of a past or future event involving that stimulus, depending on the task at hand and the aff ordances and cue properties of the stimulus and context. Many accounts of memory involve (at least in part) assumptions that sound similar to those just stated. However, the SCAPE account makes two radical claims. Th e fi rst is that current cognitive processing is always the product of a constructive act. One implication is that, although a prior episode can, in part, control the shape and ease of constructing a mental model of a current stimulus, that prior episode is not itself retrieved. Th at has major implications for understanding the nature of remembering, as documented below. A second departure is the account's insistence that the production function is always accompanied by the operation of the evaluation function, although that is oft en diffi cult to detect (see Kronlund & Whittlesea, 2005, for a demonstration of this point). Th e evaluation function consists of chronic monitoring of the integrity and coherence of ongoing performance;

it also makes inferences about unexpected successes or apparent failures of coherence. In the words of Marcel (1983), it consists of an attempt to "make sense of as much data as possible at the most functionally useful level" (p. 238). It is this act of inference which gives rise to the phenomenology accompanying performance. In attempting to make sense of apparent disparities between two aspects of a current stimulus, or between what is expected and what occurs, the evaluation function makes an attribution to some plausible source of infl uence. Th e apparent disparity may be resolved by an attribution to the stimulus, the situation, the person, or the past; these unconscious attributions give rise to conscious feelings such as desirability, impending danger, unusual mood, or familiarity. THE CONSTRUCTIVE NATURE OF AWARENESS According to separate systems accounts, explicit and declarative knowledge is thought to be accessed by retrieval. In contrast, the SCAPE account assumes that information is never retrieved, but constructed. Th is idea was originally proposed by Bartlett (1932), and with some exceptions (e.g., Janiszewski, Noel, & Sawyer, 2003; Braun-LaTour, LaTour, Pickrell, & Loft us, 2004),1 it is hardly considered in the consumer literature. As an example, imagine that a recognition study begins with a study phase consisting of paired associates, such as onion-carrot, milk-cheese, bread-cake, etc. At test, when asked "Did you see MILK in the earlier list?", one subject may reply "MILK......oh yeah, CHEESE. Yes, I do remember seeing MILK." Th at performance seems to demonstrate that the person has used MILK as a cue to retrieve the episodic representation of the earlier experience, and that, in doing so, they have become aware of a prior experience. Th at description of the process is too simple, however. Another subject might respond "MILK, um, CHEESE, um, no, that's just a common associate. I don't remember MILK." Th at subject's initial performance duplicates that of the fi rst subject's. However, although the content of the earlier experience comes to mind, this person has not become aware of the prior experience. Another subject might say, "MILK — oh right, DAIRY. Yes, I do remember seeing MILK." Th is person's performance is infl uenced by a source other than the specifi c prior experience, yet this person is experiencing awareness of encountering that item. Th ese examples demonstrate that becoming aware of a prior experience is caused by two interlinked processes: the production of a response, and an evaluation of the signifi cance of that production. Th e coming-to-mind of an item in a remembering task is thus not one and the same as awareness of the prior event. Awareness of the source of the production comes about by an evaluation of the signifi cance of that production, which results in an attribution to a source that seems most likely. As another illustration of the diff erence between these two aspects of construction, Leboe and Whittlesea (2002) presented subjects with pairs of items: one-third contained two strong associates (e.g., LION-TIGER), one-third contained two unrelated words (e.g., ROAD-NAVY), and onethird contained one word and four Xs (e.g., TABLE-XXXX). Each associate in the former two cases occurred only once in the study phase, whereas XXXX occurred on many study trials. At test, subjects were provided with a word stem (e.g., LION-?) and were required to recall the item with which it was paired earlier, and provide a confi dence rating about their performance. Subjects performed accurate recall on 48% of the trials involving strong associates, on only 13% of the trials involving unrelated words, and on 41% of the trials involving XXXXs. In contrast, subjects' confi dence ratings for those trials were 78% for recall of the strong associates, 91% for recall of the unrelated words, and only 45% for recall of XXXXs. Leboe and Whittlesea concluded that the diff erential rates of recall accuracy and confi dence refl ect the interaction of two operations: the coming-to-mind of a response (i.e., a strong associate, an unrelated word, or XXXX), and the subject's resulting evaluation of the signifi cance of each of those types of responses coming to mind. For example, subjects were unimpressed with the coming-to-mind of XXXX, because they were aware that they could easily generate it because of their knowledge that one-third of studied items were paired with XXXX. Th us, they oft en produced XXXX correctly, but even when accurate, they were not convinced that they were actually recalling. In contrast, recall of an unrelated word was diffi cult, in part because the association formed during study would oft en be of low quality (e.g., the association between ROAD and NAVY). Consequently, accurate recall was low in this condition. However, when an unrelated word did come to mind, subjects were very impressed because they could think of no other reason why that word would come to mind other than that it had been presented in study. Such productions were thus experienced as accurate recall, and were associated with high confi dence ratings. Th erefore, the conclusion that one is now aware of an aspect of the past is always a decision: an adoption of an attitude toward current processing. Awareness of the contents of previous experiences does not comprise direct access to a representation of the past. It is the product of a heuristic decision. People are chronically having to infer the nature of their past from the quality and content of their current processing. Th ere are always multiple possible reasons why a particular mental event occurs: because it actually occurred in one's past, because one experienced a similar event with a diff erent stimulus, because that event occurred in the life of someone else who has told you about it, or because one has experienced many similar events, which in parallel contribute to the ease of processing the current mental event. Th is inferential relationship between awareness and experience is not limited to remembering. It is also true of knowledge in general. In the next section, we will demonstrate analogous performance in remembering and classifi cation judgments, but that people claim awareness of the basis of their performance in the fi rst but not the second. Th e diff erence appears to be only due to the adoption of an appropriate attitude and theory to understand their performance in the fi rst case and a lack of doing so in the latter.2 SEPARATE SYSTEMS APPROACHES TO MEMORY Separate-systems accounts of memory, including the episodic/semantic (Tulving, 1983, 1985), declarative/procedural (Cohen & Squire, 1980), and explicit/implicit (Graf & Schacter, 1985) dichotomies, are based on the notion that memory performance is sustained by distinct modules of memory. Th e modules support diff erent functions of memory, each of which is based on specifi c types of knowledge, and thus have specifi c principles for acquiring and applying each type of knowledge. Each type of knowledge is also selectively cued by diff erent types of tasks, and preserved in distinct stores. Evidence for such dichotomies in memory has come from dissociations that have been observed in both intact and amnesic subjects. We provide an in-depth description of the episodic/ semantic and implicit/explicit dichotomies, as they have dominated how consumer researchers conceptualize memory.3 We provide empirical evidence for each distinction, and examples of consumer behavior studies which have embraced or relied on each. We focus primarily on studies on consumer memory published since the review by Alba et al. (1991). THE EPISODIC/SEMANTIC DICHOTOMY According to this account, memory can be subdivided into an episodic system which preserves details of particular experiences and supports remembering tasks (i.e., recall and recognition), and a semantic system, which preserves conceptual and categorical knowledge and supports nonremembering activities (i.e., perception and identifi cation). Th e semantic system thus preserves the abstract, context-free, summary properties of all prior experiences (Tulving, 1983, 1985). Th e fundamental distinction is between remembering, which depends on event-specifi c information, and knowing, which depends on the abstracted summary of prior experiences. Event-specifi c information can take on the form of tokens (Kanwisher, 1987); abstractions can take on the form of types (Anderson, 1980, 1983; Kanwisher, 1987), prototypes (Rosch, 1978), rules (Reber, 1989, 1993), or logogens (Paap & Noel, 1991). Th e process of acquiring knowledge occurs by automatic abstraction or implicit learning; the process of accessing knowledge is thought to be mediated by the principles of activation and inhibition. Although not always made explicit, numerous consumer researchers appear to assume an episodic/ semantic distinction of memory. A set of studies have examined how brand or product category schemas are formed and organized. For example, Meyvis and Janiszewski (2004) investigated how breadth of brand categories aff ects brand associations and perceptions of brand extensions (see also Gurhan-Canli, 2003); Wood and Lynch (2002) examined the eff ects of expertise or prior knowledge about products on learning of new information and subsequent memory; and Roedder-John and Sujan (1990) studied product information organization and categorization in young children.

Th e strength and extensiveness of information held in memory and how it aff ects consumers' judgments and decisions are almost always considered to be a direct or indirect function of person-related (e.g., motivation, ability), stimulus-related (e.g., distinctiveness, visual vs. verbal), and situational factors (e.g., time delay, usage situation). For example, Park and Hastak (1994) have examined how involvement aff ects product memory, and how the product memory aff ects judgments. Peracchio and Tybout (1996) have also investigated how product category schema aff ects product evaluations. In particular, they examined the eff ects of schema incongruity on product evaluations. Th us these consumer studies share commonalities with some aspects of the SCAPE framework. For instance, the production part of construction processes posited by the SCAPE assumes an interaction of stimulus, task, and context that is in line with the approach taken by consumer researchers. However, there is no accompanying acknowledgement in the studies that the signifi cance of the production is, in turn, evaluated. Other studies have also investigated the manner in which organization of brand information or prior knowledge aff ects how and what information is processed and remembered by consumers. Th e way that prior knowledge infl uences judgments or choice has been of interest to a number of consumer researchers (e.g., Crowley & Mitchell, 2003; Hutchinson, Raman, & Mantrala, 1994; Nedungadi, 1990). Th ese studies, however, largely assume that "retrieval" occurs as the result of a spreading activation process. A threshold level of activation of a particular concept, such as a brand, is assumed to be facilitated through the use of cues such as attribute information. Th is in turn results in retrieval of the target brand. Spreading activation models have also been applied to models of brand equity (e.g., Aaker, 1991; Keller, 1993, 1998). In the following sections we describe assumptions made by the episodic/semantic approach that separate principles are involved in remembering and knowing, that acquisition of knowledge occurs by automatic abstraction, and that access to knowledge structures is mediated by activation and inhibition. We consider further examples of consumer behavior studies which have embraced each assumption. We also provide predictions made by SCAPE for each observation discussed. ACQUIRING KNOWLEDGE STRUCTURES One observation that suggests the use of abstracted information is implicit learning (Dienes & Berry, 1997; Knowlton & Squire, 1994; Reber & Allen, 1978; Reber, 1989, 1993). As an example of what takes place during an implicit learning study, brand logos (e.g., the Hello Kitty picture) are shown to subjects in their regular and opposite orientations (e.g., Hello Kitty with a bow in her hair above her right ear instead of her left ear). Subjects are above chance at choosing the correct orientation, suggesting automatic, incidental learning of regularity in such stimuli (Kelly, Burton, Kato, & Akamatsu, 2001). Such results have also been found in controlled laboratory settings, where attention is directed to stimuli that follow a rule. At test, subjects are above chance at discriminating between legal and illegal items (i.e., they demonstrate sensitivity to the abstract structure of the domain) without having awareness of the rule (e.g., McGeorge & Burton, 1990). Such performance is taken as evidence that the subjects must have abstracted information about the rule during the exposure phase. Because they are unaware of doing so, that abstraction must be automatic. Th e phenomenon of implicit learning is thus argued to demonstrate the existence in memory of an autonomous abstraction mechanism that proceeds independent of conscious intention or awareness, and supports performance in tasks such as classifi cation and identifi cation. Th e suggestion of automatic abstraction has been criticized on the grounds that test items that are legal are highly similar to each previously encountered legal (studied) exemplar of the given class, therefore, if a subject simply memorizes one or more of the study items, and uses the perceived similarity of test items to those memorized instances as a basis for their decision, they will perform above chance (Brooks, 1978, 1987; Dulany, Carlson, & Dewey, 1984; Neal & Hesketh, 1997; Perruchet & Pacteau, 1991; Shanks & St. John, 1994; Vokey & Brooks, 1992). Th is provides a situation whereby the same processes that are involved in showing sensitivity to prior individual experiences (episodic) are also involved in showing sensitivity to general, abstract properties of classes (semantic). Th e SCAPE account is in agreement, but adds that memory preserves processing experiences, and the type of processing experience that occurred on a prior encounter with a stimulus will infl uence later processing of the same (or a similar) stimulus to the extent that later processing matches the earlier processing experience (i.e., transfer appropriate processing: henceforth TAP; Morris et al., 1977). Th e SCAPE account suggests that TAP will apply to both remembering and non-remembering tasks (Whittlesea & Dorken, 1993, 1997). To demonstrate that TAP applies to non-remembering activities such as classifi cation, Wright and Whittlesea (1998) developed a set of four-digit stimuli, each which followed the rule oddeven-odd-even (e.g., 3412, 8954, etc). Th ey presented these items to subjects in a study phase, and encouraged them to read them as bigrams (e.g., "thirty-four, twelve," etc). At test, no studied items were shown, however, half corresponded to the odd-even-odd-even rule, half violated the rule (e.g., 4613, 8723, etc). Subjects were asked to discriminate legal from illegal items, and they accurately did so 68% of the time, although they were unable to state the rule. Th is type of fi nding is usually interpreted as providing evidence for automatic abstraction and subsequent use of a rule in semantic memory. In another study, the same study phase was used. At test, studied (e.g., 3412) and new (e.g., 1374) items were presented; subjects were asked to discriminate studied from unstudied items (i.e., they performed recognition); they accurately did so 71% of the time. Th is type of fi nding is usually interpreted as acquisition and use of episodic memory. In a subsequent study, half the subjects were given the identical study and instructions as outlined above (i.e., to read digits as bigrams), the other half were encouraged to read stimuli as individual digits (e.g., "three-fourone-two"). Th e bigram group classifi ed legal from illegal test items with 70% accuracy, however the digit group had only 58% accuracy. Th is result demonstrates that representations of particular experiences are determined by the type of task used, and are preserved and demonstrate transfer to both recognition and classifi cation tasks. In their fourth experiment, they showed subjects digits in a study phase, and encouraged them to read them as bigrams. At test, subjects were able to discriminate legal (odd-even-odd-even) from illegal items at 65% accuracy, but could not state the rule, again suggesting automatic abstraction of the rule. In this study however, the study items all consisted of combinations of odd-odd or eveneven bigrams with odd-even bigrams (e.g., 3714, 8432, 6897, etc). Th us, if subjects were abstracting a rule of some sort, it would be "either odd-odd or even-even as one of the two bigrams." In this case, Wright and Whittlesea attempted to demonstrate that subjects could appear to show sensitivity to a rule (i.e., to a non-existent odd-even-odd-even rule). To achieve this end, they constructed the test items such that both bigrams in the "legal" test items (e.g., 1432) had occurred in several study items (e.g., in 3714, 8432, 7514, etc), whereas the bigrams of the "illegal" items (e.g., 3154) never occurred in any of the study items. Th us subjects could successfully classify the items if and only if they had encoded the instances from study rather than if they had automatically abstracted a rule. Th e ability of subjects to show above-chance performance at classifying according to the non-existent odd-even-odd-even rule demonstrates that subjects used the similarity of the test items to study instances to classify them. Th e important lesson to be learned from these studies is about the nature of awareness. In the initial recognition study, when subjects were told about their above-chance scores, they were unimpressed: when asked for an explanation of their success, they said something like, "Well, I just remembered them, you know?" In contrast, subjects in the remaining studies were quite mystifi ed when told about their above-chance success. Having not been told any rules, and having not consciously worked out any rules, they could think of no basis for above-chance success, and agreed that they must have learned the rules unconsciously. In fact, the set of experiments taken together suggest that the subjects performed on exactly the same basis in classifi cation as they did in recognition. Why, then, should they not be aware of the basis of their success? We suggest that they adopted an inappropriate theory (as did the original investigators of this eff ect): that success in classifying according to a rule can occur only if one has the rule. Th is adoption of an inappropriate theory prevented the subjects from achieving awareness of the basis of their performance. In turn however, that conclusion changes the nature of what is meant by awareness. Rather than being aware or unaware of what we are doing, the question is whether we are aware or unaware of the eff ect of what we are doing now with respect to some unanticipated decision in the future. Viewed in that way, "awareness" is an attribution, based on an inference, about the signifi cance of our current processing. Th ought of in this way, "accessibility" and "diagnosticity" (Feldman & Lynch, 1988) are very complicated processes, which, according to the assumptions of SCAPE, may be based on a person's intuitive theories of cause and eff ect, the salient aspects of the current situation, and the current task, which selectively cues prior experiences, both individually and in parallel.

4

Consumer Learning and Expertise

To structure our review of research on consumer learning and expertise, it is useful to note a perspective that is seldom explicitly endorsed or rejected, but is lurking behind the scenes in the literature on consumer knowledge. In the normal course of everyday life, people have many experiences that involve products (i.e., goods and services), and they become increasingly familiar with those products. Also, over time people learn from these experiences and gain true expertise in a variety of product domains. Following Alba and Hutchinson (1987), we use the term familiarity to refer to the accumulated level of product-related experiences and expertise to refer to the ability to perform product-related tasks successfully. We will refer to the general hypothesis that increased familiarity leads to increases in expertise as learning from experience (H1). Also, it seems reasonable that as expertise increases, people become better and more effi cient in their roles as consumers. We will refer to this general hypothesis as inproved consumer welfare (H2). As will become evident as we proceed, these hypotheses are not always supported, and sometimes opposite results obtain (i.e., increased familiarity leads to less expertise or increased expertise leads to lower welfare), but most people would agree that the world would be a better place if it worked according to H1 and H2. Hence, we have dubbed this pair of hypotheses the "perfect world" perspective. Independent of whether the perfect world perspective is valid or not, one result of research in this area has been to show that the key constructs—product familiarity, consumer expertise, and consumer welfare—are multidimensional in nature (see Figure 4.1). Product familiarity can arise from a wide variety of experiences, including information search, repeated decision making, repeated product usage and consumption, and deliberate practice. Each of these types of experience has been found to increase expertise in some cases, but not in others. However, high levels of expertise are seldom obtained without successful information search, or without clear and immediate feedback about the outcomes of decisions, usage, and consumption. In consumer domains that include competitive performance or creative expression, deliberate practice is oft en essential. Similarly, there are a number of benefi ts that could arise from product familiarity through the development of consumer expertise. First, consumers could become more completely and perfectly informed because expertise allows consumers to comprehend, retain, recall, and infer more information with lower levels of error. Second, consumers could make more optimal decisions because they learn more successful strategies, rely less on simple heuristics, are able to reason further into the future and conform more to traditional conceptualizations of "rational," utility-maximizing behavior. Th ird, consumers could incur lower costs of information search, product usage, and consumption because they become faster and better at these activities or because they learn new, more effi cient strategies and behaviors. Th ese costs would include time, money, and mental and physical eff ort. Finally, consumers could obtain more or better outcomes from information search, product usage, and consumption because the ultimate utilitarian and hedonic results of these activities are produced in part by consumers themselves, and expertise could create more eff ective production functions. Th e multidimensionality of consumer expertise has been frequently noted (Alba & Hutchinson, 1987, 2000; Brucks, 1985). In the remainder of this section, we will specifi cally consider changes resulting from product familiarity in cognitive structure, memory, elaboration, analytic processing, knowledge calibration, cognitive eff ort/automaticity, and skilled behaviors, and the benefi ts that arise from these changes. For each dimension, we will summarize the status of learning from experience (H1) and improved consumer welfare (H2). Our discussions will highlight what we see as key results and ongoing issues and will refer readers to more comprehensive treatments of the topics. Aft er this overview, we will continue assessing the perfect world perspective as we review theory and method in the area of consumer learning and expertise. COGNITIVE STRUCTURE Cognitive structure refers to the way in which factual knowledge is organized in memory. Th e most common forms of cognitive structures studied in consumer research are naturally occurring, taxonomic categories because the mappings onto the marketing concepts of product categories, brand families, and market niches are fairly direct. Several stylized facts from cognitive psychology are commonly adopted. First, most product categories exhibit the characteristics of basic level categories (e.g., objects are named at this level and processing is faster to identify objects as belonging to a basic level; Rosch, Mervis, Gray,. Johnson, & Boyes-Braem, 1976). Th e central claim about basic level categories is that within-category similarity and between-category dissimilarity are maximized at this level. It is easy to see how market forces make product categories the basic level insofar as product categories are defi ned as collections of substitutes that compete with each other to fulfi ll the same consumer needs. Moreover, as expertise increases, knowledge about subordinate categories increases and information at this level is processed as effi ciently as (but not more effi ciently than) at the basic level (Johnson & Mervis, 1997). Second, product categories exhibit a graded structure that can be indexed by measures of typicality (Medin & Smith, 1984; Rosch & Mervis, 1975). A central issue from the perspective of consumer research is the extent to which the most typical products are also the best products (in general or for specifi c consumers). Th ird, the ad hoc and goal-derived categories that consumers oft en use in shopping (e.g., things to by for a camping trip, my favorite restaurants, etc.) also exhibit graded structure (Barsalou, 1985). Several researchers have confi rmed that as product familiarity increases, especially from nonuser to user of a product, cognitive structure is acquired (e.g., Hutchinson, Raman, & Mantrala, 1994; Nedungadi & Hutchinson, 1985). Mitchell and Dacin (1996) provide a particularly thorough analysis of the cognitive structures found for motorcycles. Th ey factor analyzed 10 measures related to product familiarity and expertise and found that subjective and objective measures of knowledge loaded on the same factor; however, number owned and magazines read formed a second factor and number owned by friends formed a third. In general, their results confi rm the perfect world perspective, but there are some cautionary notes. Self-rated familiarity loaded on the same factor as measures of subjective and objective knowledge, supporting learning from experience (H1). However, the independence of number owned and magazines read (which clearly indexes the number of product-related experiences) from the knowledge measures does not support H1, or at least suggests that mere ownership does not lead to knowledge. Moreover, while the knowledge measures were strongly related to measures of the organization of knowledge, ownership was only weakly related, at best. Also, a separate experimental session assessed choices among hypothetical motorcycles for which there were objectively correct answers. Th e knowledge factor was strongly related to correct choices and correct reasons for the choices, supporting improved consumer welfare (H2). However, ownership was not predictive of choice, further weakening the simple view of familiarity leading to expertise leading to better decisions. Th ese results suggest that not all types of product experiences increase learning and expertise. Interestingly, ownership of motorcycles by friends was also highly predictive of choice quality. Th is suggests a social dimension to consumer expertise that has not been explored in detail. MEMORY Th e hallmark of expertise in all domains is greater memory for domain facts. Th e classic studies of chess experts showed that grand masters could remember game confi gurations much better than novices, but only for confi gurations that were possible in real games (Chase & Simon, 1973). Memory for random confi gurations was the same for experts and novices. Similar results have been obtained in a wide variety of fi elds (see Vincente & Wang, 1998, for a discussion of theories that account for expert recall superiority). While little of this research has been called consumer research, many (arguably most) of the domains involve consumer markets (mainly for entertainment of various sorts) that become professions at the highest levels of expertise. Games (chess, bridge, and go), sports (baseball, basketball, football, fi gure skating, and fi eld hockey), computer programming, and even medical diagnosis exhibit this type of continuum and have empirical evidence for expert recall superiority. Superior memory has also been found in explicitly consumeroriented research (Mitchell & Dacin, 1996). Memory superiority, almost by defi nition, leads to more completely and perfectly informed consumers, and in that sense these results support both learning from experience (H1) and improved consumer welfare (H2). In addition to greater recall, the cognitive structures that are acquired infl uence the recall of brands and attributes, which ones are recalled and in what order (Hutchinson, Raman, & Mantrala, 1994; Mitchell & Dacin, 1996; Nedungadi, Chattopadhyay, & Muthukrishnan, 2001; Ratneshwar, Peckman, & Shocker, 1996; Ratneshwar & Shocker, 1991). Cowley and Mitchell (2003) found that when novices were exposed to product information in the context of a specifi c usage situation, they could not reorganize that information in memory and successfully recall products appropriate for a diff erent usage situation. Expert consumers were able to retain more information and better recall information that was appropriate for a new situation. Cowley and Janus (2004) found that high product familiarity consumers had better memory for a product experience and were more resistant to the biasing eff ects of misleading advertisements about that experience than were low familiarity consumers. Th us, in addition to information being more complete and perfect, there is evidence that decisions will be better (see also Mitchell & Dacin, 1996), supporting the perfect world perspective. In contrast, Wood and Lynch (2000) found that, compared to novices, experts were less likely to encode and remember new product information that made older information obsolete. However, experts did learn better than novices if they were cued that their knowledge might be out of date or if they were given incentives to carefully attend to all information about the new product. ELABORATION In addition to better organization and memory for information acquired directly from product experiences, experts sometimes exhibit higher levels of reasoning and problem solving in their domains of expertise. Alba and Hutchinson (1987) referred to these abilities as elaboration new knowledge that is internally generated from old knowledge). Arguably the most frequent and important type of elaboration for consumers is the ability to infer the ultimate benefi ts and costs of a product based on its objective features and technical specifi cations and use these inferences to solve the problem of satisfying specifi c needs. For example, expert consumers in the domain of computer products can accurately assess the price, size, weight, CPU, RAM, cache, and I/O ports of various laptops, and choose the machine that best suits their need for out-of-offi ce computing. Novices are less able to engage in this type of elaboration. However, novices are more likely to elaborate by simplifi cation (e.g., many technical features are interpreted as implying performance superiority, regardless of the match between those features and their specifi c needs). Evidence for accurate feature-to-benefi t inferences by expert consumers and increased simplifi cation by novices can be found in the results of an extensive experiment on mass customization conducted by Dellaert and Stremersch (2005). In this experiment a probability sample of consumers shopped for hypothetical computers using confi gurations of mass customization that varied in extent of customization, heterogeneity in levels of product attributes, pricing format, and presence and type of default option. Th ese factors created large diff erences in the degree of success consumers had in constructing their most preferred computer (as measured by the rated utility of the fi nal product design) and the amount of complexity they perceived in the customization process. Importantly, expertise was shown to reduce perceived complexity, increase product utility, and reduce the negative eff ect of complexity on product utility. Th ese results are also supportive of the perfect world hypothesis. ANALYTIC PROCESSING A number of researchers in diff erent areas of cognitive psychology have argued that there are two fundamentally diff erent types of information processing and decision making (e.g., Hammond & Brehmer, 1973; Jacoby & Brooks, 1984; Sloman, 1996). One corresponds fairly closely to normative, logical reasoning. It is analytic and rule-based. A central characteristic of this type of thought is identifying and using only the information that is relevant and diagnostic, ignoring other information that may be salient but irrelevant. Th e second is associative, similarity-based, intuitive, and holistic in the sense that all salient information is integrated in some way to form an overall judgment or choose among options. Because this second type has been given so many diff erent names and defi nitions, we will simply refer to it as non-analytic processing. In consumer research, this diff erence has been related to situational factors. Hutchinson and Alba (1991) found that intentional learning (e.g., deliberately trying to understand the product attributes that infl uence price) increased the likelihood of analytic information processing; however, incidental learning (e.g., learning about price when one's explicit goal is forming overall preferences), complexity, and memory load were all found to increase the likelihood of non-analytic processing factors. Importantly, several researchers have reported evidence that experts are more likely to engage in analytic processing than are novices (Alba & Hutchinson, 1987; Dillon, Madden, Kirmani, & Mukherjee, 2001; Spence & Brucks, 1997). Dillon et al. developed a psychometrically sophisticated model of brand ratings and found that the ratings of high experience consumers were more infl uenced by brand specifi c attributes and less infl uenced by general brand impressions than were the ratings of low experience consumers. Spence and Brucks compared professional appraisers (experts) to undergraduates (novices) in a task that required participants to estimate the market value of houses based on multi-attribute descriptions. Th ey found that experts used fewer but more diagnostic attributes compared to novices. Both of these results are consistent with the hypothesis that processing shift s from holistic to analytic as product familiarity increases (i.e., H1, learning from experience).

5

Categorization Theory and Research in Consumer Psychology

To make sense of the myriad new and existing products and services in the marketplace, consumers construct and use categorical representations to classify, interpret, and understand information they receive about these products and services. We defi ne a consumer category as a set of products, services, brands, or other marketing entities, states, or events that appear, to the consumer, related in some way. We defi ne a categorical representation as information that becomes stored in the cognitive system for a consumer category, and that is later used to process it.1 One important use of category representations is during categorization, when consumers use these representations to assign a particular product or service to a consumer category, so that they can understand and draw inferences about it. Consumers might classify a new product as an MP3 player on the basis of prior knowledge about physical or functional features of MP3 players, for example, that MP3 players store music effi ciently, are small in size, and are rectangular in shape. Once the new product is categorized, prior categorical information about MP3 players may also be used to make inferences about unknown attributes or features of the new product, or to form an evaluation of the new product. From a marketing perspective, a number of questions about categorization have been examined that have implications for marketing decision making. For example, how should a new product be positioned so that consumers can identify it as belonging to a particular product category? How can it be diff erentiated from competitors in the same category? How should the structural aspects of a product or consumer-relevant category be measured? What factors increase category fl exibility and acceptance of new category members? If a new product is introduced with an existing brand name (e.g., Kraft microwave popcorn), how will the existing brand image (e.g., Kraft) aff ect its categorization? How will the image aff ect its acceptance? What contextual, environmental and individual diff erence variables infl uence acceptance of a new category member (e.g., a brand extension)? Will a brand (e.g., Kraft) be perceived diff erently if it includes a very diff erent category (microwave popcorn) than prior existing members of the category (macaroni and cheese, cheese slices, etc.)?

In the present chapter, we build on the 1987 reviews by addressing theoretical and empirical research in consumer psychology in the subsequent two decades. Th e organization of this chapter uses a framework that refl ects the structure of the basic science underlying the reviewed research, in particular addressing two general areas of study, category representation and category-based inferences. Within each of these sections, we discuss the types of consumer research questions that have been addressed. In the fi rst general section, on category representation, we describe theory and research that addresses the nature, structure, and functional location of category representations. We provide a brief overview of the three prominent historical views of category representation, including the prototype, exemplar, and connectionist views (for more extensive discussion of these views, in cognitive psychology, see Barsalou, 2003a,b; Murphy, 2002; Smith & Medin, 1981; for further discussion of prototype and exemplar views in consumer psychology, see Cohen & Basu, 1987, Alba & Hutchinson, 1987). Next we discuss the dual roles of category representations as both stable and fl exible. Flexibility of category representations has been shown in recent literature of consumer psychology in the context of consumer goals and research on malleable self (and cultural) views. We also discuss consumer research that addresses the question of the conditions under which a specifi c category representation will be activated in a given context. Finally, we close the topic of category representations by addressing an emerging research direction within cognitive psychology on the functional location of category representations in consumers' memory. We introduce Barsalou's (1999) proposition that representations reside in the brain's modality-specifi c systems. Th is work is important because the assumptions underlying the nature and neural location of category representations in Barsalou's theory departs signifi cantly from the assumptions underlying previouslydeveloped theories. We review consumer research that is consistent with this theory and call for future research that demonstrates and tests the theory in a variety of consumer contexts and across diff erent sensory modalities. In the second general section of this chapter we examine the role of category-based inferences in consumer judgments, particularly with respect to brand categories. Brand categorization research emerges as a prominent research direction of the prior two decades, with researchers studying the conditions under which category-based inferences are generated and used in judgments, particularly when a brand extension (a new category member) is introduced to the consumer. We examine the role of similarity (e.g., between a category and a new category member) in forming category inferences, together with when and how new instances of a category (e.g., new brand extensions) impact existing category representations and vice versa. Also in the context of brand categories, consumer researchers have examined factors that increase category expansion and acceptance of new category members, or fl exibility in category structure. We demonstrate that factors that increase category expansion and fl exibility oft en work through their impact on consumer perceptions of similarity. Building on research that addresses category structure and similiarity, we analyze the important relationship between prototypicality and aff ect, and alternative theoretical explanations for the conditions under which a positive relationship will be demonstrated. Finally, we conclude this chapter by summarizing the methodologies and analytic techniques that categorization researchers in this area typically use, and then off er some fi nal conclusions about research on category representations and category-based inferences. HISTORICALLY SIGNIFICANT VIEWS OF CATEGORY REPRESENTATION Prototype, exemplar, and connectionist theories represent three prominent accounts of how categories are represented in memory. Th e prototype view assumes that categories are represented by abstract composites, called prototypes, based on central tendency information. Th ese summary representations are based on the most likely features of the category's instances, based on a person's experiences with category members (e.g., Rosch & Mervis, 1975). Th e features in a prototype need only be probable of the concept, not necessary and suffi cient. Categories are assumed to have graded structure, such that some category members are more representative, or typical, of a category than other category members. For example, popcorn is more representative than yogurt of the snack food category. Th e brand iPod is more representative of MP3 players than the brand Rio Sport. Within brand categories, the product Diet Coke is more representative of the Coca-Cola brand than Vanilla Diet Coke. In general, greater feature overlap with common features of the category is presumed to increase a category member's prototypicality. A new stimulus is classifi ed as a category member to the extent that it is more similar to the category prototype and less similar to competing category prototypes. Th e exemplar view assumes that categories are represented by specifi c, stored instances of the category, rather than by general, abstracted prototypes. An exemplar is oft en viewed as a representation of a specifi c category instance (e.g., a specifi c MP3 player, such as iPod). Some exemplar theorists, however, assume that an exemplar can also be a subset of a category (e.g., sedans as a subset of automobiles), its representation consisting of other exemplars or a conceptualization of the subset's features. According to exemplar theorists, a new stimulus (e.g., an ad for a new MP3 player) acts as a retrieval cue to access similar exemplar representations (e.g., iPod) in memory. The stimulus is classifi ed as a member in the category to which it has the most similar stored exemplar representation (Medin & Schaff er, 1978). Finally, the connectionist approach (McClelland & Rumelhart, 1985) views categories as attractors in dynamic feature spaces. Th is view assumes that people establish correlations of features that co-occur for a category (e.g., MP3 players) by tuning associations between features in a network to represent these feature confi gurations. A new stimulus then activates the most similar feature confi guration in the network (i.e., an attractor), which then captures the stimulus, and assigns it to the associated category. STABILITY AND FLEXIBILITY IN CONSUMER CATEGORY REPRESENTATIONS Regardless of the approach taken to representing categories, category representations must be both stable and fl exible if they are to explain the information processing activity that underlies consumer behavior. Th e consumer environment is complex and ever changing. Th ousands of new products are introduced in the marketplace each year. To keep up with these changes, consumers need two types of information processing capabilities. On the one hand, they need stable representations of products and brands in memory that relate veridically to their environment. Th ese stable representations provide a foundation upon which consumer information processing can take place. Th ey are important for recognizing, interpreting, and evaluating both objects and events in a wide variety of consumer environments. Simultaneously, however, these object and event representations require considerable fl exibility, as consumers adapt them to an unlimited number of situations and unexpected changes in the environment. We address stability and fl exibility further in turn. Stability of Category Representations Structure and stability of product categories. A number of consumer studies have sought to understand the determinants of prototypicality and the underlying structure of product categories. Some of these studies have assessed degree of prototypicality through analysis of a category's features or attributes, using measures such as family resemblance (Rosch & Mervis, 1975; in the consumer literature, Loken & Ward, 1990; Viswanathan & Childers, 1999), ideals (Barsalou, 1985; in the consumer literature, Loken & Ward, 1990; Viswanathan & Childers, 1999), attribute structure (Loken & Ward, 1987, 1990), and fuzzy set-based measures of category membership (Viswanathan & Childers, 1999; for a more complete discussion of these measures, see Barsalou, 1985; Loken & Ward, 1990; and Viswanathan & Childers, 1999.) Implementing these attribute-based measures oft en requires obtaining preliminary data to determine the attributes or ideals that are salient or accessible for a particular product category. Attribute-based measures are then correlated with various measures of prototypicality (e.g., Barsalou, 1985; Loken & Ward, 1987, 1990; Viswanathan & Childers, 1999). Across many studies, these attribute-based measures have been found to predict prototypicality measures well (Barsalou, 1985; Loken & Ward, 1990). For example, Loken and Ward (1990) found that a global typicality measure was signifi cantly (p < .05) correlated with both an attribute structure measure (r = .68 for 8 subordinate and r = .33 for 8 superordinate product categories) and an ideals measure (r = .64 and .51, p < .05, for the same 8 subordinate and 8 superordinate categories). Viswanathan and Childers (1999), almost a decade later, made small modifi cations to the Loken and Ward (1990) attribute and exemplar lists, and recomputed the correlations for 8 of the original 16 categories with an updated sample. For categories at both the superordinate and subordinate levels, signifi cant correlations again occurred between global typicality measures and attribute structure (r = .47 for the 4 subordinates, and r = .42 for the 4 superordinates); signifi cant correlations also occurred between global typicality measures and ideals (r = .69 and .64, for the 4 subordinates and 4 superordinates, respectively). Th ese correlations show that predictions with the ideals measure were very stable from 1990 to 1999.

Prediction with the measure of attribute structure changed somewhat from the 1990 to the 1999 study, which may refl ect expected changes over the course of a decade in category composition, or even in minor changes of attributes across the nine-year period. Viswanathan and Childers (1999) also found that two fuzzy-set measures that assessed representativeness at the attribute level also predicted typicality very well (reverse scored, with global typicality, r = .72 and .55 for the four superordinates and .75 and .93 for the four subordinates). As these results illustrate, the structure of product categories, both at the superordinate and subordinate levels, appears quite stable over time and across diff erent product categories. Structure and stability of emotion categories. One might expect emotion categories (e.g., anger) to be more unstable than other types of categories. However, research in consumer and social psychology suggests that even emotion responses exhibit stability. Over time, people provide reliable measures of emotion categories, as shown in Richins' (1997) review and development of scale descriptors for thirteen emotional states in consumption situations. Ruth (2001) further fi nds that when the description of an emotion in the tagline of an advertisement (e.g., aff ection) is congruent with a description of an emotion expressed in the ad (aff ection), people prefer the ad to one in which the emotions described are incongruent (aff ection and joy). Furthermore, emotionally-valenced product attributes that are bipolar opposites appear to be related in memory, such that priming one (e.g., healthy) can activate the other (unhealthy), as demonstrated through how product information is interpreted (e.g., "more sweeteners" is interpreted as unhealthy) and how it impacts brand evaluations (Park, Yoon, Kim, & Wyer, 2001). Together, these fi ndings indicate that emotionallyvalenced attributes of product and brand categories exhibit properties of stability. Flexibility of Category Representations Consumer goals and category fl exibility. Research also supports the conclusion that category representations are fl exible. Categories do not take the same form across diff erent contexts or situations; the perceived structure of a category depends on goals that are salient at a particular time or in a particular context (Barsalou, 1982). Evidence in consumer psychology also supports this conclusion. For example, Ratneshwar and Shocker (1991) found that prototypical "snack foods" diff ered from prototypical "snacks that people might eat at a Friday evening party while drinking beer." Th e contextual information relevant in the latter judgment focused consumers selectively on goal-relevant attributes of the product (e.g., saltiness or convenience) that diff ered from attributes underlying snack food judgments more generally (e.g., saltiness, sweetness, portability, convenience). Data on brands and types of beverages (Hutchinson, Raman, & Mantrala, 1994) also support the need to consider consumer usage situations when asking consumers to recall relevant brands. Barsalou (1983, 1985, 1987, 1989) argued that individuals actively construct cognitive representations toward achieving goals. Multiple goals associated with a category may coexist within a single individual (Sengupta & Johar, 2002). Ratneshwar, Pechmann, and Shocker (1996) found that when consumers could not meet the needs of two diff erent goals that were salient with a single product, or when they experienced goal ambiguity, they were more likely to consider alternatives from diff erent product categories. In other words, members of a goal-derived category crossed traditional product category boundaries (also, cf. Johnson's, 1989, research on noncomparable alternatives). In this study, consumers who experienced goal ambiguity chose consideration sets on the basis of brand names, whereas consumers who experienced goal confl ict chose consideration sets

.

on the basis of mixed categories to meet diff erent goals (and postponed confl ict resolution to a fi nal stage). Ratneshwar, Barsalou, Pechmann, and Moore (2001) argued that similarity perceptions are infl uenced, not only by surface-level resemblances, but also by salient personal and situational goals. Although surface resemblance was important—for example, a granola bar was perceived as more similar to a candy bar than to fruit yogurt—goals were also important. Individuals for whom a personal health goal was salient rated the granola bar as more similar to fruit yogurt than to a candy bar, as long as other situational goals (convenience) were not also salient. Individuals for whom the situational goal of convenience was salient, and for whom a personal health goal was not salient, rated an apple as more similar to a donut than to an orange. Contextual factors and category fl exibility. Evaluations of category members also have been found to depend on contextual factors. Wanke, Bless, and Schwarz (1997, as reported in Wanke, Bless, & Schwarz, 1998) found that when consumers' task instructions encouraged them to place two disparate concepts (wine and lobster) in the same (versus diff erent) category, the evaluations of these category members varied. For example, wine was rated more favorably when it was categorized together with lobster than when it was categorized separately. When a really new product is introduced to the market, information from multiple categories may be relevant. Moreau, Markman, and Lehmann (2001) demonstrated that changing the salience of these categories infl uenced the extent to which they were used in making inferences about the new item. Information about the category that was encountered fi rst, or cued by an ad, infl uenced consumers' categorizations, expectations, and preferences for the new product to a greater extent than category information encountered subsequently. Flexible cultural and other self-views. A fundamental way of organizing information received from the environment is with respect to the self (Markus, 1977). Th e self category can be viewed as fl exible or malleable (Aaker, 1999; Markus & Kunda, 1986). In consumer psychology, diff erent self-views can be retrieved from memory and used in judgment, depending on situational cues. For example, an individual may view oneself as having several diff erent personality traits, and when situational cues make a particular trait salient, brands that match the trait will be better liked (Aaker, 1999). Th us, diff erent views of the self (see, also, Reed, 2004) can cue diff erent categories, which are then used in subsequent processing. When consumers are bicultural, they more easily retrieve and use both cultural views, as compared with monocultural consumers (Lau-Gesk, 2003). Situational cues can make diff erent cultural views salient (e.g., independent versus interdependent views, Briley, Morris, & Simonson, 2000; Aaker & Lee, 2001) leading to diff erent outcome eff ects (e.g., Forehand & Deshpande, 2001; Briley & Wyer, 2002; Mandel, 2003). For example, diff erent views of the self (independent versus interdependent) have been found to vary in terms of category representations that are accessible for each. Interdependents, who were asked to describe their thoughts in response to an advertisement, listed more specifi c category exemplars than did independents (Ng & Houston, 2006). Situational cues can also make both cultural and subcultural schemas salient, which may confl ict with one another even though they are both linked to the self (Brumbaugh, 2002). Summary. In summary, research increasingly views categories as fl exible representations. Th is fl exibility has been demonstrated in research directed toward goal-derived categories, contextual infl uences on category structure, diff erent self-views, and diff erent cultural categories. Activation of a Category Representation Because much consumer knowledge can belong to multiple categories, it is important to understand factors that aff ect whether a specifi c category representation will be activated in a given situation.

When a consumer is exposed to information in an environment, a specifi c category representation may be activated, not activated, or even inhibited (see Macrae & Bodenhausen, 2000, for a more thorough discussion of activation of social categories). In the consumer psychology literature, evidence for accessibility generally includes measures of increased recall, increased use of the representation in subsequent judgments, and faster response times on either memory or judgment tasks. Priming of a category also increases its later use (Herr, 1989; Hoch & Ha, 1986; Yi, 1990), unless people are aware of the priming manipulation (Herr, 1989; Meyers-Levy & Sternthal, 1993). In a branding context, Morrin (1999) analyzed whether exposing consumers to a hypothetical brand extension (e.g., Crest mouthwash) increased accessibility of the parent brand (e.g., Crest), as demonstrated by the speed with which the consumer indicated whether the parent brand was a member of the correct product category (e.g., toothpaste). Th e logic here is that if a person responds rapidly to a connection between Crest and toothpaste, then the brand extension (Crest mouthwash) also activates the parent brand (Crest) category. Morrin found that exposure to the brand extension increased accessibility of the parent brand, with the increase being less for typical than atypical brands in the category (e.g., Crest increasing less than Gleem in the toothpaste category). A prototypical brand (e.g., Crest) is already highly accessible in the context of its category (toothpaste), such that further increases in accessibility are unlikely to occur. In contrast, the atypical brand is not already accessible, such that exposure to it increased the parent brand's accessibility. Morrin also found that when the brand extension was a good fi t for the brand category (e.g., breath mints, mouthwash, or dental fl oss), it increased the parent brand accessibility further (e.g., Gleem toothpaste), relative to when the brand extension was a poor fi t (e.g., soft drinks, dishwashing liquid). Again, this facilitating eff ect occurred for the atypical brands (e.g., Gleem) more than for the typical brands (e.g., Crest). Th ese eff ects replicate earlier consumer research indicating that prototypical category members are chronically more accessible than atypical category members (cf. Nedungadi & Hutchinson, 1985; Boush & Loken, 1991), and that priming a category increases its accessibility (Herr, 1989). In general, atypical category members stand to gain more from priming tasks. A similar fi nding for accessibility and priming occurred in a diff erent context, when ninth graders were primed with either cigarette ads or nonsmoking ads (Pechmann & Knight, 2002). Because most ninth graders have negative perceptions of smoking, anti-smoking beliefs should be chronically accessible whereas pro-smoking beliefs should not. Indeed, the authors found that priming pro-smoker beliefs (with cigarette ads) led to increases in pro-smoking responses (e.g., smoking intentions), whereas priming anti-smoker beliefs (with anti-smoking ads) led to no changes. Priming with both anti- and pro-smoking ads also led to no changes; the anti-smoking prime counteracted the pro-smoking one. Research in comparative advertising fi nds analogous eff ects. Specifi cally, comparative ads (showing a target brand along with a competitor) benefi t an atypical brand such as Shasta cola, more than they benefi t a typical brand such as Coke (e.g., see Grewal, Kavanoor, Fern, Costley, & Barnes, 1997), and a comparative ad between an atypical brand and leading brand may benefi t the atypical brand more than no comparison at all (Hutchinson et al., 1994). Priming a category has also been found to infl uence the type of processing in which consumers engage. Priming category information increases relational processing, or the extent to which consumers elaborate on the relationships or similarities between the category and the target object, relative to processing specifi c attribute information of the target object alone (Malaviya, MeyersLevy, & Sternthal, 1999). Research also suggests that perceptions of a category as accessible (i.e., easy rather than diffi cult to recall) infl uence category use (Schwarz, 2004). When people are asked to recall few (versus many) exemplars of a category (e.g., behaviors that increase one's risk of heart disease), they experience the exemplars as easy (rather than diffi cult) to retrieve and infer that the exemplars are more typical (e.g., perceptions of heart disease risk increased, Rothman & Schwarz, 1998). Even imagined easeof-retrieval infl uences judgments (Wanke, Bohner, & Jurkowitsch, 1997). In general, consumers utilize accessible experiences in evaluation and decision making, unless the relevance or information-value of these experiences is called into question (Schwarz, 2004). Consumer research on these meta-cognitive theories is increasing and provides an interesting focus for future research. Modality-Specifi c Representations in Conceptual Processing: Where Do Categories Reside? An important recent development in cognitive psychology is an increased empirical and theoretical interest in the interplay between cognitive systems (e.g., category representation) and the brain's modality-specifi c systems (e.g., for vision, action, aff ect) systems. In contrast to the traditional approach of viewing cognitive and modality-specifi c systems as functionally separate, recent research in cognitive psychology and cognitive neuroscience suggests that representations in modality-specifi c systems underlie conceptual knowledge (for reviews of relevant empirical fi ndings, see Barsalou, 2003b; Barsalou, Niedenthal,

Barbey, & Ruppert, 2003; Martin, 2001; Pecher & Zwaan, 2005). According to this view, the perceptions, actions, and mental states active while processing a category's members are captured in the respective modality-specifi c systems of the brain. For example, consumers' knowledge about colors is represented in their perceptual mechanisms that perceive and process colors; consumers' knowledge about sounds is represented in their perceptual systems that perceive and process sounds. Later, when representing a category in the absence of any members, the brain reenacts or "simulates" these perceptions, actions, and mental states. Barsalou (1999, 2003a) argues that these simulations can implement the central symbolic operations that underlie the human conceptual system, including categorical inference, the type-token distinction, predication, and conceptual combination. For example, in classifying a perceived category member, a simulation of the category is retrieved that is grounded in the modalities. In this way, the conceptual representation of a category (a modality-specifi c simulation) is similar to the perceived representation of the category, rather than being diff erent (an amodal representation), thereby facilitating comparisions between them. Barsalou and Wiemer-Hastings (2005) further extend this approach to the representation of abstract concepts. Prior consumer research. Consumer research is consistent with the view that modality-specifi c and conceptual systems are linked. Unnava, Agarwal, and Haugtvedt (1996) presented consumers with advertising information that was high in imagery-provoking ability (either high in visual imagery or high in auditory imagery) and then engaged them in a perceptual task involving either reading or listening to the information. Th ey found that when mental images were activated, they competed with available cognitive resources if consumers were asked to perform perceptual processing in the same modality. Th e learning of visual information was reduced if the consumer read, rather than listened to, the information; the learning of auditory information was reduced if the consumer heard, rather than read, the information. Also, when information had high, rather than low, levels of visual imagery, it was learned better when it was presented auditorally, but less well when it was presented visually. Th ese results provide support that imagery processing draws on the same mental resources as perceptual processing. Although imagery interferes with perceptual processing of the same modality (visual, auditory), generating visual imagery has been found to facilitate cognitive operations that are compatible with it. For example, visual images may serve as spatial representations (MacInnis & Price, 1987) that facilitate information processing. Along these lines, Keller and McGill (1994) found that visual imagery was eff ective when it was compatible with other aspects of the communication process. Attributes that were easy to imagine had more impact on judgments when consumers engaged in imagery processing than when they engaged in analytical processing.

Sometimes pictures can increase imagery and thereby spur processing. Information presented in a narrative format (e.g., stories) tends to be more eff ective than information presented in a disorganized list format, but only when accompanied by pictures or by instructions to image (Adaval & Wyer, 1998). Similarly, narrative information is easier to process when it is physically integrated with relevant picture information, rather than being placed below it (Peracchio & Meyers-Levy, 1997). It seems clear that pictorial information is processed both perceptually and conceptually (e.g., Kim, Allen, & Kardes, 1996; Mothersbaugh, Huhmann, & Franke, 2002; Scott, 1994; Unnava, Agarwal, & Haugtvedt, 1996). Languages that rely on pictures or symbolic fi gures (logographic script) have been found to rely more on visual processes than languages based on alphabetic script (Schmitt, Pan, & Tavassoli, 1994; Tavassoli, 1999, 2001; Tavassoli & Han, 2001). Type of imaging also infl uences the perceptual or cognitive processing in which consumers engage. Imaging and thinking about one's past experiences tends to produce more contextual details than anticipatory thinking about future events (Krishnamurthy & Sujan, 1999). Yet, when consumers were asked for information relevant to designing new products, they produced more innovative and eff ective information when imaging new uses for the product (anticipatory) than when thinking about past experiences, which limited visualization to retrieved memories (Dahl, Chattopadhyay, & Gorn, 1999). Summary and Future Research Research on category representations is increasingly focused on the fl exibility associated with goal-derived and other types of categories, and we anticipate this focus to continue in consumer research. Also, although the literature covers category activation rather extensively, category inhibition has been less thoroughly considered (e.g., Macrae & Bodenhausen, 2000). For example, the question of how consumers become cognizant of stereotypical (categorical) bias and then correct for it (e.g., stop unwanted thoughts) are both newer areas of research. Finally, new research on the link between modality-speci fi c and cognitive processing in categorical representations is a promising new direction for researchers. Consumer research shows a strong link between conceptual and modality-specifi c systems in the brain. Perception, imagery, and higher cognition, share representational mechanisms. Pictures tend to facilitate imagery as well as to facilitate cognitive processing. Th e quality of imagining (e.g., anticipating the future versus refl ecting on past experiences) also infl uences the specifi c objects and events that are processed. Future research could examine the links between conceptual and modality-specifi c systems within particular modalities (e.g., touch, smell, taste, action) not previously examined in consumer psychology, and also in the context of diff erent types of consumer categories (e.g., perception of brand categories and goal-derived consumer categories). Further research based on the nature of specifi c descriptive and aff ect-laden information associated with this link would also be worthwhile. In addition to uncovering interesting fi ndings about category representations in the previous two decades, consumer research on category-based inferences has also increased dramatically. In the next section, we examine this research, the second major topic addressed in this chapter. SIMILARITY?BASED CATEGORY INFERENCES: THE INFLUENCE OF A CATEGORY ON A NEW CATEGORY MEMBER A primary reason category information is useful to consumers is that it can be used in making judgments about new category members, which are traditionally referred to as category inferences or inductions. Much of the consumer research on category inferences has been performed with brand categories, examining the extent to which beliefs (and aff ect) associated with a brand category are used to draw inferences about a new brand extension. Although many other marketing categories are relevant, this focus on brand categories is understandable. Marketing practitioners oft en manage their companies' products as brand categories; many companies are organized by brands. Given the continuing popularity, for a variety of economic and strategic reasons, of brand leveraging strategies (e.g., brand and line extensions, licensing) the number of products associated with many brand names has continued to grow. As a result of this, it is common to see new products launched with existing brand names and increasingly, the promotion of the full range of products under a brand name in a single communication. In this environment, consumers will be more inclined to think about brands as categories when considering new products introduced with an existing brand name, when considering the specifi c image or evaluating a particular brand name (Loken, Joiner, & Peck, 2002), or when attending to marketing communications for an existing brand and product. In this literature, a typical research scenario is one that examines the extent to which brand category inferences extend from the original brand category (e.g., Lexus) to a new brand extension (e.g., Lexus Hybrid, usually a hypothetical extension of the brand). Measuring the extent to which the new extension is similar to the brand category is the most standard approach for determining whether these inferences will occur. For example, in learning about the new Lexus Hybrid, consumers may infer that it shares similarities with both the traditional Lexus (e.g., high performance, prestige, and leather seats) as well as other hybrid automobiles (e.g., good for the environment, high gas mileage, and expensive). A key factor that determines whether category inferences are extended in this manner is the similarity or match between the representation of the brand category and the representation of the new brand extension. Consumers use prior knowledge about the category and the new category member to judge the relationship between them. When the relationship is perceived to be high, inferences are likely to be drawn from the category to the new member. When a new category member is viewed as dissimilar from the category, the relevance of category information is diminished, decreasing belief and the transfer of aff ect. In the sections that follow, we review fi ndings that aff ect the perceived similarity of two categories in the context of induction. In addition to the important role of prior knowledge about categories, we examine two other consumer psychological factors that aff ect perceived similarity: accessibility and relevance. Consumers selectively attend to only a subset of knowledge available about the category and the category extension, and this selective focus is infl uenced by: (a) the accessibility of information either retrieved from memory or in the environment, and (b) the relevance of information in achieving specifi c goals. In contexts that include both brand and product categories, researchers have also examined the alignability of attributes and the circumstances that increase contrast eff ects (rather than assimilation to the category). In the sections that follow, we review how these various factors aff ect category inferences. Accessibility and Similarity-Based Inferences Brand category accessibility and similarity-based inferences. Th e accessibility (or salience) of information pertains to the ease with which category information is retrieved from memory, or the ease with which it is perceived in the environment. A brand category, such as Snickers, can be viewed as consisting of a set of brand attributes (e.g., peanuts, chocolatey, tastes good), or as a set of exemplar products (e.g., Snickers candy bars, Snickers miniatures, Snickers ice cream bars), or both. In any given context, information about either brand attributes or exemplar products of a brand, or both, may vary widely in accessibility, with some being much more accessible than others (Loken, Joiner, & Peck, 2002; Meyvis & Janiszewski, 2004). Th e highly accessible information for a new category member (e.g., Snickers ice cream topping) may include its product category (ice cream topping), its brand name (Snickers), its connection to the brand name (e.g., strong or weak connection), and/or its individuating attributes (e.g.,its texture when used as a topping for ice cream is creamy). Increasing the salience of specifi c attributes can have a very strong eff ect on category membership judgments and processing of new brands (Hutchinson & Alba, 1991). When accessible information about the brand category and accessible information about the brand extension are similar, category inferences are more likely to occur. An abundance of research supports the idea that the properties of the brand category (e.g., cognitions and aff ect regarding the brand Snickers) transfer to the properties of new exemplars (brand extensions such as"Snickers ice cream topping), to a greater extent as the perceived similarity between the brand category and the brand extension increases (Aaker & Keller, 1990; Bottomley & Holden, 2001; Boush & Loken, 1991; Boush et al., 1987; Hansen & Hem, 2004; Zhang & Sood, 2002). Research also demonstrates that changing the focus of the similarity comparison oft en changes the perception of similarity between the two representations. Depending on what type of information is accessible and/or selectively attended to about the brand (brand image attributes; product categories of the brand) or about the extension (product category of the extension; individuating information; relationship-to-category information), similarity judgments can vary widely. For example, Lane (2000) found that when consumers were exposed repeatedly (fi ve times) to information about a new brand extension, and that when the information focused on the extension's positive connection to the brand, people's perceptions of extension similarity increased relative to a single-exposure condition. Th e key mechanism that produced this change was an increase in positive thoughts about the extension as exposure increased. Th is eff ect even occurred when the exposure information included brand associations not strongly related to the brand. Just focusing on positive attributes of these peripheral associations was suffi cient to trigger positive thoughts about the extension. In general, repeated exposure directed the focus of attention, the focus of elaboration, and consequently the inferences that consumers made about an extension, leading to an increasingly positive evaluation.

Klink and Smith (2001) found, too, that multiple exposures (three versus one) increased the acceptance of a moderately dissimilar extension, in this case when only the brand name and extension category information were provided. Lane (2000) found, however, that when the extensions were highly dissimilar to the brand category, and when the ad evoked associations that were not strongly related to the brand, repeated exposure did not lead to more acceptance of the extensions. Meyvis and Janiszewski (2004) found that properties of the brand category, specifi cally whether it included a narrow or broad array of products, infl uenced the type of information to which consumers selectively attended. Th ey reasoned that narrow categories (e.g., a brand such as Campbell's, which makes mostly soups) will have accessible associations that include the product category (soup), more oft en than will broad categories (e.g., Healthy Choice, which makes a variety of products), for whom product category associations are more diff use and weaker (cf. Boush & Loken, 1991). Th e product category associations of narrow (versus broad) brands (e.g., soup) are therefore stronger and more likely to compete and interfere with associations pertaining to brand image attributes (e.g., tastes good). When assessing new brand extensions, the narrow brand focus is more likely to include product category information (e.g., soup) as a basis for similarity perceptions, leading to greater acceptance of close category extensions (e.g., new soups) and lower acceptance of far category extensions. Th e broad brand, in contrast, for which product category associations are weaker and brand attribute associations are stronger, leads consumers to show less extreme responses to close and far extensions, and more acceptance as a function of whether the brand attributes are broadly similar (e.g., do the brand attributes transfer easily to the new extension?). Finally, Klink and Smith (2001) found that when individuating attribute information is available, it can become the focus and reduce the emphasis on the parent brand category and on its relationship to the extension. Specifi cally, the eff ects of brand similarity on extension evaluations diminished when individuating information conveying novel features for the extension (e.g., Timex bicycle and a unique gear system) was accessible. Brand name accessibility and similarity-based inferences. In the same way that narrow (versus broad) brands trigger specifi c (versus general) category associations, the name of a brand can vary in whether it triggers specifi c (or general) category associations and/or specifi c (or general) brand attribute associations. Keller, Heckler, and Houston (1998), for example, found that the name of a new extension was remembered better when it suggested superiority on a specifi c brand attribute (e.g., PicturePerfect televisions), than when it suggested superiority on a general attribute (e.g., Emporium). Focusing on a specifi c attribute of a brand can also diminish the emphasis placed by the consumer on the brand category (and its broad array of attributes), but it can also diminish consumers' acceptance of new brand extensions (van Osselaer & Alba, 2003). For example, the specifi c (versus general) name inhibited memory for brand attributes unrelated to the specifi c attributes. Co-branding strategies and similarity-based inferences. When two brands are combined in a cobranding strategy (e.g., Slimfast chocolate cake mix by Godiva) or brand alliance (e.g., Northwest Airlines and Visa), associations of each brand category, as well as the relationship between the two brands, may be triggered. Park, Jun, and Shocker (1996) found that a co-branded extension (e.g., Slimfast chocolate cake mix by Godiva) led to more favorable attribute inferences when the header brand (Slimfast) was combined with a complementary brand (Godiva) than when combined with a noncomplementary brand (e.g., Haagen-Dazs). Complementary brands were those that contributed along attribute dimensions that the other brand lacked. Also, complementarity of brands was more eff ective in benefi ting the co-branded extensions than simply combining two equally favorable brands. In addition, because a co-branded (versus monobranded) extension creates the perception of diff erence between a parent brand and the brand extension, countermoves made by a competitor in response to the extension are perceived less favorably (Kumar, 2005). However, co-branding with two well-known brand names also increases consumers' expectations for the co-branded product. For example, ingredient branding using a well-known brand name weakened brand quality inferences because of overexpectations, an outcome described by van Osselaer and Janiszewski (2001) in terms of connectionist models of adaptive learning (also, van Osselaer & Alba, 2000). When two brands are combined, and when consumers are more familiar with one than with the other, consumers' inferences from one brand to the other are unidirectional, from the familiar to the unfamiliar brand (Simonin & Ruth, 1998). Similarly, when two (hypothetical) restaurants are linked, and only one of the restaurants is well defi ned, the well-defi ned brand restaurant serves as a context for making inferences about the ambiguously-defi ned restaurant (Levin & Levin, 2000). Relevance to a Specifi c Consumer Goal As noted earlier, when a specifi c goal is salient, exemplars that accomplish the same goal will be perceived as more similar than exemplars that are physically similar but do not accomplish the same goal (Ratneshwar, Barsalou, Pechmann, & Moore, 2001). Furthermore, goal-relevant information is more likely than goal-irrelevant information to be used during comparison judgments when evaluating a new category exemplar. In the context of brand categories, consumers generate increasingly positive category inferences about a new brand extension as the perceived similarity between the extension and the parent brand on "image" and other goal-related attributes of the brand increases (e.g., Park, Milberg, & Lawson, 1991; see also Chakravarti, MacInnis, & Nakamoto, 1990; Herr, Farquhar, & Fazio, 1996; Keller & Aaker, 1992; Smith & Park, 1992). Consumers also generate more positive inferences as the perceived relevance of the brand's attributes to the new extension increases (Broniarczyk & Alba, 1994). Broniarczyk and Alba (1994) found that even when an extension is in a dissimilar product category, it can be viewed as acceptable if the attributes of the brand category are relevant to the new extension. Th e Ralph Lauren brand image, for example, has transferred successfully to product categories that are low in physical similarity to its core product base of apparel (e.g., perfume, paint), but that share a prestige image of the brand. An extension that is physically similar to a parent brand product (e.g., Nike dress leather shoes), but that is incongruent with the brand category's goals, may not be successful. Martin and Stewart (2001) found that when an extension is moderately incongruent with the goals of the parent brand category, the attitudes toward the category have less impact on attitudes toward the brand extension (and purchase intent) than when the extension is congruent with the goals of the parent brand category. When the extension was extremely goal-incongruent, the attitudes toward the parent brand category had no impact on attitude toward the extension (or purchase intent). Further, when two products shared a set of goals, consumers' elaborations about those products were more detailed and focused on a link between attributes of the extension and the parent brand. When two products were less goal-congruent, consumers' elaborations about them were less detailed and focused on why the extension was not a good fi t. Finally, Martin and Stewart (2001) found that when both product category similarity and brand attribute similarity refl ected a common goal, they both predicted extension acceptance. If the consumer had multiple goals that were incongruent with one another, then other factors, such as a similarity heuristic, predicted extension acceptance (Martin & Stewart, 2001). Similarity as a Heuristic Using categorical information oft en simplifi es judgment and decision-making, because consumers produce useful inferences by comparing current information about a perceived product to relevant category information. Similarity between a parent brand and an extension has also been viewed as a heuristic used in making extension-related judgments under certain conditions. For example, category inferences that simplify decision-making (e.g., evaluation-based inferences, similaritybased inferences, and correlational rules) are more likely to occur when cognitive resources are low, when people are unmotivated to process detailed information, when they lack the ability to do so, when the category information is suffi ciently relevant and accessible for use, or when there is no suffi cient justifi cation for accuracy in judgment (e.g., Alba & Hutchinson, 1987; Alba, Broniarczyk, Shimp, & Urbany, 1994; Maheswaran 1994). In contrast, when resources, ability, and/ or motivation are abundant, people are more likely to elaborate more on the details of the new category member and its idiosyncrasies. In their research examining consumers' classifi cation learning, Hutchinson and Alba (1991) distinguished between analytic and holistic processing. Analytic processing was operationalized as those categorization decisions that were based exclusively on features diagnostic of category membership (i.e., "criterial" attributes). Nonanalytic or "holistic" classifi cation was operationalized as those involving membership decisions based on overall brand similarity. Hutchinson and Alba (1991) found that perceptual salience of attributes enhanced analytic learning if the attributes were criterial but inhibited learning if they were not. Both analytic and nonanalytic processing tended to be multiattribute in nature, but nonanalytic processing was limited to a smaller subset of available attribute information as compared with analytic processing. Research further suggests that similarity is used as a heuristic when similarity information is accessible and when more relevant information is unavailable. For example, when the relationship between the category and the new category member is made accessible through repeated exposure, increased elaboration, or instructions to elaborate on relations between them, similarity will be more likely to be used as a heuristic (and when other information is not accessible). As noted earlier, similarity was used when product category information about the parent brand (Meyvis & Janiszewski, 2004), or product category information about the brand extension (Klink & Smith, 2001), was the only information available or accessible to the consumer. When individuating information about the brand extension was available, the individuating information, rather than a similarity heuristic, was used (Klink & Smith, 2001). Alignability of Attributes Another type of similarity-based comparison, generally studied outside the domain of brand categories, involves the alignability of attributes between the new category stimulus and the existing category representation in memory (Gentner & Markman, 1997; in the consumer literature, Gregan-Paxton, 2001; Moreau, Lehmann, & Markman, 2001; Roehm & Sternthal, 2001). Alignable diff erences focus on the structural properties of attributes and the degree to which attributes from one object can be "mapped onto" another object. Research fi nds that alignable diff erences (versus diff erences that are not alignable) are more accessible from memory (Zhang & Markman, 1998), are perceived as more useful inputs in judgments (Markman & Medin, 1995; Zhang & Fitzsimons, 1999), and increase brand evaluations in comparative advertising (Zhang, Kardes, & Cronley, 2002). When two diff erent brands were paired in a comparative advertising setting, the more the attributes of the target brand could be mapped onto (or compared with) those of the comparison brand, the higher the target brand evaluations (Zhang, Kardes, & Cronley, 2002). When two brands were not alignable, the brands were more diffi cult to compare, and transfer of aff ect was less likely to occur. Assimilation and Contrast in Consumer Contexts Th e research on similarity-based inferences fi nds that the lower the similarity between the new category and an existing category, the lower the likelihood of category-based inferences. Assimilation and contrast theories in psychology (e.g., Herr, Sherman, & Fazio, 1983; Martin, 1986; Mussweiler, 2003; Schwarz & Bless, 1992) make a diff erent set of predictions. Th ey suggest that if, at encoding, the domains or categories for the context and target match (or are at least similar), assimilation will likely occur, and there will be a positive transfer of beliefs between the two. Th ese theories suggest that the assimilation of information to a target results under conditions in which the information is included in a temporary representation of the target, whereas contrast eff ects result from exclusion of the information from the representation, and the use of the target as a standard of comparison from which to judge the information (Schwarz & Bless, 1992). When the similarity between the new instance and the existing category are high, an assimilation eff ect occurs, such that beliefs and aff ect are more likely to transfer to the new instance. But conditions that produce contrast eff ects show how the theories are diff erent from theory and research discussed earlier that predict category-based inferences. In particular, under certain conditions, consumers' judgments show contrast eff ects for extremely dissimilar (atypical) category instances. In these cases, not only may

beliefs fail to transfer from a familiar brand (Ralph Lauren) to an extremely atypical new brand extension (Ralph Lauren toaster oven), but contrast eff ects may produce a negative impact of the brand on the new product (evaluations and beliefs about the toaster oven may be more negative as a result of the brand name). Seemingly, category information should be viewed as irrelevant for judgments about a new category member that is extremely atypical, or when people are skeptical that an atypical instance is a category member. For example, a consumer may simply discount the Ralph Lauren toaster oven as an anomaly. If so, atypical instances should not aff ect category perceptions, and category knowledge should not be used to form inferences about the atypical instance (Fiske & Neuberg, 1990). As Wanke, Bless, and Schwarz (1998) suggest, however, if an atypical instance is perceived as excluded from the target category (the toaster oven is not included in the Ralph Lauren brand category), then judgments pertaining to it may refl ect contrast eff ects (see, also, Stapel, Koomen, & Velthuijsen, 1998, for an alternative explanation for contrast eff ects). Research fi nds some evidence for contrast eff ects. In the consumer domain, researchers have attempted to determine the conditions under which advertising information will be assimilated versus used as a standard of comparison and contrasted with the target category or representation. Assimilation eff ects, viewed as the default, occur more oft en than contrast eff ects, and are more likely to occur under conditions of category or domain similarity. Contrast eff ects are more likely under conditions of category or domain mismatch or dissimilarity (Hafner, 2004; Mussweiler, 2003). Contrast eff ects are also likely when substantial cognitive resources are available for processing comparison information (Meyers-Levy & Sternthal, 1993), when the individuals are high (versus low) in need for cognition (Meyers-Levy & Tybout, 1997), when remembered information is recounted analytically, rather than episodically (Bickart & Schwarz, 2001), and when situational cues include dissimilarities, rather than similarities (Hafner, 2004). SUMMARY AND FUTURE RESEARCH In sum, research shows that the degree to which inferences from a category are extended to a new category member refl ects three factors: (1) What information is accessible? As information that triggers similarity associations between the brand category and new brand extension becomes more accessible, the greater the likelihood that category inferences are drawn (e.g., when product category information is the only information available; when the relationship between the brand category and new brand category member is salient; when attributes of the extension are the same as the category's attributes). (2) Is the accessible information appropriate? If accessible information pertains to the category in which an object is being judged, then that information will probably be viewed as relevant or appropriate. (3) What information is elaborated upon? To the extent that elaboration (e.g., due to repeated exposure to the extension) increases the perception that a connection exists between the category and extension, similarity-based inferences are more likely to occur. Future research could analyze how similarity or typicality relations benefi t from frequency (e.g., Barsalou, Huttenlocker, & Lamberts, 1998) apart from feature similarity. Future research could also examine how category inferences are infl uenced by the number and typicality of exemplars retrieved when a category judgment is made. In a context in which a larger number of exemplars, or a broader array of exemplars, is retrieved, consumers may be more confi dent in making inferences based on those exemplars than in a context in which a small number of exemplars, or a narrower array of exemplars, is retrieved. Individual diff erences may also exist in sampling exemplars from memory, such that some consumers retrieve more representative exemplars than other consumers, due to motivational, ability, and contextual factors.

A factor that could infl uence the perceived relevance of category information is the degree to which category information is stable or unstable for a given individual. When the same representations (e.g., prototypes, exemplars) are retrieved across multiple occasions and contexts (cf. Lord, Paulson, Sia, Th omas, & Lepper, 2004), the stability of these representations may facilitate category inferences that lead to more stable beliefs and attitudes, as compared with exemplars that are unstable or vary signifi cantly across occasions and contexts. Also, when a consumer retrieves and uses unstable exemplars as bases for an attitude toward a category, that category attitude may be more vulnerable or susceptible to change. On the other hand, such attitudes, because they are based on unstable or changing exemplars, may be more fl exible and less rigid in the face of disconfi rming information. THE INFLUENCE OF NEW CATEGORY MEMBERS ON EXISTING CATEGORY REPRESENTATIONS Not only can category knowledge be used to make inferences about new category members, the reverse fl ow of infl uence can also occur. Information about new category members can infl uence existing category beliefs and attitudes, and thereby alter the representation of the existing category. Brand Categories and New-Member Eff ects In the consumer psychology literature, these new-member eff ects have been examined chiefl y in the context of brand categories, where they can either have a positive (enhancement) eff ect or a negative (dilution) eff ect on people's general beliefs about the category. Loken and John (1993) examined whether information about a new inconsistent category member (brand extension) infl uenced beliefs about the brand category negatively. Th ey found that, for the brand category Johnson & Johnson, negative information about a brand extension's gentleness rating infl uenced consumers' beliefs about both the extension and the general category, that is, the parent brand Johnson & Johnson. John, Loken, and Joiner (1998) found that, in addition to aff ecting the parent brand category negatively, a moderately inconsistent brand extension can infl uence consumers' beliefs about prior existing products of the brand. For example, a new Johnson & Johnson brand extension (e.g., hand lotion) that was rated low on the gentleness attribute impacted consumers' beliefs about the parent brand, Johnson & Johnson, as well as beliefs about prior existing exemplars of the brand (e.g., Johnson & Johnson dental fl oss). Interestingly, Johnson & Johnson's fl agship product, Johnson & Johnson baby shampoo, was most immune from dilution eff ects, presumably because gentleness beliefs about this product were fi rmly established and more resistant to change. A key factor that determines extent of dilution is the similarity between the parent and new brand extension, or, alternatively, the perceived typicality of the new brand extension of the parent brand category. Milberg, Park, and McCarthy (1997) found that the more the brand extension was either inconsistent with the parent brand image or dissimilar from the parent brand's product categories, the greater the amount of dilution (i.e., negative transfer of association from the extension to the brand category). However, negative information had no eff ect on parent brand beliefs when the extension was viewed as extremely atypical and these atypical perceptions were salient (Loken & John, 1993), or when the extension was introduced using a sub-branding strategy (Milberg, Park, & McCarthy, 1997). Th ese modifi ed dilution eff ects are consistent with prior research in social categorization (Rothbart & Lewis, 1988). A moderately inconsistent brand extension (e.g., a Johnson & Johnson facial tissue that was rated low on the gentleness attribute) was viewed as moderately atypical of the parent brand (Johnson & Johnson). An extremely inconsistent brand extension (e.g., a Johnson &

Johnson facial tissue that was rated low on both gentleness and quality attributes) was viewed as extremely atypical of the parent brand. When these typicality judgments were made salient, consumers used them in forming judgments about the parent brand, such that moderately atypical extensions had a negative eff ect on the parent brand beliefs and extremely atypical extensions had no eff ect (cf. Rothbart & Lewis, 1988). Th us, people appear to discount inconsistent extension information when the extension is viewed as extremely inconsistent (versus moderately inconsistent) of the category and, importantly, the atypicality (or typicality) of the extension is salient (Loken & John, 1993). In a diff erent applied domain, within U.S. culture, beliefs about social reality (e.g., occupational categories) have been shown to be caused in part by television viewing, especially among heavier viewers, who failed to discount TV-based exemplars in forming their beliefs (Shrum, Wyer, & O'Guinn, 1998), perhaps because these exemplars are moderately, but not extremely, inconsistent with prior category beliefs. Th e dilution eff ects of Loken and John (1993), as well as positive extension eff ects on the brand (brand enhancement), were replicated by Gurhan-Canli and Maheswaran (1998) under conditions of high motivation, when people were more likely to use detailed, thoughtful processing to evaluate the brand category and its members. Under low motivation, the modifi ed, heuristic-based dilution eff ects of Loken and John were replicated; that is, more (versus less) typical extensions diluted the parent brand evaluations. According to the authors, people used less analytical processing (Gurhan-Canli & Maheswaran, 1998), and the Rothbart and Lewis predictions applied. In a follow-up study of brand enhancement and dilution, Ahluwalia and Gurhan-Canli (2000) predicted that negative information would be more diagnostic than positive information when evaluating close (typical) new brand extensions, but that positive information would be more diagnostic than negative information when evaluating far (atypical) brand extensions. Ahluwalia and Gurhan-Canli also predicted, however, that these eff ects would occur only when other relevant brand extension information was not accessible. Results of their research were supportive. When brand extension information was highly accessible, positive extension information created more positive parent brand category evaluations, and negative extension information created more negative parent brand category evaluations. When extension information was lower in accessibility, negative extension information induced dilution eff ects for close (but not far) categories, and positive information induced enhancement eff ects for far (but not close) categories, supporting the idea that negative information is more diagnostic for close (versus far) categories, whereas positive information is more diagnostic for far (versus close) categories. Th e brand extension literature illustrates the conditions under which moderately typical but not extremely atypical extensions will impact parent brand beliefs. In these conditions, when typicality information is salient or accessible, extremely inconsistent brand extensions are viewed as implausible, or exceptions, and their information content is discounted. Employees of a Firm and New-Member Eff ects Folkes and Patrick (2003) reported analogous fi ndings when the employees of a fi rm were the category members being evaluated. Negative information about a particular service employee was less diagnostic about other employees of the same fi rm when that service employee was viewed as atypical of the company overall. In these cases, information about the employee was discounted in evaluating the service category as a whole. Positive information about an atypical employee, however, did have an eff ect (and more eff ect than negative information) on evaluations of a related subgroup in the fi rm. Matta and Folkes (2005), too, demonstrate more discounting of information about atypical than typical employees of service providers, and further demonstrate that employing a positively-rated atypical provider increased brand diff erentiation (i.e., the perception that the fi rm was diff erent from competing fi rms) compared with those employing a positively-rated typical provider. Summary and Future Research Th e literature on brand extensions has provided much insight into the possible infl uence a new category member can have on the overall category, and also on individual category exemplars. First, researchers have assessed when new category members will aff ect the category's representation. Empirical fi ndings show that they aff ect it when they are viewed as at least somewhat typical of the category. If they are viewed as very atypical, then information about the new category member is discounted, and has no eff ect on the category. Th e diagnosticity of the atypical new category member varies depending on how related it is to the category, whether the information about the new category member is positive/negative, and the extent to which the information is accessible. Brand extension research has also demonstrated that a new category member can infl uence beliefs or evaluations of a particular existing category member, but that central category members (e.g., fl agship products) are least vulnerable to change. Additional areas to be examined in the future include developing a better understanding of the potential impact a new member has on individual category members. For example, what factors infl uence the diagnosticity of this information? Does diagnosticity refl ect the characteristics of the existing category member (e.g., familiarity, strength of beliefs, linkage to the category) or of the new category member (e.g., plausibility of the information, confi dence in the information, knowledge of the product category, salience of category membership) or of some other factor (e.g., availability of competitor information). Future research could also explore the conditions that make category membership appear relevant to the task. Does relevance depend on subjective experiences of the consumer, or on some form of meta-cognition? Having considered the roles that similarity and related processes play in category-based inferences, we next turn to literature that addresses how similarity-based processes contribute to the fl exibility of category structure described earlier. FACTORS THAT INFLUENCE CATEGORY FLEXIBILITY AND EXPANSION As described earlier, category representations are characterized by a degree of fl exibility and expansiveness. In addition to the fl exibility of category boundaries and category membership demonstrated through goal-derived category research, a number of motivational, ability, and contextual factors have been found to increase category expansiveness, usually by changing perceptions of category similarity. Emotional states, discussed next, are an example of motivational states that infl uence category fl exibility. Emotional States A positive mood state has been found to increase category fl exibility (Isen & Daubman, 1984). In the consumer psychology literature, researchers have found that people in a positive mood showed increased relational elaboration (elaborating on the interrelationship between items), which included greater clustering of brands by product category membership, greater recall of brand names when they were in the same categories as stimulus brands (Lee & Sternthal, 1999), increased categorization of nontypical items as belonging to a category, and increased optimism about the success of a stimulus product (Kahn & Isen, 1993). Barone and Miniard (2002; Barone, Miniard, & Romeo, 2000) showed positive mood eff ects on category fl exibility in the context of brand categories. Specifi cally, they suggested that increased fl exibility might consist of rating moderately dissimilar extensions (e.g., Nike basketball nets) as more acceptable under certain aff ective conditions. When consumers were in a positive mood (relative to a negative mood), and when they received information about a new category member (brand extension), they were more likely to transfer positive evaluations from the category (parent brand) to the new category member (brand extension), even if the new category member (brand extension) was moderately dissimilar from the category (parent brand) attributes (Barone & Miniard, 2002; Barone et al., 2000). Th e categories of people in a negative mood were more rigid. Th ese researchers also examined extensions in very similar and extremely dissimilar categories. Th e category fl exibility of people in a positive mood did not occur when the membership of a category exemplar was viewed as implausible (e.g., for a distant, extremely dissimilar extension), and was not needed when the categories were highly similar (e.g., for near extensions). Another motivational variable found to infl uence willingness to expand category boundaries is a person's feelings of commitment to the category. For example, a study done among South Korean homemakers (Park, Kim, & Kim, 2002) found that feeling trust and commitment toward a brand increased the acceptability of an extension when the attribute claims of the extension were atypical (versus typical) of the brand category, as long as the extension product category was not too dissimilar from the category. Expertise Expertise in a domain is an ability factor that has been found to increase fl exibility in categorization. Cowley and Mitchell (2003) found that experts (relative to novices) were more likely to organize information by product subcategories, and to store information about alternatives in a way that increased fl exibility when evaluating the same product across diff erent usage occasions (Mitchell & Dacin, 1996), or when retrieving diff erent brands for diff erent usage occasions (Cowley & Mitchell, 2003). Owners (versus nonowners) of a brand were more likely to accept brand extensions that "stretch" a nonprestige brand's price line upward or downward, and that stretch prestige brands upward (e.g., American Express platinum card; Kirmani, Sood, & Bridges, 1999). Owners were less accepting of downward stretches of prestige brands (e.g., a new BMW for $11,990), because of owners' preferences for brand exclusivity, such that a sub-branding strategy (e.g., Ultra by BMW) was preferred. Cognitive psychologists have argued further that, early during the development of expertise in a domain, conceptual knowledge increases the salience or importance of certain perceptual distinctions. Perceptual knowledge serves as the data to which conceptual theories originally pertain (Barsalou, 1999; Smith & Heise, 1992). As people's expertise increases, so does their ability to attend selectively to perceptual aspects that are relevant to precise categorization (Johnson & Mervis, 1997). In other words, experts are not simply able to think more abstractly conceptually. Th eir knowledge allows them to attentionally select increasingly subtle perceptual distinctions relevant to categorization (Johnson & Mervis, 1997). Further research has found that teaching consumers strategies can increase their ability to process categories fl exibly. For example, when consumers were taught decompositional strategies (e.g., unbundling credit card expenses into diff erent subcategories), they exhibited both increased accessibility of information and reduced biases in memory and estimation (e.g., Menon, 1997; Srivastava & Raghubir, 2002). Coverage/Diversity of Category Members As noted earlier, brand names can be suggestive of broad or narrow categories. When an ingredient in a brand was branded (e.g., Tide with Irish Spring scent), and the change to the brand was relatively minor, consumers were more likely to accept the brand extension in the short-term. Using a new ingredient name (e.g., Tide with EverFresh scent), however, improved long-range expansion into new product categories (Desai & Keller, 2002). Th e exception to this eff ect is when the ingredient represented a signifi cant attribute change. Under these conditions, the extension fares better when the ingredient is co-branded than when it has a new name, conceivably because the branded ingredient enables consumers to view the brand extension as a plausible extension (assuming that the brand connection to the ingredient is credible). In these cases, the branded ingredient provided additional associations that the existing brand did not originally possess (i.e., broadening the brand category), which proved benefi cial in the new category. More diverse or broad categories (as compared to narrow categories) also have brand associations that allow for a broader range of new acceptable category exemplars to which parent category aff ect and associations can be assimilated (Boush & Loken 1991). Brand diversity or coverage also explains why sequential brand strategies can increase brand acceptance over a nonsequential strategy (Dawar & Anderson, 1994; Keller & Aaker, 1992). Introducing new category members in a sequential strategy (i.e., moving from products that are more to less similar), increases the likelihood that extension categories will be viewed as moderately rather than extremely dissimilar, thereby increasing the chances of consumer acceptance. For example, if a brand category that makes only cameras moves into cell phones, consumers would view this product extension as more dissimilar to the brand than if the brand had instead initially introduced camera cell phones followed by regular cell phones. When Ralph Lauren expanded their product line to designer paints, they followed a sequential strategy that fl owed from designer apparel to designer bedding (and home furnishings) to designer wall coverings (including paints), rather than moving directly from designer apparel to designer paints. A sequential expansion that progresses to more and more dissimilar categories slowly increases perceptions of brand coverage, which in turn increases perceptions of similarity and brand extension acceptance. A nonsequential strategy does not have these benefi ts, as the perception of similarity is too implausible for the perceiver, such that they reject the new extension. According to Osherson, Smith, Wilkie, Lopez, and Shafi r's (1990) similarity-coverage model, premises from diverse categories that exhibit greater coverage lead to stronger arguments than premises from categories that are very similar to one another. Diversity per se (i.e., having a greater number of products under the parent brand umbrella), however, does not translate into greater consumer confi dence in the brand (Dacin & Smith, 1994). Sometimes diversity leads to uncertainty about category attributes. Folkes and Patrick (2003), for example, found that inferences from one category member to other category members were less likely to occur when the category members were heterogeneous than when they were homogeneous. PROTOTYPICALITY AND AFFECT: HOW ARE THEY RELATED? In addition to fl exibility, another characteristic of categories that has been widely researched is the concept of graded membership. Many models of category representation suggest that membership is graded, with members ranging from very good (typical) members of the category to very poor (atypical) members of the category. One reason that this characteristic has been researched extensively in consumer psychology is because of its relationship to aff ect. For example, fi rst movers in a consumer category are generally thought to have advantages of category prototypes such as being preferred to second or third movers in the category (Carpenter & Nakamoto, 1989). In this section we present an overview of the relationship between prototypicality and aff ect, and we address the signifi cance of this relationship in consumer research. Many studies in consumer psychology have reported a positive relationship between the prototypicality of a category member and the evaluation or attitude associated with it. For example, Loken and Ward (1990) found that, although the correlations between typicality and attitude ranged from .00 to .92 for 16 diff erent product categories, it was positive and signifi cant overall across the 16 categories ($r = .58$, $p < .01$). More typical items were better liked. For instance, among fast food outlets, the more prototypical ones (e.g., McDonald's) tended to be more preferred or better liked relative to less typical ones (e.g., Church's Chicken or Taco Bell). Other research, too, supports a positive, linear relationship between prototypicality and attitude (Carpenter & Nakamoto, 1996; Folkes & Patrick, 2003; Simonin & Ruth, 1998; Veryzer & Hutchinson, 1998). Several explanations have been off ered for this linear relationship. One explanation is based on the concept of perceptual fl uency. By this account, more typical members of a category also tend to have greater perceptual fl uency, which is aff ectively pleasing (e.g., Schwarz, 2004). Perceptual fl uency increases over time, as familiarity with a stimulus increases. A related concept is frequency of instantiation, or the frequency with which an item appears as an instance of the category (Barsalou, 1985). Researchers have found that both the extent to which a category member is instantiated, and also the person's perceived familiarity with the category member, are signifi cant predictors of category member typicality, and also tend to predict attitudes toward the category (e.g., Barsalou, 1985; Loken & Ward, 1990; Viswanathan & Childers, 1999). A second explanation for this linear relationship is that typical category members are more likely than atypical category members to have valued attributes, as the category has evolved over time (Loken & Ward, 1990). New category members tend to include attributes that are valued by consumers, and these attributes tend to overlap with attributes that are more common for typical than for atypical category members. If the value of attributes underlies this relationship, then categories with negatively valued attributes should show the opposite eff ect, and they do (Ward & Loken 1988). Th is explanation might also explain why earlier research on taxonomic categories did not fi nd a positive relationship between typicality and attitude (Rosch, 1973). Because some categories had a positive relationship and other categories had a negative relationship, these patterns averaged to zero. In the context of brand categories, as noted earlier, new category members (new brand extensions) are better liked when they are similar to, or typical of, the parent brand (Aaker & Keller, 1990; Boush & Loken, 1991; Boush et al., 1987; Broniarczyk & Alba, 1994; Zhang & Sood, 2002; see also, Chakravarti, MacInnis, & Nakamoto, 1990; Herr, Farquhar, & Fazio, 1996; Keller & Aaker, 1992; Park, Milberg, & Lawson, 1991; Smith & Park, 1992). Hence, in this context, too, greater typicality is related to more positive aff ect. While the nature of the criteria used for establishing similarity, typicality, or "fi t" between the new extension and the parent brand varies for these studies, the conclusion is the same: In the absence of any relevant negative information about the brand extension, a greater fi t contributes to more acceptance and stronger aff ect toward the new extension. In these studies, the brand categories examined were ones associated most with positive (rather than negative) features.

Aesthetic product design evaluations, in addition to being infl uenced by prototypicality, are also infl uenced by whether the visual elements of the design appear to belong together in a unifi ed or Gestalt-like fashion (Veryzer & Hutchinson, 1998). In an advertising context, when the components of a communication process are congruent and seem to belong together, people's attitudes toward the brand increase (Kirmani & Shiv, 1998). Wanke, Bless, and Schwarz (1998) found that when the name of a sports car extension suggested continuation rather than discontinuation of prior models of the brand, people evaluated the new extension positively (as they would a typical sports car). Conversely, when the name suggested discontinuation, contrast eff ects occurred, particularly among nonexperts. Research on alignable diff erences produces analogous eff ects as similarity and typicality. Alignable (versus nonalignable) diff erences have been found to increase brand evaluations in comparative ads (Zhang, Kardes, & Cronley, 2002). A diff erent research stream fi nds that the linear relationship between typicality and attitude breaks down in certain contexts, and shows that moderate levels of typicality induce more positive aff ect than low or high levels of typicality. According to this view, when consumers have abundant cognitive resources and are highly motivated to process information, the thought processes generated under a moderate level of incongruity are more pleasing than under a low level of incongruity. Meyers-Levy and Tybout (1989) argue, based on Mandler's (1982) moderate incongruity eff ect, that the process of resolving incongruity is pleasing, as long as people have the necessary resources and the incongruity is not too great. If the category is extremely similar, elaborative thought is less likely to be generated, resulting in more mildly positive aff ect. Meyers-Levy and Tybout found that the resulting positive aff ect deriving from the eff ort does indeed transfer to the target stimulus. Other research replicates the moderate incongruity eff ect (Meyers-Levy, Louie & Curren, 1994; Stayman, Alden & Smith, 1992). Peracchio and Tybout (1996), however, argue that for the moderate incongruity eff ect to occur, people need to have low prior knowledge of the category. Specifi - cally, people with low prior knowledge will be more sensitive to category-inconsistent information, whereas people with high prior knowledge will be more likely to rely on their prior knowledge about salient category attributes. Peracchio and Tybout's fi ndings support these predictions. Other research fi nds that the eff ect disappears under conditions of risk aversion (Campbell & Goodstein, 2001), or for people high in dogmatism (Meyers-Levy & Tybout, 1989). Finally, under some circumstances, novelty and variety increase aff ect (Woll & Graesser, 1982). To the extent that a novel or unusual category member is more atypical of the category, typicality and aff ect are related negatively (Ward & Loken, 1988). In this case, the atypical members of the category are positively valued for their novel attributes. An area for future research is to investigate under what conditions these attributes are considered novel and positive, and under what conditions they appear atypical and less positive. In sum, however, most studies support a strong positive, linear relationship between typicality and aff ect, as long as the category has valued attributes. In more limited contexts, a nonlinear or even a negative relationship may exist. METHODOLOGY AND ANALYTIC TECHNIQUES In examining the extensive roles that category representation and category inference play in consumer information processing, researchers have had to draw on a diverse set of traditional methodologies, but have relied primarily on two. Many studies of category structure (e.g., category stability/fl exibility and graded structure) have relied on correlational methods. As mentioned in an earlier section, various measures (ideals, attribute structure, fuzzy-set measures) are correlated with global measures of prototypicality (e.g., Barsalou, 1985, Loken & Ward, 1987, 1990; Ward & Loken, 1986; Viswanathan & Childers, 1999). Similar correlational studies have been used in studying the roles that context and goals play in altering category representations (e.g., Barsalou 1982; Ratneshwar & Shocker 1991), and in altering the relationship between prototypicality and aff ect (Loken & Ward 1990; Ward & Loken 1988). One pertinent question is whether some of the measures discussed earlier (e.g., ideals, attribute structure, fuzzy set-based measures) can accommodate both taxonomic categories (which oft en have surface-level resemblances) and situational, goal-derived categories. Th e ideals measure captures the common goal(s) for both taxonomic and goal-derived categories (Barsalou, 1985; Loken & Ward, 1990). Th e attribute structure measure (Loken & Ward, 1990; Viswanathan & Childers, 1999) and fuzzy set measures (Viswanathan & Childers, 1999) capture the central tendency of categories, and feature elements can include both physical and nonphysical features of the category, as well as goals and/or image attributes. In the case of all three measures, the underlying attributes and goals are accessed via representations that are accessible for the category. Furthermore, because the attributes accessible in one context may diff er from those accessible in another, the measures can accommodate and allow researchers to predict category fl uctuations as a function of context. Th e majority of the research in consumer categorization has relied not on correlational methods, but on experimental methods. When investigating category inferences in the context of brand categories and brand extensions, for example, researchers have typically presented consumers with information about a new category member (the extension) and then asked them to provide one of several conceptually relevant responses (e.g., choice, purchase intention, evaluation, beliefs, cognitive responses, see Aaker & Keller, 1990; Gurhan-Canli & Maheswaran, 1998; John, Loken, & Joiner, 1998; Lane, 2000; Loken & John, 1993; Meyvis & Janiszewski, 2004; Milberg, Park, & McCarthy, 1997). In these experiments, stimuli (extensions) and context information (brand category characteristics) are sampled or created such that the factors of interest that are being tested vary (e.g., presence of brand specifi c associations, Broniarczyk & Alba, 1994; brand breadth, Meyvis & Janiszewski, 2004; brand variability, Dacin & Smith, 1994; extension-category similarity Park, Milberg, & Lawson, 1991). Similar experimental methods have been used to examine the role of concepts in memory (e.g., Keller, Heckler, & Houston, 1998; Zhang & Markman, 1998) and inferences in induction (Levin & Levin, 2000; Park, Jun, & Shocker, 1996). Research on category expansion and fl exibility has utilized measures of clustering and categorization/grouping as dependent variables (e.g., Isen & Daubman, 1984; Kahn & Isen, 1993; Lee & Sternthal, 1999), as has research on expertise and category structure (e.g., Cowley & Mitchell, 2003). Finally, researchers who have focused on the question of category activation have used priming as a means of gaining insight into the relative accessibility of concepts for information processing. Morrin (1999), for example, used a priming and response time methodology to investigate what impact brand extensions had on the accessibility of parent brand associations (see also e.g., Pechmann & Knight, 2002; Grewal et al., 1997; Forehand & Deshpande, 2001). An interesting question is whether a greater future focus on the modality-specifi c representation view of conceptual knowledge proposed by Barsalou (1999) will require a broadening of the methods used to examine concepts and categorization. CONCLUSIONS Consumer research that borrows from theories of categorization dates back to the mid-1980s. During the subsequent two decades, consumer researchers have identifi ed applications beyond traditional product categories that include brand categories, goal-related categories, cultural categories, and service employee categories, among others. Research has found that the categories typically examined in consumer psychology have both stability and fl exibility of structure, and that they are used across diverse environmental contexts. Also, consumers oft en adopt categories on the basis of goal-based criteria, rather than on more traditional structural and taxonomic criteria, and these goal-derived categories, as well as categories based upon one's self-view, are quite malleable and membership depends on the consumer context. Research that further examines the roles of the brain's modality-specifi c systems in higher cognition is needed. Barsalou's (1999) conceptualization of categories as residing in these systems could be a fruitful direction for future research. Future research could aim to increase our understanding of how modality-specifi c processing and simulation aff ect consumers' perceptions of new category members, their representations of categories, and their inferences about new and existing category members. Research has also furthered our understanding of factors that infl uence category inferences, specifi cally, inferences from category beliefs and attitudes to new category instances. Much of the work on category inferences has been conducted in the context of brand categories. Early research on the global construct of similarity gave way to more thoughtful analyses of the various dimensions of similarity relevant to understanding inferences from brand categories to new category members (e.g., similarity to the brand product categories, similarity to the brand's beliefs or image), along with important moderating variables (e.g., accessibility, diagnosticity) that increase perceived similarity and category inferences. Most research has examined category inferences pertaining to new category members (brand extensions), with relatively little research being conducted on factors that impact inferences between existing category members. For example how might advertising of Healthy Choice soups aff ect inferences about Healthy Choice frozen dinners? Or, if one branded product (say, Healthy Choice soups) increases in quality over time, how will this aff ect inferences about the quality of other branded products (e.g., Healthy Choice frozen dinners)? Consumer research on inferences has also found that information about new category members (e.g., brand extension failures) can impact category beliefs, as long as the information about category members is accessible and relevant to the original category beliefs. Future research could also examine whether existing category members that are accessible and perceived negatively impact perceptions of the category as a whole. Also, the conditions under which representations of current category members are stable or unstable (e.g., if retrieved consistently across settings vs. inconsistently) may also infl uence the ability of category representations to resist change. Consumer research has also examined conditions under which a new category member (typically a brand extension) is likely to be accepted as a category member of a favorably viewed category. Research that examines category expansion fi nds that certain motivational (e.g., positive mood), ability (e.g., product expertise), and contextual (e.g., category diversity) factors increase acceptance of new category members. Th e extensive research on the relation between similarity (typicality) and aff ect generally shows a positive linear relationship between the two. Exceptions to this positive relationship occur, however, and a greater understanding of these contingencies would be useful. In particular, how prevalent and important are these exceptions? What is the impact of these exceptions on marketing decisions? In conclusion, in the past two decades, consumer research on category representation and category inferences has yielded important theoretical and managerial insights. Consumer researchers have found categorization concepts useful for a variety of types of consumer-driven categories and for a variety of marketing applications. Consumer categorization research has used insights from cognitive and social psychology to further understand consumer applications such as branding and goal-derived categories. Th ese fi ndings, in turn, increase our basic understanding of how categories are represented, the nature of retrieval of category representations, the functional location of category representations, the conditions under which category inferences are generated, and contextual factors that infl uence fl exibility of category boundaries.

6

Effects of Sensory Factors on Consumer Behavior

As Colleen arrives at the entrance of the store, she scans the inside noticing the layout of merchandise, where the sales racks are located, and the table of sweaters just to the left of the entrance. She then hears the screaming of a baby in a stroller and the customer complaining to a sales person that a blouse she had purchased was the wrong size. At the same time, Colleen takes a sip of coff ee from the Caribou store next door, notices the scent of fl owers in the air, while she moves toward the table of sweaters. Picking up the pale blue sweater she strokes the collar and is impressed by the soft ness of the cashmere fabric. All of Colleen's impressions occur within seconds as she makes decisions about whether to remain in the store or move along to another shopping experience. Yet contained in those brief seconds was an integration of her "windows to the world" through her fi ve senses. Our judgments about a store, its products, and even its personnel, are driven in part by the smells we encounter (our olfactory system), the things we hear (our auditory system), the objects we come into physical contact with (our tactile system), our taste experiences (the gustatory system), and what we see (the visual system). Consumer research has approached the study of consumer behavior from a wide and varying set of perspectives. Th e chapters in this book provide a synthesis of these perspectives and the research that has followed. Among these perspectives is how information in the environment relates to the forms in which it is received and processed by individuals. Particularly for the latter, is how the perceptual system is organized to receive inputs in diff erent forms or senses. Th e primary human senses consist of smell, taste, hearing, touch, and sight. Although each of these is a potentially important system for the processing of information, the sense of sight has perhaps received the greatest amount of attention and is discussed in a separate chapter (see Petrova & Cialdini, chapter 19 of this volume). In this chapter, we narrow our focus on the varied eff ects of the remaining four senses. In psychology and the cognitive sciences, perception is the process of acquiring, interpreting, selecting, and organizing sensory information (Grohol, 2005). Perception is one of the oldest fi elds within scientifi c psychology. Many cognitive psychologists hold that, as we move about in the world, we create a model of how the world works. Th at is, we sense the objective world, but our sensations map to percepts, and these percepts are interpreted within the context of the environment we fi nd ourselves in, such as the atmospherics of our store example. As we acquire this new information and consider it relative to the knowledge we have in memory from prior experiences, our perceptions shift as we select further pertinent information to aid our judgments and purchase decisions. In this chapter, we examine research in the fi eld of consumer behavior published over the past twenty fi ve years on four of the senses. We fi rst examine research on smell and the olfactory system, followed by a discussion of past research on the sense of taste (gustatory), then research on hearing, particularly music, (auditory), and fi nally research on touch (tactile and haptic system). We then discuss areas where future research might be directed, particularly in terms of implications for the study of individual diff erences, the role of mental imagery, the promise of more neurocognitive approaches, and the need for more consideration of the multi-sensory interactions of our senses on consumption behavior METHODOLOGY A search of articles concerning the senses of taste, hearing, smell and touch was performed through an examination of seven journals that are primarily, or in part, focused on the study of consumer behavior. A total of 81 articles were compiled from the Journal of Consumer Research (24 articles), the Journal of Marketing Research (15 articles), Journal of Marketing (9 articles), Journal of Consumer Psychology (10 articles), the Journal of Business Research (14 articles), the Journal of Retailing (7 articles) and Psychology & Marketing (2 articles). Th e most researched sense is the auditory sense (33 articles) with the majority of this research examining some form of music. Taste follows with 24 articles, smell with 14 and fi nally, touch with 10 articles. Interest in sensory research appears to be growing, with only 6 of the research articles published before 1980, 18 articles published in the 1980s, 29 in the 1990s and 28 articles in the last 5 years. REVIEW OF PAST RESEARCH ON SENSORY FACTORS Sense of Smell Th e olfactory sense, or the sense of smell, has been the subject of study in several papers published in the marketing fi eld. While some previous studies have looked at the scents of specifi c products (e.g., Schmitt & Shultz, 1995, men's fragrances; Schneider, 1977, package fragrance), research in the past ten years has focused on ambient scent. Ambient scent is defi ned as a scent that is present in the environment but not emanating from a particular object. In general, various scents have been classifi ed by the aff ective quality of the scent (e.g., how pleasing the scent is), the arousal level of the scent (how likely it is to evoke a physiological response) and the intensity of the scent (e.g., how strong it is). Spangenberg, Crowley, and Henderson (1996) extensively pretested 26 individual scents and separated them into the aff ective dimension and the arousing or activating dimension and found that the aff ective dimension explained most of the variance. In this same paper, Spangenberg et al. (1996) manipulated the scent aff ect (neutral vs. pleasing) and scent intensity (low, medium, high) with an additional control group. Th e authors found that whether the scent was neutral or pleasing did not matter, nor did the intensity of the scent, compared to the control, no scent condition. Subjects in the scent condition perceived that they had spent less time in the store compared to the no scent condition. In addition, subjects in the no scent condition perceived having spent signifi cantly more time in the store than they actually did. Subjects in the scented condition did not show this discrepancy. Evaluations of the store overall and of the store environment were more positive when the store was scented versus not scented. Authors found mixed evidence of scent on specifi c product evaluations and suggest that the congruency of product and scent may be an important dimension for further study. Th is notion of congruency has been pursued by other researchers. Mitchell, Kahn, and Knasko (1995) manipulated whether the ambient odor was congruent with a product category. In the congruent conditions, a chocolate scent was paired with a candy assortment choice and a fl oral scent with a fl ower arrangement choice. When the odor was congruent with the product class, subjects spent more time processing the data, generated more self references, were more likely to make additional inferences and were more likely to exhibit variety seeking behavior. Interestingly, the researchers found no main eff ect of scent versus no scent. In general, cognitive elaboration was greater in the congruent conditions. Scent and Music In another variant of congruency, two studies concerning the interaction of scent and music have been conducted. Mattila and Wirz (2001) manipulated scent arousal (no scent, pleasant low arousal, and pleasant high arousal) and music arousal (no music, pleasant low and high arousal music) and examined whether scent and music were matched on arousal level or mismatched. When scent and music matched in terms of arousing qualities, consumers satisfaction with the shopping experience, approach behavior and impulse buying were signifi cantly higher then in the mismatched conditions. Th is was true of both the high arousal match (scent of grapefruit and fast tempo music) and low arousal match (scent of lavender and slow tempo music). Spangenberg, Grohmann, and Sprott (forthcoming) also examined the eff ects of ambient scent and music by using a Christmas theme. Th ey set up a lab experiment and manipulated scent (no scent vs. Christmas scent) and the type of music (non-Christmas music vs. Christmas music) in a mock retail store. Similar to previous research, they found that the matched condition of Christmas scent and Christmas music resulted in more favorable evaluations for the store, its merchandise, the store environment, and intentions to visit the store. When music and scent did not match, evaluation and behavior intentions were not aff ected, or, in some cases, negatively aff ected. Scent and Other Moderators Michon, Chebat, and Turley (2005), in the context of a fi eld experiment varied scent along with retail density (how crowded the mall was) and examined shopper's perceptions of product quality, mall environment and positive aff ect. Th e authors found a u-shaped relationship in that the positive eff ect of ambient scent on shoppers' perceptions of the mall atmosphere was observed only at the medium retail density level. Further, a favorable perception of the retail environment infl uenced the perception of product quality. Shoppers' mood did not have a signifi cant direct eff ect on the perceptions of product quality.

Morrin and Ratneshwar (2000, 2003) crossed ambient scent (unscented, pleasant) with brand familiarity (familiar, unfamiliar) and examined the evaluation, attention, and memory for familiar and unfamiliar brands. Th e authors (Morrin & Ratneshwar, 2000) found that a pleasant ambient scent improved evaluations for objects that were not as familiar or well liked. However, they were concerned about potential ceiling eff ects for the familiar brands as well as allowing only a 5-minute delay before the memory measures. In their subsequent research (Morrin & Ratneshwar, 2003), the authors examined the memory eff ects in more detail to determine if ambient scent infl uences memory of brands at encoding, retrieval, or both. In a two-phase experiment, 24 hours apart, the authors manipulated ambient scent (no scent, scent congruent to household cleaning products (geranium), scent incongruent to household cleaning products (clove)) and brand familiarity. In Study 1, the same scent was used at encoding and retrieval and it was found that ambient scent improved recall and recognition of familiar and unfamiliar brands. Th is was true whether or not the scent was congruent with the product category. In Study 2, the authors manipulated whether the scent was present at encoding or retrieval and found that the enhancement of brand memory was due to the presence of an ambient scent at encoding rather than retrieval. Th e ambient scent increased attention in terms of longer viewing times. Process Explanations Why does ambient scent infl uence consumer behavior? Th e two explanations most oft en used can be separated by whether scent primarily infl uences aff ect such as mood or whether a scent primarily infl uences cognition. In the area of retail atmospherics, Mehrabian and Russell (1974) discuss mood as a mediating factor between environmental cues and behavior. Th e environmental psychologists assert that shoppers react to environmental cues with approach (e.g., desire to stay in the environment, explore, etc.) or avoidance (e.g., desire to leave) behaviors and that mood mediates this relationship. However, in the marketing literature, this explanation has not received strong support. Bone and Ellen (1999), in a review article, found that only a small percentage of studies (16.1%) showed any infl uence of scent on mood. Another process explanation is that scent infl uences cognitive processes. Morrin and Ratneshwar (2003) found no eff ect of scent on mood, but found that scent increased attention to brands as measured by viewing times of various brands (Morrin & Ratneshwar, 2000, 2003). Mitchell et al. (1995) found that scent infl uenced the extent of information processing and cognitive elaborations. Chebat and Michon (2003) tested various process theories and concluded that cognitions pertaining to product quality and the shopping environment are infl uenced by scent, which in turn infl uenced the mood of the shopper. Hirsch (1995) examined the eff ects of ambient odors in a Las Vegas casino. While the specifi c odors used are not identifi ed in the research, the author found that an ambient odor signifi cantly increased slot-machine usage. Th e author suggests (but does not test) a cognitive process whereby the odor may have induced nostalgic recall of memories which enhanced the gambling mood. Th ere seems to be more support for the infl uence of scent on cognitive processes but, given the interaction between cognition and aff ect, this is clearly a complicated question. Bone and Ellen (1999) suggest that accessibility and availability theories may be a more useful theoretical basis for understanding ambient scent research. We next turn to a discussion of past research in consumer behavior and marketing on the sense of taste. Sense of Taste Research on the sense of taste (or the gustatory sense) is quite varied and includes administration of taste tests, changes in taste as it relates to new product formulations, store-sampling, branding, packaging and taste as a form of direct product experience. Each of these topics will be discussed in turn. Taste Discrimination At the most basic level, some researchers have examined various methods of administering taste tests (e.g., Buchanan, Givon, & Goldman 1987). One of the key issues is to identify which type or method of taste test can best determine an individual's ability to discriminate between diff erent tastes. Th is is important to marketing for several reasons. In some instances, a manufacturer may want to test the similarity of two alternative product formations to assess the consistency of taste from batch to batch of a product. Oft en, these tests involve in-house trained experts (Greenhalgh, 1966). Also, a taste test may be used to identify consumers who have greater ability to discriminate products by taste or to test alternative formulations. A common test, termed the triangle test asks consumers to identify the one sample of three that is diff erent from the other two, which are identical. Researchers (Morrison, 1981; Moskowitz, Jacobs, & Firtle, 1980) have examined whether subjects who do well on this type of test are actually discriminating between the tastes or are simply guessing. Th e authors make statistical suggestions for improving the quality of the results of triangle tests. Another common taste discrimination task involves consumers making several paired comparisons and noting their preferred choice following each comparison. Once subjects have completed several paired comparisons, the consistency of their choices is used to determine their discrimination ability. Finally, a preference rank procedure is used where subjects are given three taste samples, one diff erent from the other two and are asked to rank the three from most to least preferred. A subject who ranks the diff erent sample as most or least preferred is judged to have made a correct choice, regardless of the preference. A subject who ranks the odd sample as between the two identical samples is judged not to have discriminated. In an empirical investigation examining the three procedures, Buchanan et al. (1987) found that the repeated pair comparison method was the most sensitive discrimination task and preference ranking was the least sensitive. Th e researchers also found that the discrimination ability measured by triangle tests was signifi cantly correlated with that measured by paired comparisons, which supports the validity of the tests. In the area of product reformulations, Villani and Morrison (1976) investigated a method for estimating demand for a new product formulation and recommended that estimates for current users and non-users be made separately for more accuracy. In arguably the most famous product reformulation, the New Coke experience is discussed by Dubow and Childs (1998). Th ese researchers explain the gradualist approach hypothesis which uses the perception and psychophysical concepts of just noticeable diff erence (when a consumer can just notice a change) and just unnoticeable diff erence (where the change is undetectable). In the gradualist approach to product reformulation, the manufacturers would change the taste of a product in a sequence of small, constant, just unnoticeable diff erence steps so that, at no point would tasters perceive the reformulation diff erences. Arguing against the gradualist approach hypothesis, the fl avor balance hypothesis suggests that a gradualist approach is impossible in a multi-ingredient formula as unexpected interaction eff ects of various ingredients may be perceptible. Using New Coke and Coca-Cola Classic, Dubow and Childs (1998) conduct an empirical test which suggests that Coke may have been better off using a gradualist approach to reformulation and not announcing the product change. Taste and Store Samples Th e area of taste and sampling food items in stores has also been researched. Johnson, Sommer, and Matino (1985) unobtrusively observed consumer behavior at bulk food bins in fourteen supermarkets. Th e most frequent problem behaviors were consumers using their hands to retrieve products and consumers snacking on products. Not surprisingly, these two problem behaviors were correlated. Besides this unsanctioned behavior of snacking, stores oft en encourage taste by off ering product samples. Steinberg and Yalch (1978) examined obese and nonobese shoppers in a supermarket, how hungry the shoppers were, and the eff ect of sales of other grocery items when shoppers were off ered an in-store sample (a doughnut in the bakery section). For the nonobese, if a shopper was hungry, the food sample seemed to satisfy some of their hunger and they reduced their additional buying compared to the nonobese shoppers who were not hungry. For the obese shoppers, off ering a food sample increased additional buying and this was only slightly moderated by their level of hunger. Th e authors conjecture that obese shoppers are not as sensitive to their internal cues of hunger so off ering a sample may have increased further the salience of food and they purchased more. Some research (Nowlis & Shiv, 2005; Shiv & Nowlis, 2004) looked at whether or not to distract shoppers as they tasted a food sample. Contrary to industry wisdom, these researchers found that distraction of the shopper increased subsequent choice for the sampled food. Th e authors explain these results using a two-component model in which the ultimate pleasure a shopper derives from tasting a food sample is a function of an informational and an aff ective component. Th e aff ective component involves the emotional responses of the shopper and is associated with relatively automatic processes. Th e informational component is a more objective feature of the tasting experience and related to aspects such as quality. Th is information component is comprised of more controlled processes. Distracting a consumer infl uences subsequent choice by increasing the impact of the aff ective component. Taste and Branding Another area of taste research concerns the relationship between and taste and brand name. In an early marketing study, Allison and Uhl (1964) found that, in a blind taste test, experienced beer drinkers (they drank beer at least three times per week) were unable to distinguish their preferred brand from other brands of beer. However, when the brands of beer were identifi ed, these same beer drinkers rated the taste of their preferred brand signifi cantly higher than in the blind taste test. Similarly, Bellizzi and Martin (1982) found that whether a brand was national or generic signifi cantly infl uenced the taste of the product (national brands ranked higher). Sprott and Shimp (2004) examined the interaction of brand status (store brand, national brand) and quality of the tasting experience. Th ey revealed that sampling a store brand substantially increased evaluation for the store brand compared to the group that did not have the opportunity to taste the product (juice) only if the sample store brand was high quality. No benefi t was demonstrated with the national brand. Th e authors theorize two explanations that may be likely. When consumers make quality judgments, they base these judgments on inherent product features, or intrinsic cues and on extrinsic cues such as price and brand name. Intrinsic cues, such as taste, tend to dominate extrinsic cues when intrinsic cues can be evaluated with confi dence at the time of purchase. When intrinsic cues cannot be evaluated (i.e., taste), consumers base their judgments more on extrinsic cues (i.e., brand name). By providing consumers with the opportunity to taste the store brand, an intrinsic cue was provided that infl uenced product perceptions. Th e other theoretical explanation used is schema congruity theory (Mandler, 1982). Schema congruity theory asserts that aff ect for a particular brand will be most positive when a person perceives moderate incongruity between the product category schema compared to extreme congruity or incongruity. Th e expected schema for store brands is that they are lower quality compared to national brands. Participants who tasted the store brand learned that the juice was of high quality and consequently their store brand schema and their actual experience were moderately incongruent, thus resulting in more positive aff ect compared to the subjects who did not have the opportunity to taste. LeClerc, Schmitt, and Dubé (1994) examined the eff ect of foreign branding (French) on product perception and attitudes. In Experiment 3, the authors crossed whether a participant could taste the product (yogurt) with whether the brand was foreign (English, French). Th ey found that with no taste test, a French brand name generated higher ratings on the hedonic dimensions of the product (i.e., pleasantness, sweet, delicious, creamy) and lower ratings on the utilitarian dimension (healthy, wholesome, nutritious). Additionally, a French sounding brand name aff ected product perception and evaluation even aft er a taste test but only on the hedonic dimension. Th e eff ect of brand awareness on sampling of brands and choice revealed that when subjects do not have any brand awareness, they tended to sample more brands and were more likely to select the high quality brand (Hoyer & Brown, 1990). If subjects were aware of one brand in a set (this study used brands of peanut butter), they tended to sample fewer brands and tended to choose the known brand even when it was lower quality than other brands in the sample. In a related area to branding, one study on product packaging and taste found that packaging infl uenced the taste of the product. McDaniel and Baker (1977) examined consumer reactions to identical potato chips placed in a wax coated potato chip bag or a "new" polyvinyl bag. In a blind taste test, subjects rated the chips as identical. However, when the taste test was conducted with the bags, even though the polyvinyl bags were extremely diffi cult to open (subjects had to use their teeth, stand on the bag and pull, etc.), the chips in the polyvinyl bags were viewed as crispier and tastier. Th e authors interpret the fi ndings that a negative packaging attribute (hard to open) can enhance product quality perceptions since consumers infer other attributes such as crispier or fresher, even when no diff erence in the actual product quality exists.

Taste, Direct Experience, and Product Perceptions Taste can be conceptualized as a form of direct product experience. Smith and Swinyard

(1983) researched product trial (tasting a salted snack product) and attitude-behavior consistency. When attitudes were based on the taste of the product, the attitude-behavior correlation was much higher then without this tasting experience. Th e authors emphasize the information value of direct product experience. Scott and Yalch (1980), using Bayesian analysis, examined consumer acceptance of experiential information about a new product. Consumers who were given a reward for sampling a new product and who were encouraged to attribute their behavior to this situational factor (and thus discount their intrinsic interest in the product) were receptive to unfavorable product information and unreceptive to favorable information. Th e authors maintain that their research demonstrates a tendency for people to accept information consistent with their perceptions about the causes of their behavior and to reject information when it contradicts these attributions. Similarly, Roberts and Taylor (1975) demonstrate that even with a tasting experience, it is diffi cult to change consumer's previously held perceptions. Some researchers consider that product trial through tasting can be diagnostic and infl uence perceptions and choice. Levin and Gaeth (1988) vary the temporal order of tasting a product (before or aft er reading a ground beef label) and the valence of the label information (positive, 75% lean; negative, 25% fat). Th e framing eff ect of the labeling was reduced when consumers sampled the product compared to when they did not. Th e authors note that product experience will have greater weight when it is unambiguous or diagnostic. Also, using diagnosticity, Pechmann and Ratneshwar (1992) varied the diagnosticity of a taste test as well as the objective correlation of price and quality. Four samples of orange juice varying in quality were used.In one condition taste was perfectly correlated with price and in another the correlation was zero. Diagnosticity of the taste test was manipulated by either allowing participants to go back and forth between the four samples (high diagnosticity) or by presenting the samples sequentially with some time in between and no opportunity to go back to previous samples (low diagnosticity). It was found that prior beliefs biased judgments of the samples less when diagnosticity was high rather than low (Study 1). When subjects were allowed to use a memory aid (Study 2), they tended to be relatively accurate in their judgments, even though they had the same constraints as the low diagnosticity subjects in the fi rst study. Th e authors conclude that the degree to which prior beliefs and actual direct taste experience are used depends on the diagnosticity of the mental representations of the taste experience. Th e higher the diagnosticity, the greater the impact of the actual taste experience relative to prior beliefs. Th e lower the diagnosticity, the greater the impact of prior beliefs relative to the actual taste experience. Braun (1999) looked at a diff erent aspect of taste and memory. She asked the question of whether advertising received aft er a direct product experience (tasting orange juice) altered how consumers remember their experience. Th is research found that consumer recall of a past direct experience with a product (tasting) was subject to distortions. Post-experience advertising made consumers think they had tasted a better tasting juice by altering their memories of the tasting experience through advertising. Altering the time between the tasting experience and the advertising exposure, this research revealed that the post experience is working at the memory reconstruction phase of recall rather than as a source confusion problem at encoding. Another study found that imagining a taste experience, even of a hedonic product (ice cream) may actually be a more aff ective experience than actually eating the product (Compeau, Grewal, & Monroe, 1998). Taste as More Incidental In some reach, the actual product tasting is not a key part of the research question yet product taste plays a role. Maison, Greenwald, and Bruin (2004) used a Coke-Pepsi taste test in a pretest to determine subjects who could identify each of the brands in a blind taste test. Th e primary focus of this research was to compare the predictive validity of implicit versus explicit preferences for brands. When separating subjects by their ability to identify Coke or Pepsi in a blind taste test, this research found that subjects who exhibited higher taste discrimination in the blind taste test had more extreme implicit preferences. Th is research suggests that implicit preference measures are more sensitive measures of preference than explicit preference measures. Kahn and Isen (1993) did not include actual tasting in their study, but rather taste perceptions. Th ey found that a positive aff ect manipulation increased variety seeking behavior relative to the control when unpleasant or negative features of the items were not made salient. However, when salient negative features were introduced into the choice set with the inclusion of products that potentially tasted bad (i.e., low salt and high fi ber crackers—Experiments 1 and 2), or by alerting subjects to the negative health risks of familiar items (Experiment 3), there was no diff erence between positive aff ect and a control group on variety seeking behavior. We next turn to the discussion of research on hearing or auditory eff ects on consumer behavior. Sense of Hearing Th e auditory sense or hearing has been studied in marketing mostly in the context of background music in advertising and in retail stores. Researchers have examined the eff ects of music on consumers' moods, product evaluation and choice, fi t with an ad or store, time perceptions, and as part of a retail store's atmosphere. A few studies have examined non-music elements such as voice pitch and the interaction between auditory information and visual information. First, the auditory sense as it relates to music in marketing will be discussed followed by studies concerning the interaction between audio and visual information. Music and Mood Bruner (1990), in a review article on music and mood, stressed the complexity of music and its infl uence on individual's moods. Bruner also provided a taxonomy of musical elements and the emotional expressions ascribed to each structural element. Th e three main structural features of music are tempo or time of the music (how fast or slow it is), pitch related characteristics (includes major, minor keys), and texture (includes volume, instrumentation). (Please see Bruner, 1990, Appendix, p. 102, for a more complete description of the elements.) Bruner stressed that people assign emotional meaning to music and experience aff ective reactions. For example, fast music is considered happier than slow music. Kellaris and Kent (1994) identify three basic musical properties similar to those of Bruner (1990) which are tempo (fast, moderate, slow), tonality (major, minor, atonal) and texture (classical, pop). Th ese authors produced original compositions with digital sound technology to provide orthogonal manipulations of the three structural properties of music. Th ey also identifi ed three dimensions of response (pleasure, arousal, and surprise) that were elicited by the three properties of music. Th ey call for a better understanding of the multidimensional nature of both musical stimuli and listener response. Similarly, Scott (1990) advocated using an interpretist approach in research to understand the complexity of consumer meaning and response to music. In one study in marketing, Gorn (1982) used classical conditioning and illustrated that hearing liked music (music from the movie Grease) or disliked music (classical Indian music) while being exposed to a product (a pen) can directly aff ect product preferences as measured by product choice. Both Kellaris and Cox (1989) and Allen and Madden (1985) attempted to replicate Gorn (1992) but failed to do so. Kellaris and Kent (1994) note that Gorn (1992) did not control for the diff erent structural properties of music. Th ey argue that when fast tempo, upbeat music is used to operationalize the positive unconditioned stimulus, the valence of the music may have been confounded with the arousing quality of the music which may have altered the level of attention of participants. In classical conditioning, music is assumed to induce a mood which is directly transferred to the product. Th e infl uence of music on mood states and new product evaluations was researched by Gorn, Goldberg, and Basu (1993). Mood was manipulated by music to induce either a good or a bad mood and subjects' awareness of the music as a source of their mood was also manipulated. When subjects were not aware of the source of their mood, their mood biased their evaluations of the product so that the product was evaluated more favorably when in a good mood than when in a bad mood. However, when subjects were made aware of the source of their mood (the music), there was no diff erence in product evaluations between those in a good or bad mood. Th e authors explained the results with a mood-based cognitive heuristic "How do I feel about it?" (Schwarz, 1990), which suggests that people observe their own feelings and draw conclusions from them. If a person is not aware of the source of their mood, they assume the feelings are information to be used in product evaluation. Music was also used to induce either a pleasant or unpleasant aff ective state and examine its interaction with the aff ective tone of an advertisement (Gorn, Pham, & Sin, 2001). While controlling for arousal (Study 1), music was used to manipulate a pleasant or unpleasant aff ective state. In Study 2, both arousal and pleasure were manipulated with music. Results showed that the valence of a person's aff ective state infl uenced judgment in a mood congruent direction especially if an ad had an ambiguous aff ective tone. Th e arousal dimension, but not the valence dimension, infl uenced ad evaluations. Ad evaluations were more polarized in the direction of the ad's aff ective tone under high arousal than under low arousal. Dubé and Morin (2001), in a fi eld setting, examined the pleasure induced by music (measured, not manipulated) and its impact on store evaluations. No main eff ect of pleasure intensity induced by music on store evaluations was found and they explain that there was no support that mood induced by music directly infl uenced store perceptions. Instead, this is mediated by attitude toward the servicescape and attitude toward the sales personnel. While the preceding studies focus on the infl uence of music on mood, some researchers have examined the cognitive processes resulting from background music. Olsen (1997) manipulated whether background music was present (2 levels, silence and music) and the amount of time between consecutive information presented in ads (0, 1, 2, 3, second) in two studies. Relative to silence, background music hindered recall when information was presented at 2 seconds or shorter but enhanced recall at 3 seconds. Using a resource matching explanation (cf. Anand & Sternthal,

1990), music had a detrimental eff ect on recall at shorter times because it distracted cognitive resources from the rehearsal of brand information thereby hindering attention. As cognitive resources increased to the point when those available matched those required, information was suffi ciently processed and a higher level of recall was exhibited. Music and Congruence Park and Young (1986) examined the eff ect of music (present, absent) and three types of involvement (low involvement, cognitive involvement, aff ective involvement) on the formation of attitudes toward a brand in the context of TV commercials. Music increased the brand attitude for subjects in the low involvement condition but had a distracting eff ect for those in the cognitive involvement condition. Its eff ect for those in the aff ective involvement condition was not clear. Th ey argue that music acted as a peripheral persuasion cue. While the notion of fi t was not specifi cally studied in Park and Young (1986), the music was selected since it was "best suited" for the commercial. MacInnis and Park (1991) examine two dimensions of music including its fi t with the ad and the extent to which it arouses emotion laden memories. Fit was defi ned as a participant's perception of the music's relevance to the central advertising message. Th ese two dimensions of music were fully crossed with two levels of involvement. Th e emotion laden quality of the music had similar eff ects on attention to the music and aff ective response for both high and low involvement participants. Yet, it had diff erent eff ects on their message based processing. For low involvement participants, the emotion laden quality enhanced message processing while it seemed to distract high involvement participants from processing the message. Similarly, while fi t had similar eff ects on high and low involvement participants by focusing attention on the music and the message, it created diff erent eff ects on their aff ective responses. Lack of fi t created more negative emotions for low than for high involvement participants. An unexpected fi nding of this research was the strong impact of fi t on both positive emotions and attitude toward the ad. Kellaris, Cox, and Cox (1993) examined the fi t or congruency of music and the message (low, high) and the attention getting value of music (low, high) along with a no music control group. Th e dependent measures consisted of recall and recognition of brand names and message arguments in the context of a radio ad. Th is research found that when background music was congruent, attention getting music increased recall and recognition of brand names. When the music was attention getting and the message incongruent, it pulled listener's attention away from the message and negatively infl uenced recall. Th e no music ads performed as well or better than the musical ads in terms of recall and recognition. Th e relationship between the fi t of the mood induced music (happy/sad) and the purchase occasion (happy/sad) and its eff ect on purchase was studied by Alpert, Alpert, and Maltz (2005). While mood induced by music did not exhibit a main eff ect on purchase intentions, its interaction with fi t was signifi cant. Th e authors conclude that when music is used to evoke emotions congruent with the symbolic meaning of the product, the likelihood of purchase is increased. Music and Tempo Music is a key element in determining the atmosphere of a service or retail environment. Numerous studies have examined the role of music in these settings. Milliman (1982, 1986) researched the infl uence of background music tempo in a supermarket and in a restaurant. In the supermarket study, Milliman (1982) varied the tempo of classical music (fast, slow) and found that the pace of the in-store traffi c was signifi cantly slower with slow tempo music compared to fast tempo music. Also, higher sales volume was associated with slower tempo music and lower sales fi gures were associated with faster tempo music. Interestingly, when shoppers were asked about their awareness of background music, the majority of participants were not sure if music was in the background or they were incorrect. In the context of restaurant dining, Milliman (1986) varied the tempo of the background music (slow, fast) and found that with slower music, patrons stayed longer, ate about the same amount of food but consumed more alcoholic beverages. Th e author conjectured that the slower, more relaxing environment created a greater approach condition for the diners. In the context of a travel agency service, participants viewed a video in which the four music conditions varied in the arousal quality through changes in tempo (Chebat, Chebat, & Vaillant, 2001). Th e classical music was pretested to be equally pleasurable. Th is research found that highly arousing music hampered cognitive activity and the authors argue that the "fi t" between the highly arousing music and their context of the message from the travel agency was low. Similar to MacInnis and Park (1991), this study showed that when highly arousing music drew attention to itself, the eff ect was to reduce cognitive resources available for information processing and also reduce recall. In contrast, the slow tempo music did not attract attention to itself and did not interfere with the cognitive resources used to process the message. However, the authors caution that the deeper the cognitive activity, the more negative the attitude toward the employee and toward the visit. Music and Atmospherics

Several studies have not simply manipulated an aspect of music but rather manipulated the image or atmosphere of a retail setting with music as an element. For example, Meyer (1981) manipulated the décor of a pizza restaurant and had an elaborate décor condition, which included live music, or plain décor condition with no music. Th e purpose of the research was not related to music but was to advance a model for the study of consumer evaluation of choice alternatives given uncertainty about the alternative and attributes. Using videotape technology, Baker, Levy, and Grewal (1992) combined music and lighting to manipulate ambient cues in a retail environment. Th ey found that ambient cues (low and high) interact with social cues (number and friendliness of employees) to infl uence shoppers' pleasure and subsequently their willingness to purchase. Again, music is confounded with lighting making the results from music alone impossible to interpret. Finally, while not the main focus of their study, Grewal, Baker, Levy, and Voss (2003) use classical music versus no classical music as one manipulation in the atmosphere of a jewelry store. (Th e number of store employees and the number of customers was also varied). Results found that classical music had a positive eff ect on store atmosphere and, in turn, intentions to shop at the store. Th e authors also point out that classical music "fi t" with the jewelry store. Schlosser (1998) manipulated music along with other components in order to operationalize a prestige and a discount condition. In the prestige condition, the store was described as having classical music, soft lighting, hardwood fl oors, and wide aisles; in the discount condition the music was top 40, the fl oors were linoleum, and the aisles were narrow. Th e primary conclusion from this research was that diff erent types of products are diff erentially aff ected by the atmosphere of a store. Products were divided by whether they have a utilitarian function (more related to product performance) or a social identity function (more related to the expression of self-concept). Store atmosphere infl uenced perceptions of social identity products but not utilitarian products.

7
Stages of Consumer Socialization

Consumer socialization occurs in the context of dramatic cognitive and social developments, which take place from birth to adolescence. A common approach is to characterize these developments as a series of successive stages, with each stage describing children's thought, reasoning, and perspectives at particular ages. Below, we describe several frameworks most relevant for our subsequent discussion of consumer socialization. Stages of Cognitive and Social Development Cognitive Development. Th e most well known framework for characterizing developments in cognitive abilities is Piaget's theory, which proposes four main stages of cognitive development: sensorimotor (birth to 2 years), preoperational (2 to 7 years), concrete operational (7 to 11 years), and formal operational (11 through adulthood) (Ginsburg & Opper, 1988). Vast diff erences exist in the cognitive abilities of children at these stages, including the preoperational, concrete operational, and formal operational stages of most interest to consumer researchers. Preoperational children tend to be "perceptually-bound" to the readily-observable aspects of their environment, unlike concrete operational children, who do not accept perception as reality but can think about stimuli in their environment in a more thoughtful way. Preoperational children are also characterized by "centration," the tendency to focus on a single dimension. In contrast, the concrete operational child can consider several dimensions of a stimulus at a time and relate the dimensions in a thoughtful and relatively abstract way. Finally, in the formal operational stage, children progress to more adult-like thought patterns, capable of even more complex thought about concrete and hypothetical objects and situations.

Information processing theories of child development provide additional explanatory power for the types of cognitive abilities evidenced by children as they mature. Several formulations of information processing theory exist, but all share a focus on children's developing skills in the areas of acquisition, encoding, organization, and retrieval of information. In the consumer behavior literature, children have been characterized as belonging to one of three segments—strategic processors, cued processors, and limited processors—based on information processing skills they possess (Roedder, 1981). Strategic processors (age 12 and older) use a variety of strategies for storing and retrieving information, such as verbal labeling, rehearsal, and use of retrieval cues to guide memory search. Cued processors, ranging in age from 7 to 11 years, are able to use a similar set of strategies to enhance information storage and retrieval, but typically need to be aided by explicit prompts or cues. Finally, most children under the age of 7 years are limited processors, with processing skills that are not yet fully developed nor successfully utilized in learning situations, even when prompted to do so. Social Development. Th e area of social development includes a wide variety of topics, such as moral development, altruism and pro-social development, impression formation, and social perspective taking. In terms of explaining aspects of consumer socialization, we consider social perspective taking and impression formation to be the most directly relevant for our consideration. Social perspective taking, involving the ability to see perspectives beyond one's own, is strongly related to purchase infl uence and negotiation skills. Impression formation, involving the ability to make social comparisons, is strongly related to understanding the social aspects of products and consumption. Developments in social perspective taking are described well by Selman (1980). In the preschool and kindergarten years, the egocentric stage (ages 3–6), children are unaware of any perspective other than their own. As they enter the next phase, the social informational role taking stage (ages 6–8), children become aware that others may have diff erent opinions or motives, but believe this is due to having diff erent information rather than a diff erent perspective on the situation. Th us, children in this stage do not exhibit the ability to actually think from another person's perspective. Th is ability surfaces in the self-refl ective role taking stage (ages 8–10) as children understand that others may have diff erent opinions, even if they have the same information. Th ey can consider another person's viewpoint, but not simultaneously with their own, an ability that does not emerge until the fourth stage of mutual role taking (ages 10–12). Th is is a most important juncture as much social interaction, such as persuasion and negotiation, requires dual consideration of both parties' perspectives. Th e fi nal stage, social and conventional system role taking (ages 12–15 and older), features an additional development, the ability to understand another person's perspective as it relates to the social group to which he (other person) belongs or the social system in which he (other person) operates. Impression formation abilities also undergo dramatic development, as described by Barenboim (1981). Before the age of six, children describe other people in concrete or absolute terms, oft en mentioning physical appearances ("Nick is tall") or overt behaviors ("Elizabeth likes to skate"). However, these descriptions do not incorporate comparisons with other people. In Barenboim's fi rst stage, the behavioral comparisons phase (ages 6–8), children do incorporate comparisons as a basis of their impressions, but the comparisons continue to be based on concrete attributes or behaviors ("Matthew runs faster than Sam"). In the second stage, which Barenboim calls the psychological constructs phase (ages 8–10), impressions are based on psychological or abstract attributes ("Rosemary is friendly"), but do include comparisons to others. Comparisons based on psychological or abstract attributes do not emerge until the psychological comparisons phase (11 or 12 years of age and older), which features more adult-like impressions of people ("Sara is more outgoing than Amy"). Stages of Consumer Socialization We propose that consumer socialization be viewed as a developmental process occurring in a series of stages as children become socialized into their roles as consumers. Changes occur as children move through three stages of consumer socialization—the perceptual stage (ages 3–7), the analytical stage (ages 7–11), and the refl ective stage (age 11–adult). Th e perceptual stage derives its name from the overwhelming emphasis that children in this stage place on perceptual as opposed to abstract or symbolic thought. Th e analytical stage is named for the vast improvements we see at this stage in children's abilities to approach matters in more detailed and analytical ways. Finally, the refl ective stage derives its name from the ability of children of this age to refl ect on the complex social contexts and meanings related to consumption.

Analytical Stage. Enormous changes take place, both cognitively and socially, as children move into the analytical stage (ages 7–11). Th is period contains some of the most important developments in terms of consumer knowledge, skills, and consumption motivations. Th e shift from perceptual thought to more symbolic thought noted by Piaget, along with dramatic increases in information processing abilities, results in a more sophisticated understanding of the marketplace, a more complex set of knowledge about concepts such as advertising and brands, and a new perspective that goes beyond their own feelings and motives. Concepts such as product categories or prices are thought of in terms of functional or underlying dimensions, products and brands are analyzed and discriminated on the basis of more than one dimension or attribute, and generalizations are drawn from one's experiences. Reasoning proceeds at a more abstract level, setting the stage for knowledge structures that include information about abstract concepts such as advertiser's motives as well as the notion of contingencies (e.g., sweetness is an appealing attribute for candy but not soup). Th e ability to analyze stimuli on multiple dimensions and the acknowledgement of contingencies brings about vast changes in children's consumer decision-making skills and strategies. Now, children exhibit more thoughtfulness in their choices, considering more than just a single perceptually salient attribute and employing a decision strategy that makes sense given the task environment. As a result, children are more fl exible in the approach they bring to making decisions, allowing them to be more adaptive. Th ese tendencies also emerge in the way children try to infl uence and negotiate for desired items. Th e approach is more strategic, based on their newfound ability to think from the perspective of a parent or friend and adapt their infl uence strategy accordingly. Refl ective Stage. Th e refl ective stage (ages 11–16) is characterized by further development in several dimensions of cognitive and social development. Knowledge about marketplace concepts such as branding and pricing becomes more mature and complex as children develop more sophisticated cognitive and social skills. Many of these changes are more a matter of degree than kind. More distinct is the shift in orientation to a more refl ective way of thinking and reasoning, as children move into adolescence and become more focused on the social meanings and underpinnings of the consumer marketplace. A heightened awareness of other people's perspectives, along with a need to shape their own identity and conform to group expectations, results in more attention to the social aspects of being a consumer, making choices, and consuming brands. Consumer decisions are made in a more adaptive manner, depending on the situation and task. In a similar fashion, attempts to infl uence parents and friends refl ect more social awareness as adolescents become more strategic, favoring strategies that they think will be better received than a simple direct approach.

n how children think, what they know, and how they express themselves as consumers. Th ese stage descriptions, similar to other stage frameworks found in child psychology, have tremendous heuristic value. Yet, it is important to keep several caveats in mind. First, the ages associated with each stage are approximations based on the general tendencies of children in that age group. To constrain the number of stages to a reasonable number, some degree of variance among children in an age range was tolerated. For example, children 7 to 11 years of age are identifi ed with the analytical stage, even though diff erences in degree clearly exist at the extremes. To deal with variations of this sort, we formulated our stage descriptions to be most representative of children in the middle to end of each age range and allowed the age ranges to overlap at transition points between stages. Second, we note that the nature of the task environment or marketing stimuli can alter the age at which certain knowledge or behaviors would occur. Tasks that are more complex, requiring consideration of more information or more in-depth knowledge, can be expected to increase the age at which children appear to have mastered a particular concept. We turn now to a review of empirical fi ndings pertaining to stages of consumer socialization. We begin our discussion by examining evidence about children's consumer knowledge, skills, and motivation for the fi rst stage of consumer socialization—the perceptual stage. PERCEPTUAL STAGE Advertising and Persuasion Knowledge Much of the concern about television advertising to children has been focused on children under the age of eight, who have been found to have a limited understanding of advertising. One of the few skills that emerge during this stage is the ability to identify television commercials and distinguish them from other forms of programming. By age fi ve, almost all children have acquired the ability to pick out commercials from regular television programming (Blosser & Roberts, 1985; Butter, Popovich, Stackhouse, & Garner, 1981; Levin, Petros, & Petrella, 1982; Mallalieu, Palan, & Laczniak, 2005; Palmer & McDowell, 1979; Stephens & Stutts, 1982; Stutts, Vance, & Hudleson, 1981). Even 3- and 5-year-olds have been shown to discriminate commercials above chance levels (Butter, et al., 1981; Levin et al., 1982). However, the ability to identify commercials does not necessarily translate into an understanding of the "true" diff erence between commercials and programs (entertainment vs. selling intent). Children under the age of six or seven usually describe the diff erence between commercials and programs using simple perceptual cues, such as "commercials are short" (Butter et al., 1981; Palmer & McDowell, 1979; Ward, 1972). Young children oft en view advertising as entertainment (e.g., "commercials are funny") or as a form of unbiased information (e.g., "commercials tell you about things you can buy"). Although preschool children may implicitly understand that commercials include mainly positive statements about advertised products (Pine & Veasey, 2003), explicit understanding of the selling intent of advertising does not emerge until many children are seven or eight years of age (Macklin, 1985; Ward, Wackman, & Wartella, 1977). For example, in a landmark study with fi rst graders (6 to 7-year-olds), only 50% described the purpose of commercials as trying to sell something (Robertson & Rossiter, 1974). Product and Brand Knowledge In addition to advertising, products and brands are the most salient aspects of the marketplace for young consumers. Products and brands are advertised on television, displayed in stores, and found in the home. Even before they are able to read, children as young as two or three years of age can recognize familiar packages in the store and familiar characters on products such as toys and clothing (Derscheid, Kwon, & Fang, 1996; Haynes, Burts, Dukes, & Cloud, 1993). By preschool, children begin to recall brand names from seeing them advertised on television or featured on product packages, especially if the brand names are associated with salient visual cues such as colors, pictures, or cartoon characters (Macklin, 1996). By the time children reach fi rst grade, most can recall at least one brand in popular child-oriented product categories, such as candy and fast food (Ward et al., 1977). During this time, children develop a preference for particular brands. Children begin to express a preference for familiar branded items over generic off erings in the preschool years (Hite & Hite, 1995), with preference for branded items escalating further as children enter elementary school (Ward et al., 1977). In a clever study analyzing children's letters to Santa, Otnes, Kim, and Kim (1994) found that about 50% of children's gift requests were for specifi c branded (toy and game) items, with the vast majority of children (85%) mentioning at least one brand name in their letter to Santa. Despite these developments, children's understanding of products and brands is limited by a focus on perceptual attributes that are visually dominant, such as shape, size, or color. Product categorization is a vivid illustration of this point. Although children learn to group or categorize products at an early age, young children rely on highly visible perceptual attributes to categorize products and discriminate brands (John

& Lakshmi-Ratan, 1992; Klees, Olson, & Wilson, 1988). For example, in a study by John and Sujan (1990), preschoolers (ages 4–5) grouped beverage products together based on having similar packaging (e.g., cans vs. bottles), label colors (e.g., green vs. red), and size (e.g., 2-liter vs. 16 oz. bottles). Older children (ages 9–10) placed more emphasis on underlying attributes such as taste (e.g., cola vs. lemon-lime) or carbonation (e.g., orange juice vs. soft drink). Shopping Knowledge and Skills A major accomplishment at this stage is an understanding of money as a medium of exchange. Early childhood is a period of rapid development in abilities to understand where money comes from, to identify specifi c coins and bill values, and to carry out transactions with money involving simple addition and subtraction (Marshall, 1964; Marshall & MacGruder, 1960; Strauss, 1952). Signifi cant jumps in knowledge occur between preschool and fi rst and second grade, with most second graders having acquired many of the basic concepts for understanding the exchange of money for goods and services. Also developing is an understanding of the basic sequence of events involved in the shopping process. Children acquire a vast amount of experience as an observer of the shopping process at very early ages, but these experiences do not result in an understanding of the basic shopping script until children reach the preschool or kindergarten years (Berti & Bombi, 1988; Karsten, 1996). Karsten (1996) illustrates this point in her study with kindergartners through fourth graders, who were asked to participate in a "shopping game." Each child was shown a small toy with a price tag and was given money to buy the item at a play store. A store area was set up nearby with a small cash register, containing visible amounts of coins and bills. Children were asked to show the interviewer how they would buy the toy in the store. Even the youngest children in the study enacted the basic shopping script. Kindergartners understood that one needed to select an item, check on the money available, place it on the cashier's counter, wait for the cashier off er change, and obtain a receipt.

Decision-Making Skills and Abilities Children assume the role of consumer decision makers at a young age. During the period from preschool to early elementary school, one of the most important skills to emerge is the ability to adjust information search according to costs and benefi ts of additional search. Preschoolers can adjust their information search according to either costs or benefi ts (Davidson & Hudson, 1988, experiment 1), but adjusting information search in line with both costs and benefi ts emerges later as children move into elementary school. In a study with 4-

to 7-year-olds, Gregan-Paxton and John (1995) found that 6- to 7-year-olds modifi ed their search behavior in line with appropriate costbenefi t trade-off s, gathering the least amount of information in the condition with the least favorable cost-benefi t profi le (high cost, low benefi t) and the most information in the condition with the most favorable cost-benefi t profi le (low cost, high benefi t). Younger children (ages 4–5) were less discerning, however, gathering the most information for one of the conditions warranting a very modest degree of search (low cost, low benefi t) and much less information for one of the conditions warranting the most extensive information search (low cost, high benefi t). Th e type of information gathered is oft en perceptual in nature, whether or not it is relevant for the decision at hand (Wartella, Wackman, Ward, Shamir, & Alexander, 1979). Once information is gathered, young children do not always utilize the information in an eff ective manner. Kindergarten children oft en rely on a single attribute or dimension in forming preferences, comparing products, or choosing one alternative from a set of options (Bahn, 1986; Capon & Kuhn, 1980; Ward et al., 1977; Wartella et al., 1979). Th e focus on perceptual data and single attributes is the hallmark of decision making in children at the perceptual stage. Purchase Infl uence and Negotiation Strategies Children infl uence purchases at a very young age. At this stage, children approach infl uence attempts from an egocentric perspective, with the goal of getting what they want instead of persuading parents who may have a diff erent viewpoint on the purchase. Toddlers and preschool children exert their infl uence in a very direct way, oft en pointing to products and occasionally grabbing them off store shelves for deposit inside their parent's shopping cart (Rust, 1993). As children become more verbal, they ask for products by name, sometimes begging, screaming and whining to get what they want (McNeal, 1992). For frequently-purchased items, such as snack food and cereal, children are oft en able to exert their infl uence simply by asking (Isler, Popper, & Ward, 1987), due to parents who become more accepting of children's preferences for such items and more comfortable with the idea of occasionally yielding to those preferences. Consumption Motives and Values Consumer socialization involves more than the acquisition of knowledge and skills related to the consumer role. It also includes the adoption of motives and values pertaining to consumption activities. Researchers have addressed these developments by focusing on the adoption of social motivations for consumption, emphasizing consumption for social expression and status, and materialistic values, emphasizing the acquisition of material goods as a means of achieving personal happiness, success, and self-fulfi llment. Research suggests that children value material goods from a very young age, sometimes favoring them above all else. Goldberg and Gorn (1978) provide an interesting illustration in a study with 4- to 5-year-old boys. Children saw an ad for a new toy ("Ruckus Raisers") and were then given a choice between two hypothetical playmates: one described as "very nice" that did not own the new toy and one described as "not so nice" but owning the new toy. A majority of the children selected the boy with the new toy. Children also made choices from two hypothetical play situations: playing alone with the new toy or playing in a sandbox with friends (without the toy). Again, a majority of children selected the play situation with the new toy. However, children's desires for material goods at this stage appear to be driven by rather simple considerations, such as novelty or quantity. Baker and Gentry (1996) provide an example in their study of collecting as a hobby among fi rst and fi ft h graders. Children of all ages collected similar types of items—such as sports cards, dolls, and rocks—but did so for diff erent reasons. First graders oft en compared their possessions to those of others in terms of quantity. Collecting appeared to be simply a way of getting more than someone else. Among fi ft h graders, however, the motivations for collecting had more social connotations. Collecting was appreciated as a way of socially expressing one's uniqueness and attaining a sense of personal achievement by having things that others do not. Th ese fi ndings are consistent with our descriptions of children in the perceptual stage, who value material goods on a perceptual dimension (quantity), and the analytical stage, who see things quite diff erently by virtue of their social comparison skills and perspective-taking abilities. ANALYTICAL STAGE Advertising and Persuasion Knowledge A full understanding of advertising intent usually emerges by the time most children are 7 to 8 years old (Bever, Smith, Bengen, & Johnson, 1975; Blosser & Roberts, 1985; Lawlor & Prothero, 2003; Robertson & Rossiter, 1974; Rubin, 1974; Ward et al., 1977). Children see the persuasive intent of commercials quite clearly, coming to terms with the fact that advertisers are "trying to get people to buy something." In a study with fi rst, third, and fi ft h grade boys, Robertson and Rossiter (1974) found that the understanding of persuasive intent increased dramatically from only 52.7% of fi rst graders (6- to 7-year-olds) to 87.1% of third graders (8- to 9-year-olds) to 99% of fi ft h graders (10- to 11-year-olds). Th is trend supports our description of children in the analytical stage, who are capable of viewing advertising from a number of perspectives, the buyer's (assistive intent) and the advertiser's (persuasive intent). Children in the analytical stage also recognize the existence of bias and deception in advertising. Children aged 8 years and older no longer believe that "commercials always tell the truth" (Bever et al., 1975; Robertson & Rossiter, 1974; Ward, 1972; Ward et al., 1977), with beliefs about the truthfulness of advertising becoming even more negative as children move toward adolescence (Bever et al., 1975; Robertson & Rossiter, 1974; Rossiter & Robertson, 1976; Ward, 1972; Ward et al., 1977). For example, Ward et al. (1977) report that the percentage of kindergartners, third graders, and sixth graders believing that advertising never or only sometimes tells the truth increases from 50% to 88% to 97%, respectively. Moreover, older children also understand why commercials are sometimes untruthful, connecting lying to persuasive intent (e.g., "they want to sell products to make money, so they have to make the product look better than it is"). Armed with an understanding of advertising's persuasive intent and skepticism about the truthfulness of advertising claims, children over the age of eight are oft en viewed as having a "cognitive defense" against advertising that shields them from being unfairly persuaded. Although this scenario seems straightforward, evidence regarding the extent to which children's general attitudes and beliefs about advertising function as cognitive defenses is quite mixed. Early survey research was successful in fi nding moderate links between children's knowledge of advertising's persuasive intent and their desire for advertised products (Robertson & Rossiter, 1974), but more recent experimental research fi nds that children's cognitive defenses have little or no eff ect on evaluations and preferences for advertised products (Christenson, 1982; Ross et al., 1984). For example, Christenson (1982) found that an educational segment on commercials was successful in increasing the awareness of advertising's persuasive intent and decreasing the perceived truthfulness of advertising, yet had little eff ect on younger (fi rst–second graders) or older (fi ft h–sixth graders) children's evaluations of a subsequently advertised product. More recent research has provided an answer for this puzzle, fi nding that children's advertising knowledge serves as a cognitive defense only when that knowledge is accessed and used during commercial viewing (Brucks, Armstrong, & Goldberg, 1988). Product and Brand Knowledge Brand knowledge escalates from early to middle childhood. Children's awareness and recall of brand names increases with age, from early to middle childhood (Rossiter, 1976; Rubin, 1974; Ward et al., 1977). By the time children reach middle childhood, they can name multiple brands in most child-oriented product categories such as cereal, snacks, and toys (McNeal, 1992; Otnes et al., 1994; Rossiter, 1976; Rubin, 1974; Ward et al., 1977) and can name at least one brand in more adult-oriented product categories such as cameras and gasoline (Ward et al., 1977). Between early and middle childhood, children also learn a great deal about the underlying structure of product categories. Children shift from using highly visible perceptual cues to more important underlying cues as a basis for categorizing and judging similarity among products (John & Sujan, 1990; John & Lakshmi-Ratan, 1992; Klees et al., 1988). By third or fourth grade, children are learning to group objects according to taxonomic relationships (e.g., belts and socks are items of clothing), attributes that indicate the relationship of categories to one another (e.g., fruit juices and soft drinks diff er on the attribute of naturalness), and attributes inherent to the core concept of categories (e.g., taste, more than color, is central to the category of soft drinks). Th ese are termed underlying, deep structure, or functional attributes because they convey the true meaning or function a category might serve. Th e shift to functional or underlying categorization cues around 8 to 10 years of age is consistent with symbolic thinking that characterizes children in the analytical stage.

8
Aging and Consumer Behavior

As people age, they experience physiological changes which, in turn, can aff ect the way they interact with the consumer environment. Problems with visual and auditory functions increase markedly with age, typically beginning in the fourth decade of life (Schieber & Baldwin, 1996; Willott, 1991). Th ese changes can have dramatic eff ects on older adults' attention and cognition. In many cases, it may not be possible to fully restore visual and auditory functions to levels of younger adults through surgery or use of prostheses (e.g., contact lenses, eyeglasses, hearing aids). Motor control also declines in older adults. Th ese declines include changes in the peripheral and central nervous system, and changes in control and coordination of motor functions that can lead to an array of behavioral decrements (Ketcham & Stelmach, 2003). Vision Approximately half of all adults over 65 years old have cataracts (Fozard & Gordon-Salant, 2001). As people age, size of the pupil declines and the lens becomes more opaque (Weale, 1961). Th e loss of transparency is particularly pronounced for short wavelengths (e.g., blue, green light) due to age-related yellowing of the lens. Moreover, age-related declines in visual acuity (an indicator of how well fi ne spatial detail can be recognized) become more severe when there is low luminance or the stimuli are low in contrast. However, color constancy mechanisms appear to remain relatively intact in older adults, possibly minimizing decrements on familiar real-world tasks performed in well-lighted conditions. Age-related changes in vision suggest that the way in which information is presented or displayed can aff ect whether or not it is processed. For instance, messages and displays that appear clear, bright, and attractive to a younger person are likely to be fuzzy, dark, and unpleasant to an older one. In most cases, better illumination, higher contrasts, and reduced glare will help older consumers.

Also because older adults tend to make less use of their peripheral fi elds than younger adults, managers may wish to place brands close to consumers' direct line of sight in retail environments.Hearing Older adults fi nd it progressively more diffi cult to detect simple, low-intensity sounds, discriminate small changes in frequency or intensity, fi lter out background noise, and identify the source of a target noise in space (Schneider & Pichora-Fuller, 2000). Older adults in conversations also have more diffi culty processing phonemes than syllables. Th ese changes are not only likely to compromise listening, but they can negatively aff ect the ability to encode information in many consumer situations. It suggests that sound and sound clutter can be problematic for older adults in consumer environments over which they do not have control. Motor Functions Motor behavior refers to muscular actions performed to fulfi ll some objective of the performer (e.g., braking a car, pushing lawn mover, hitting a golf ball). Normally aging people are capable of performing many motor behaviors in everyday life well into their 80s. However, they have much slower reaction times, in some cases as much as 50% slower on complex tasks (Cerella, 1990; Salthouse, 1996). Age-related changes in motor functions have important implications for product design and usability in consumer domains. For example, individual programming of devices becomes increasingly diffi cult due to declines in vision and poorer ability to handle very small objects. Use of a computer mouse has been found to pose a major impediment to computer usage among older adults (Walker, Philbin, & Fisk, 1997). It is thus important that there be development of more userfriendly means by which older adults can interface with smaller gadgets including items such as hearing aids and cell phones. A few studies have investigated the benefi ts of devices that improve the speed and accuracy of movements as well as coordination and balance in older adults (e.g., Maki et al., 1999). However, much work remains to be done in the design and development of assistive devices and technologies. MEMORY Another arena in which there is a great deal of age-related changes is memory processes. Although there is widespread agreement that aging negatively aff ects performance on most memory tasks, there is not as much consensus about when and why age-related diff erences in memory occur (Craik & Jennings, 1992; Kausler, 1994; Light, 1991; Schaie, 2005). Memory impairments that have been documented in the laboratory may not necessarily extend to everyday domains of behavior (Zacks, Hasher, & Li, 2000). In addition, not all aspects of memory are impaired (e.g., Rahhal, May, & Hasher, 2002; Schacter, Kihlstrom, Kaszniak,

& Valdiserri, 1993). In this section we review the literature with respect to changes in memory. Th eoretical Perspectives Th ree main theoretical perspectives have been advanced to account for age-related memory changes: speed of processing (e.g., Salthouse, 1996), reduced processing resources (e.g., Craik, 1986), and diminished inhibition (e.g., Hasher & Zacks, 1988). Although the theoretical accounts do share substantial conceptual overlap, they have tended to be discussed separately in the literature. Each is considered in turn, along with a discussion of empirical studies from psychology, neuroscience, and marketing that shed light on cognitive functioning of older adults.

In one series of studies, it was found that people in whom positive aff ect had been induced showed more intrinsic motivation than controls, but also responded well to extrinsic motivation when the work-task needed to be done (Isen & Reeve, 2005). Intrinsic motivation was measured in a free-choice situation by (1) choice of a more interesting task, over a dull task that had a very small chance of paying a small amount of money; and (2) increased amount of reported enjoyment of the enjoyable task (but not the dull task). Th ese are standard measures used in the intrinsic motivation literature (e.g., Deci & Ryan, 1985). However, when participants were informed that there was some work that needed to be done (no money was involved this time), and again they had the choice of what activity to do during the 20-minute time period, they chose to do the work that needed to be done, but spent the rest of their time with the more enjoyable task, and thus spent more time than controls on the interesting task (even though they got their work done and did not make any more errors than the control group—both had very low error rates). Th ey again liked the enjoyable task more than controls, but showed no diff erence from controls on the dull work task. Th us, they displayed self-control in the sense that that term is normally used—they did not like the work task as much as the puzzle task, but they engaged it as much as was necessary. EXPECTANCY MOTIVATION Th e other set of studies on motivation that relates to self-control that I want to mention are two showing that positive aff ect infl uences the three components of expectancy motivation (see, e.g.,Ilgen, Nebeker, & Pritchard, 1981; Kanfer, 1990, for discussions of the theory of expectancy motivation). In a moderate range of performance (but not at extremely high or extremely low performance levels), people in positive aff ect saw more connection between how hard they tried and how well they would do, resulting in greater motivation that is based on their realistic expectations in the situation (see Erez & Isen, 2002 for more detail and discussion). Th is is not just a matter of motivation in the sense of "trying harder," but refl ects how eff ective the person expects to be if he or she tries moderately hard. Th e results indicate that people in the positive-aff ect condition have greater expectation that their eff ort will pay off (where it is likely to pay off , but not where it is not), and this is the source of trying. Th is is important for self-control, because it prompts people to put forth eff ort and stay at tasks, in the expectation that trying will lead to success and the desired outcome. OMISSION DETECTION Another matter of very great theoretical importance is omission detection, which of course has been investigated extensively in the consumer literature (e.g., Kim et al., 1996; Sanbonmatsu, Kardes, Houghton, Ho, & Posavac, 2003). I did not mention this topic as a focus within this chapter at the outset precisely because it has been investigated extensively within the fi eld of consumer behavior, and in fact many of the most important advances in understanding its determinants and eff ects have been explored in those contexts. It is also investigated in the theoretical Psychology literature, most recently by Dunning and his students and colleagues (e.g., Caputo & Dunning, 2005), who have pointed out the damaging and problematic consequences of not realizing what we do not know. However, I do want to bring the topic of omission detection up in this chapter, because based on much of the discussion in this chapter, it seems possible for positive aff ect to play a role in enabling people to see what is missing, what they are not considering, and thus for positive aff ect to link these two streams of research (e.g., Mantel et al., 2006). Th at is, if positive aff ect leads people to be more fl exible thinkers, as has been widely demonstrated in the literature—to solve problems requiring a creative or innovative approach to looking at the functions or aspects of stimulus elements available for solving the problem; to think of unusual associates to stimuli; to categorize more fl exibly; to understand and welcome mildly unusual brand extensions—as well as the newer eff ects that have been proposed to result from such fl exibility and discussed in this chapter (broad focus of attention, broadened and built-up approaches, resources, and skills; improved incidental learning and ability to divide attention among tasks; and increased cognitive monitoring ability and tendency to check)—then it also seems likely that positive aff ect could lead people to notice missing information or material that they are not considering that they should be considering. Th is link has not yet been explicitly made between these two streams of research. However, the role of aff ect in infl uencing omission detection has recently begun to be studied (e.g., Mantel et al., 2006). It is clear, from the foregoing discussions of the critical predictions for each of the phenomena described so far that follow from the fi ndings on positive aff ect, that positive aff ect should improve omission detection. Th at is, the fl exibility that has been demonstrated to result from positive aff ect should lead to noticing when one is not considering all of the important relevant aspects of a situation or problem. A recent series of studies is off ering indication that, indeed, positive aff ect may help to reduce the problem, in judgment and decision making, of not realizing that there is important information that is missing (Mantel et al., 2006). In one study, those authors have found that people in positive aff ect, when given only a small number of product attributes as a product description for a product they are asked to evaluate, are more likely than controls to ask for additional information, and without the additional information, are less extreme in their evaluations of the product. A second study, based on the Ellsberg (1961) paradox, found that where the risk in the situation was undeclared, people in the positive aff ect condition were less likely than controls to take the risky option. As noted earlier, we know from previous research that people in positive aff ect are less likely to take a risk if the risk is high and real (e.g., Isen & Patrick, 1983; Isen & Geva, 1987). But in the case under discussion, the results indicate that they are less likely to take the risky option when the risk is unspecifi ed. Together, these results suggest that people in positive aff ect are more likely to notice when important information is missing from a decision situation. Th is line of work is just beginning, and much more needs to be done, but it is an exciting area for development, because the ability to notice missing information has so many important implications, both theoretically and in understanding the choices and behavior of consumers. CONCLUSION It is well-known that theoretical issues can have important practical implications, which is as it should be. Such implications have been discovered in the area of aff ect and cognition, where basic fi ndings regarding aff ect's infl uence on thought processes have been explored in applied contexts such as consumer behavior, managerial decision making, and medical decision making, and found to contribute to our understanding of the processes that underlie important phenomena in applied domains. For example, the fi nding that positive aff ect leads people to consider more aspects of situations and integrate that material is relevant for many fi elds, from consumer decision making to managerial decision making to physician diagnostic processes. Current developments in theoretical research domains off er exciting new directions for applied work relating basic processes to consumers' behavior and decision processes, and we can look forward to continued new applications of this and other work. At the same time, the applied research has a history of contributing back to theoretical development itself, in part because the richness of the contexts in which the applied work takes place off ers the opportunity to add shadings, detail, nuances, and specifi cs that help to expand and refi ne the theoretical work. We can all look forward to these developments as well.

9

The Nature and Role of Affect in Consumer Behavior

Th ere is still some carryover from the use of the term "aff ect" to also refer to what is, in essence, the evaluative aspect of attitudes. Th is stems from the classic tri-partite depiction of attitudes: cognitive, aff ective, and conative (see Eagly & Chaiken, 1993) and a failure to adequately diff erentiate between evaluative measures (e.g., favorable/unfavorable) and antecedent or subsequent processes, which might be feeling-based. Consistent with most recent scholarly discussions, we reserve the term "aff ect" to describe an internal feeling state. One's explicit or implicit "liking" for some object,person, or position is viewed as an evaluative judgment rather than an internal feeling state. As Russell and Carroll (1999a) put it: By aff ect, we have in mind genuine subjective feelings and moods (as when someone says, 'I'm feeling sad'), rather than thoughts about specifi c objects or events (as when someone calmly says, 'Th e crusades were a sad chapter in human history'). (pp. 3–4) Th is chapter maintains the separation of aff ect as a feeling state that is distinct from either liking or purely descriptive cognition. So when we use the term "aff ect" to describe stimuli, internal and overt responses, it is only in relation to evoked feeling states. Imagine, in contrast, an advertisement whose words or images connote a happy (i.e., successful) outcome. Aff ective processes cannot merely be assumed. Alternative explanations (e.g., the advertised product seems likely to produce favorable outcomes) for so-called "aff ective" infl uences on subsequent evaluations and behavior must be ruled out before implicating aff ect. Th ese include semantically associated changes in object meaning or construct accessibility. Th is defi nition also raises both philosophical and empirical questions about whether such a feeling state must be consciously experienced or whether we can be unaware that we are experiencing aff ect. Research where subliminally presented smiling or frowning faces were used to prime aff ect (outside of awareness) and bring about subsequent evaluative responses (Winkielman, Zajonc, & Schwarz, 1997), is a case in point. Aff ective experience in the absence of an identifi ed basis for that experience has been a staple of psychological research since Zajonc's (1980) early work on "mere exposure." In that program of research, repeated subliminal exposure to unfamiliar stimuli having neutral valence such as Chinese ideographs has been shown to generate some degree of liking for the stimuli, possibly as a result of a primitive reward mechanism associated with increasing familiarity or a reduction in uncertainty. Another standard paradigm for investigating precognitive aff ective processes is to present (outside of awareness) a stimulus known to evoke either a negative or positive aff ective response (e.g., a sad face). Following that exposure, people are asked to indicate how they are feeling (to rule out more conscious aff ective responses including inferences) and to rate the emotional quality of a semantically unrelated object, such as a piece of music. Using such a procedure, for example, Strahan, Spencer, and Zanna (2002) found that aff ective stimuli can infl uence positive/negative assessments even without producing a measurable eff ect on people's aff ective experiences (i.e., reported feelings). In a particularly sophisticated study (Schimmack, 2004), subjects received masked subliminal presentations of pleasant and unpleasant pictures, followed by supraliminal presentations of an identical picture (the target) paired with a foil whose valence was either the same as the target or opposite. If the initial subliminal target exposure produced a spontaneous aff ective experience, participants should be better able—and they were—to discriminate the target from the foil when they had a diff erent valence because only one object should match the originally experienced aff ect. Diff erent results have frequently been observed for pictures and words when used as subliminal stimuli (Schimmack & Crites, 2005). Words have been found to elicit a skin-conductance response under conditions of very short exposure (suggesting aff ective experience), whereas pictures have not. However, this fi nding may also be due to the greater inherent polarity of the selected words relative to pictures, since the interpretation of pictures may require more cognitive resources than words having relatively fi xed aff ective associations. Most consumer research on aff ect deals with moods (e.g., Barone, Miniard, & Romeo, 2000; Cohen &

Andrade, 2004; Gorn, Goldberg, & Basu, 1993; Pham, 1998), although there has been growing interest in the study of specifi c emotions (e.g., Lerner, Small, & Loewenstein, 2004; Raghunathan & Pham, 1999; Raghunathan, Pham, & Corfman, 2006). Moods are usually thought of as low intensity and diff use aff ective states that generally lack source identifi cation.1 Th e individual, prompted either by physiological or hormonal/chemical activity (such as changes in levels of serotonin and dopamine) or by external stimuli (music, weather, exposure to happy versus sad information), experiences a vague sense of feeling good or bad without necessarily knowing quite why. Some days or aft er certain experiences, we are aware of feeling good or bad, optimistic or pessimistic, up or down, relaxed or restless, alert or drowsy. Mood states also track our bodily energy levels (e.g., blood glucose levels), our daily circadian rhythm, and our general wellness or illness, thereby guiding relatively automatic self-regulatory responses as well as more conscious decisions, as we shall discuss later on. Emotions, on the other hand, are much more diff erentiated and hence provide more attitude- and behavior-specifi c information. Feeling anger, for example, will oft en lead to target and context-specifi c responses rather than more general displays of unhappiness (Bushman & Baumeister, 1998). It should be noted, however, that specifi c emotions can produce mood-like eff ects (e.g., being angry or sad can aff ect a pattern of behavior) oft en without realizing that one has transferred the emotional response (to an identifi ed target) to unrelated behaviors. Recent studies show that the degree of transfer will be a function of two factors: (1) the salience of the source of the emotional state—transfer is more likely when the actual source of the aff ect is not salient; and (2) the domain similarity between the actual source of the aff ective state and the objectively unrelated behavior (Raghunathan, Pham, & Corfman, 2006). Moods have been shown to be easily manipulated through exposure to aff ectively charged stimuli such as music, videos, and pictures, or through the recall of emotionally involving experiences (e.g., Cohen & Andrade, 2004). Note that the use of low intensity emotion manipulations, such as sadness, displeasure, or happiness, to create positive or negative mood states tends to blur the line between emotions and moods, especially when the source is made salient. Because aff ect is oft en used as information (Schwarz, 1990; Schwarz & Clore, 1983), the misattribution of incidental aff ect may play a powerful role in everyday life. Even experimentally-induced proprioceptive feedback of head nodding or shaking can lead a person to conclude that messagerelated thoughts are positive or negative (Brinol & Petty, 2003). Th e duration of mood changes is typically assumed to be short, from a few minutes to a couple of hours (Isbell & Wyer, 1999), although this duration probably varies with the method of instigation (Ehrlichman & Halpern, 1988; Isen, Clark, & Schwartz, 1976). Experimental manipulation of aff ective states Multiple techniques have been used to manipulate individuals' transient aff ective states. In most experiments, participants are exposed to a sequence of ostensibly unrelated studies, where the fi rst study is meant to manipulate people's feelings while the second assesses the dependent variables of interest. In the fi rst study, participants might be exposed, for instance, to false positive or negative performance feedback (Barone, Miniard, & Romeo, 2000; Swinyard, 1993), cheerful or depressing movies (Andrade, 2005; Cohen & Andrade, 2004), pleasant or unpleasant music (Gorn, Goldberg, & Basu, 1993), or positive or negative aff ective self-referential statements such as the Velten procedure (Velten, 1968), unexpected gift s (Barone, Miniard, & Romeo, 2000; Isen & Simmonds, 1978). Alternatively, participants may be asked to recall and describe an aff ectively-charged experience in writing (Pham, 1998). Due to their transient and mild, hence, short-lived nature, experimentally induced moods may dissipate relatively fast (see Isen, Clark, & Schwartz, 1976). Th erefore, regardless of the mood induction procedure, the dependent measure usually is collected not long aft er the manipulation. Sometimes the mood manipulation and dependent measures co-occur. Mood manipulations using background music or physical ambience, like scent, for instance, allow for a simultaneous assessment of dependent variables (Grunberg & Straub, 1992; Schwarz, Strack, Kommer, & Wagner, 1987). Th ere is no single best option among all potential techniques. Diff erent techniques raise different issues in terms of potential confounds, control for intensity levels, reliability, demand characteristics, and motivational requirements. For instance, receiving an unexpected gift , a common manipulation of positive mood (Isen, Shalker, Clark, & Karp, 1978; Kahn & Isen, 1993), can activate norms of reciprocity independently of aff ective changes (e.g., "Th e experimenter was nice to me, I'll be nice to him/her"). Similarly, false performance feedback can infl uence self-esteem or self-effi cacy along with desired changes in aff ective states (Hill & Ward, 1989). Such unwanted eff ects might be confounded with the aff ect manipulation depending on the research question and other aspects of the procedure. Asking participants to report an aff ectively charged personal experience can avoid some of the above-mentioned concerns. A major advantage of this method is that because each participant recruits his or her own personal experience, there is a lesser chance of confounding with the content of the aff ect-inducing event. Content-related confounds are much more likely with manipulations that involve exposure to a common aff ect-inducing stimulus across participants, such as watching a happy or sad movie. On the other hand, the personal experience method requires relatively high participant motivation; otherwise, the manipulation tends to be weakened. A second drawback of this method is that participants usually are explicitly directed to write about experiences that lead them to feel good or bad, which may enhance the likelihood of hypothesis guessing and demand artifacts. Th is concern is heightened if a salient mood manipulation check is administered before the dependent measures are collected. In addition, there may be extra variability in emotional states induced—hence higher experimental error—because participants may have diff erent interpretations of the type of experience they are supposed to report. Some respondents may interpret "an event that made you feel bad" as one that made them feel angry, whereas others may interpret it as one that made them feel sad. It is therefore important that the instructions be very precise when using this manipulation. Music does not require highly motivated participants, does not direct participants to specifi c feelings, and has been shown to produce signifi cant eff ects on judgment and behavioral measures (Gorn, Goldberg, & Basu, 1993; Gorn, Pham, & Sin, 2001). However, there is signifi cant variance in the population when it comes to music tastes, which can compromise reliability. Exposure to aff ectively charged videos has proven to be quite successful due to the general appeal of these stimuli (low motivation required), their easy-to-determine valence, and their higher intensity, compared to written or audio stimuli. However, as mentioned before, using a common video across participants within a given mood condition raises the possibility of confounding between aff ective experience and the semantic or episodic content of the video. To try to mitigate this problem, one can consider using diff erent stimulus replicates across conditions or experiments. Another potential drawback of video-based inductions is that, compared to other procedures, exposure to videos may also facilitate hypothesis guessing and, consequently, demand artifacts. To avoid such concern, the cover story must be convincing and, also importantly, the aff ect manipulation check disguised. For example, Cohen and Andrade (2004) used a combined technique of video plus personal experience, in which participants were informed that the university, in order to augment its web-based teaching environment, attempted to assess the impact of audio and video stimuli transmitted through the web. Students were informed that they would watch fi ve minutes of a video and then would perform memory and judgment recall tasks. Aft er the video, the "memory task" instructed them to write a personal story related to the scenes watched in the clip. Aft er the "memory task," a "judgment task" (in fact, the manipulation check) asked participants to assess ten items related to the video. Only three of them were aff ect-related. Th e other items were in line with the general cover story. Th is manipulation has shown strong and reliable eff ects on people's feelings and, importantly, very low incidence of hypothesis guessing (see also Andrade, 2005). Videos have also been used to manipulate specifi c emotional states, such as anger (Andrade & Ariely, 2007; Phillipot, 1993) sadness and disgust (Lerner, Small, & Loewenstein, 2004), and fear (Andrade & Cohen, 2007b). Restricting the eff ect to one specifi c emotion may be challenging; some video manipulations can enhance more than one specifi c aff ective state at the same time. For instance, Gross and Levenson (1995) showed that an anger manipulation tended to increase disgust levels as well. As they pointed out, "With fi lms, it appears that there is a natural tendency for anger to co-occur with other negative emotions" (p. 104). Still, videos and some combined techniques (video and personal story writing) are relatively successful aff ect manipulations (Westermann, Spies, Stahl, & Hesse, 1996). Physiological and cognitive antecedents of emotion Th e infl uential James-Lange theory (James, 1884) held that emotional stimuli elicited bodily responses, that is, peripheral activity such as changes in heart rate, blood pressure, and skin conductance, and that these bodily responses were translated fairly directly into conscious diff erences in emotional experience (e.g., fear versus anger). While there was modest success relating "energetic" physiological responses to higher arousal negative aff ect (compared to lower arousal states such as sadness and guilt), there was no consistent translation of bodily responses into diff erential positive aff ect. More generally, such physiological measures do not appear to refl ect essential diff erences in the valence of emotion (Bradley, Cuthbert, & Lang, 1993; Schimmack & Crites, 2005). One response to the failure to support the James-Lange theory was to search for other, more sensitive indicants of emotional response that could then be interpreted as particular types of emotion. Facial feedback theories identifi ed patterns that corresponded to happiness, surprise, sadness, fear, anger, and disgust (Ekman, 1973; Izard, 1977; Kleinke, Peterson, & Rutledge, 1998). However, a meta-analysis of these studies (including those where participants were induced to adopt musculature associated with smiling and frowning) indicated that these eff ects were too weak to perform the central function ascribed to bodily responses in the James-Lange theory (Matsumoto, 1987). A more basic challenge to the original theory was to question the central role of bodily response to subsequent emotional experience. Schachter and Singer (1962) made signifi cant inroads by showing (via injections of either epinephrine or a placebo) that peripheral arousal only diff erentiated an emotional response from merely cognitive responses. In their two-factor theory, cognitive processes played the decisive role in interpreting the arousal that was being experienced. A substantial challenge to the bodily arousal component of this theory can be seen in other research conducted at about the same time. Lazarus and Alfert (1964) asked people to watch a fi lm depicting a tribal ritual involving what appeared to be genital mutilation. However, half of those watching were given misinformation that the experience was actually not painful and that adolescents looked forward to this initiation into manhood, and signifi cant cognitive control over arousal was observed. Subsequent research on spinal cord injured patients best supports the view that peripheral arousal is not necessary to the experience of emotion, but can intensify it (Mezzacappa, Katkin, & Palmer, 1999). However, the importance of emotional intensifi cation should not be minimized. Recent research on memory, for example, demonstrates the importance of such emotional experience to memory consolidation, and is, thus, consistent with evolutionary underpinnings of classical conditioning (Cahill & McGaugh, 1998). More generally, emotional response was shown to be far more under cognitive control and appraisals of experience than had been imagined.

Th ere is considerable evidence that the arousal intensity of an aff ective experience increases people's immediate and long-term memory for this experience (Bradley, Greenwald, Petry, & Lang, 1992; Kroeber-Riel, 1979; Th orson & Friestad, 1989), especially with respect to the central elements of this experience (Christianson, Loft us, Hoff man, & Loft us, 1991). Th is appears to be the case even when the source of arousal is unrelated to the material to be learned and comes aft er the learning has taken place, which suggests that the phenomenon may be due, in part, to a better consolidation of memory traces under high emotional arousal (Nielson, Yee, & Erickson, 2005). Emotional intensity is no guarantee of memory accuracy, however. Biases due to changes in cognitive appraisals of the events or revised standards of judgment (e.g., looking back, a person may have a diff erent perspective on the emotion-eliciting event) as well as a desire to see things diff erently (e.g., when anticipating a recurrent experience such as childbirth) may intrude on people's memory (Levine, 1997; Levine, Prohaska, Burgess, Rice, & Laulhere, 2001). Retrospective assessments of aff ective experiences also seem to be more impacted by intensity at both the peak and the end of the experience, with duration playing a less signifi cant role (Ariely & Loewenstein, 2000; Fredrickson & Kahneman, 1993; Kahneman, Fredrickson, Schreiber, & Redelmeier, 1993). Th e Structure and Assessment of Aff ect Th ere are two separate research traditions among those whose work involves the assessment of aff ect. Th e fi rst is to identify the underlying dimensions of aff ect by analyses of judged similarities and semantic diff erential ratings of mood terms, as well as facial and vocal emotional expressions. Th e second combines a more functional/ motivational analysis with evidence from studies of neurophysiological and hormonal processes. Th e fi rst body of work supports the existence of two general dimensions: pleasantness versus unpleasantness and activation/ arousal/engagement (see Remington, Fabrigar, & Visser, 2000; Russell & Carroll, 1999a; see Russell & Carroll, 1999b; Watson, Wiese, Vaidya, & Tellegen, 1999). Research in this tradition is heavily measurement-based and has been extended into several practical domains to classify aff ective responses to stimuli of interest, such as pictures and advertisements, as well as to provide a more general basis for delineating categories of emotional response (Watson & Tellegen, 1985). Aff ect taxonomies in consumer research Researchers with a primary interest in aff ective aspects of stimuli, such as advertisements and how people describe their aff ective responses to them, have been less interested in the underlying dimensionality of aff ect and oft en prefer to think in terms of aff ect taxonomies that correspond to more macro-level constellations or prototypes (Shaver, Schwartz, Kirson, & Oconnor, 1987). Th ey rely on specially constructed inventories of mood and emotion terms, as well as scales that have been developed for other purposes (e.g., to represent appetitive and aversive motivational systems). In research on advertising, for example, Holbrook and Batra (1987) began with over 90 items that combined emotional responses and evaluative reactions to advertising content, and Edell and Burke (1987) used a 69-item inventory of feelings. In such research, investigators typically attempt to reduce the individual items to distinct clusters using techniques such as factor analysis and hierarchical cluster analysis (Shaver, Schwartz, Kirson, & Oconnor,

1987). At times, claims are made about underlying structure, but the generality of such claims is questionable because of the arbitrary selection of items and stimuli, the ambiguity of hierarchical confi gurations of emotion terms, as well as measurement issues to be discussed below (see also Mano, 1991; Schimmack & Crites, 2005). Nevertheless, such research may serve the investigator's needs in diff erentiating between types of aff ective responses to content and situations (e.g., store settings) of particular interest. Much of the earlier aff ect taxonomy research in consumer behavior, at least through 1990, was reviewed by Cohen and Areni (1991), and so it will not receive explicit attention here. An extremely comprehensive analysis of many of the emotion measures used in consumer research was carried out by Richins (1997), who identifi ed shortcomings in their ability to address a greater variety of consumption experiences. Th ese included the contemplation, purchase, use, and subsequent reactions to a broad variety of products and services from the mundane to the important and sentimental (see also Derbaix & Pham, 1991). She identifi ed a list of 175 emotion terms that had been used in consumer research and that satisfi ed criteria developed by Ortony, Clore, and Collins (1988) to screen out nonemotion terms focusing on bodily states such as "sleepy," subjective evaluations such as "feeling confi dent," behaviors and action tendencies such as "crying" and "hesitant," and cognitive states such as "interested." She supplemented this list by prompting open-ended self reports of positive and negative feelings (most commonly, the positive affective terms "happiness," "relief," and "excitement," but also "worry," "sadness," and "guilt") to a variety of consumption experiences. Although the underlying dimensionality of the resulting "Consumption Emotion Set" (CES) is somewhat ambiguous (beyond the traditional positive-negative axis), the instrument appears to be quite useful for those who wish to assess consumers' aff ective responses to a more comprehensive set of consumption experiences. Underlying dimensions: Th e bipolarity of aff ect More basic research on the structure of aff ect attempts to identify relationships among two primary components of aff ect, pleasantness, and arousal/activation. Russell (1980) originally proposed that these two dimensions be viewed as a circumplex, that is, a model in which individual mood and emotion descriptors are systematically arranged around the perimeter of a circle. Data from Russell and Barrett (1999) indicate that aff ective structure actually falls somewhere between a classic simple structure in which the variables cluster in dense groups around labeled axes and a true circumplex, as in Figure 11.1, in which the variables are more evenly spaced and defi ne a complete circle. Within this measurement tradition, there has been a debate over the bipolarity versus independence of positive and negative aff ect. When people experience and report high negative aff ect, does that mean that positive aff ect is low (i.e., bipolarity)? When thinking about implications of bipolarity, it is important to diff erentiate between "core aff ect" (Russell & Barrett, 1999) and evaluative outcomes of aff ective processes. Th e latter are the result of cognitive appraisals and clearly allow for mixed assessments (i.e., positive in some respects and negative in others). Core affect, on the other hand, refers to how a person is feeling emotionally at a point in time. Also, when the analysis is performed at an aggregate-level across emotional experiences over time, bipolarity assumptions do not necessarily predict independence. People who are asked to report emotional states using experience sampling diaries are just as likely to have self reports indicating high average negative (positive) aff ect, regardless of their average levels of positive (negative) aff ect (Diener & Irannejad, 1986; Diener, Smith, & Fujita, 1995). A general consensus has emerged that a bipolar structure dominates (see Russell & Carroll, 1999a), as acknowledged even by original proponents of the independence assumption (see Watson & Clark, 1997; Watson, Wiese, Vaidya, & Tellegen, 1999). While interested readers should consult the extensive literature directly, several key issues must be noted. First, tests of independence versus bipolarity require truly independent measures of positive and negative aff ect. Using bipolar items (e.g., -3 = sad, 0 = neutral, $+3$ = happy) artifi cially promotes bipolarity. On the other hand, using unipolar items oft en leaves the lower endpoint of the scale ambiguous. For example, if respondents are asked to rate their happiness on a 1–5 scale going from "not at all" to "extremely," does a "1" mean a mere absence of happiness or an opposite state such as sadness? In addition, where does neutrality lie in such a scale? Such measurement issues can have major infl uences on the factor structure of the resulting scale. Even assuming independent measurement of positive and negative aff ect, the bipolarity of specifi ed circumplex axes (corresponding to particular aff ective states shown in Figure 11.1 and measured by various scales) has proven to be far more problematic. A primary reason is the confounding caused by variations in arousal/engagement that prevent the semantic opposites in Figure 11.1 from lying along a 180° angle. Across a number of such studies, positive and negative aff ect have been found to be moderately negatively correlated (typically around r = $-.44$) rather than nearly perfectly negatively correlated, implying bipolarity, or nearly perfectly uncorrelated, implying independence (Diener, Smith, & Fujita, 1995; Watson, Clark, & Tellegen, 1988; Watson, Wiese, Vaidya, & Tellegen, 1999). However, the correlation increases dramatically when people report aff ect in the presence of strong, intense emotion (Diener & Irannejad, 1986), demonstrating the bipolarity of strong emotional states. On the other hand, feelings originally characterized as low positive aff ect (hence low in activation/arousal) and that correspond to quietude and calmness are not far removed from low negative aff ect states (e.g., sluggish) characteristic of mild depression. Consider a person who views himself as experiencing a lack (or loss) of pleasure or lack of response to pleasurable stimuli. At low levels, then, self reports of positive and negative aff ect can be positively correlated (Watson, Wiese, Vaidya, & Tellegen, 1999), suggesting independence. Underlying neurophysiological processes clearly register and potentiate positive and negative aff ect simultaneously. Th ough confl ict and/or ambivalence would seem to be logical consequences of events and stimuli that simultaneously prompt fear and excitement, making eff ective reactions diffi cult, emotional paralysis in not the norm. A great deal of current research beyond the scope of this chapter is providing substantial insight about how these underlying neurophysiological processes translate into more molar responses. We will discuss some relevant work on "mixed emotions" a bit later.

10
Self-Regulation

Self-regulation can be understood as the process by which one response is overridden, allowing for a diff erent response to take its place. To regulate something is to bring it under the control of rules or laws, and in the process to change it, and so self-regulation is a matter of bringing one's own behavior into line with standards such as laws, goals, morals, ideals, or rules. Essentially, the person's initial impulse may be to act, feel, or think in a particular way that goes against these personal or social standards, and so self-regulation enables the person to resist that impulse so as to respond in a more appropriate or desirable manner. Self-regulation is most commonly seen in the struggle between impulses and restraints (cf. Hoch & Loewenstein, 1991). Oft entimes, a person will have a goal that requires inhibiting one response and perhaps replacing it with another. Situations that require self-control are those in which an urge that goes against the person's overarching goal is stimulated and therefore restraints to change, modify, or otherwise alter the impulse are required. We use the terms "self-regulation" and "self-control" interchangeably, although other authors may use them to refer to diff erent constructs. Th e main distinction that is sometimes made is to equate self-control with conscious, eff ortful processes, whereas self-regulation is a broader term that also encompasses nonconscious regulating processes such as how the body maintains a constant temperature or heartbeat. Our focus in this chapter will be exclusively on the conscious, eff ortful processes by which the self exerts control over its responses, and hence any distinction between conscious self-control and nonconscious self-regulation is irrelevant to this discussion. Th e word "self" in self-control refers both to the fact that it is the self (the "I") that is doing the operating and that the self is what is being operated upon (the "me"). Impulses and urges are two terms also used interchangeably and they refer to a state that arises typically from the interaction between an underlying motivation (e.g., to increase good feelings) and a stimulus in the environment (e.g., a shiny piece of jewelry that is available for purchase). Th ere are four broad domains in which self-control can be exercised (Vohs & Baumeister, 2004a). Mental control encompasses regulating cognitive processes, ranging from controlling attention (e.g., trying to concentrate) to suppressing unwanted thoughts (e.g., Wegner, 1994) and even guiding one's reasoning process toward a desired conclusion (Baumeister & Newman, 1994). Emotion control is essentially the eff ort to induce, suppress, or prolong an emotional state. Impulse control typically involves keeping oneself from acting on desires or appetites deemed unsuitable, whether these be food cravings, addictive yearnings, sexual or violent inclinations, or other temptations. Last, performance management encompasses the attempt to perform at a certain (usually high) level, such as persistence in the face of failure or fatigue, speed/accuracy tradeoff s, or trying not to choke under pressure. We start with an example that illustrates the ingredients of self-regulation. A young man wants to buy a pickup truck but cannot aff ord it. He assesses how much money he has and how much money he needs to buy the truck, which indicates how much more money he needs to have. Accordingly, he forms a plan to save some money from his weekly paycheck, which will enable him to aff ord the truck in time for, say, a planned camping trip next summer. Along the way, however, he may have to resist temptations to spend his income on a new stereo system. His success depends on monitoring his progress at saving money while also resisting these intervening temptations.

Th e example of saving up to buy includes the four main ingredients of self-regulation. First, one has to have a goal, in this case to save enough money to buy the truck. Second, one has to be motivated to reach the goal: the more he wants the truck, the more likely he is to be willing to make the eff orts and sacrifi ces required to save. Th ird, he has to monitor progress toward the goal, rather than just vaguely stuffi ng a few bucks into various envelopes scattered in his desk and sock drawer now and then. (In particular, he has to keep track of how much he has saved and how much he needs, plus ideally whether he is on schedule of saving enough to get the truck in time for the camping trip.) Last, he will need the willpower to resist other temptations in order to keep saving toward his goal. STANDARDS Standards are the ideals, norms, goals, or other rules or guidelines that provide the endpoint of the regulatory chain. Akin to the idea that the fi rst step in the buyer's decision process involves consumers recognizing that they have an unmet need, self-regulators' fi rst step is to recognize that there exists a standard that they want to meet. Typically, this step is accompanied by an almostimmediate comparison to see where one is located with respect to the standard. (We return to the idea of monitoring in a subsequent section.) Assuming there exists a diff erence between current and goal states, the person needs self-control. If there is no discrepancy, there is no need for selfcontrol. Much of the strain on self-regulation can sometimes be alleviated by modifying standards. For example, whereas many people struggle to lose weight so as to conform to social standards of fashionable thinness, some instead join the so-called size-acceptance movements that essentially say it is okay to be fat. In the same vein, recent decades have witnessed a marked reduction in the social stigma associated with bankruptcy and with out-of-wedlock reproduction, thereby reducing the demand on people to regulate their behavior as tightly as they may have in past decades to avoid those outcomes. Th e more specifi c the standard, the better able people are to reach the goal. Specifi city in setting the goal helps at two levels. One, being specifi c about the goal reduces the goal's abstractness, which clarifi es the steps needed to reach the goal (see Gollwitzer, 1999; Gollwitzer & Brandstätter, 1997). Instead of trying to reach the abstract goal to "save money," the consumer who sets the more concrete goal of "forgoing a latte three times a week" is better positioned to reach the ultimate goal of saving more money. Two, specifi c goals (or the creation of subgoals) allow for better monitoring of progression toward the goal. With a precise endpoint, one can see how to measure current states and distance to the goal. Grocery shopping with a list makes it easy to see which foods still need to be acquired by looking at which foods are already in the cart. In addition to having a specifi ed goal, having only one goal makes self-regulation more successful than when people have two or more confl icting goals. Research on children similarly shows that when adults give diff erent and inconsistent rules to children, the children behave inconsistently (Maphet & Miller, 1982). In general, having clear standards is a benefi t to goal attainment, but new research suggests that holding highly rigid standards can at times lead to worse self-regulation. Research by Soman and Cheema (2004) found that when people violated a standard they had set for themselves, their subsequent goal-directed behavior faltered—with the result being even worse than the performance of people who held no performance standards. Th e researchers found that a feeling of failure from the violation of standards was key, especially when goals were perceived as being "all of none." Th is deleterious outcome is best avoided by choosing moderate standards: Standards that are too low may not motivate people, but those that are too high may demotivate people via the potential for perceptions of standard violations and concomitant feelings of failure. Baumeister, Heatherton, and Tice (1994) compared the stringent, so-called "zero tolerance" standards to a military tactic of putting all one's troops on the front line. It off ers the best chance of preventing any breach, but it leaves nothing in reserve to cope when a breach does occur. Th ey suggested, for example, that the zero tolerance approaches help explain the seeming paradox that the United States has relatively high rates of both teetotalers and alcoholics, in contrast to other cultures that emphasize controlled drinking as the standard. One motivational theory that has had widespread success in predicting consumer behavior centers on diff erences in behavioral guides. Promotion behavior pursues positive outcomes, whereas prevention behavior avoids negative outcomes (Higgins, 1997). Promotion behavior is aimed at achieving ideal standards, such as hopes, wishes, and dreams. Prevention behavior is geared toward goals that people feel obligated to achieve, such as duties and responsibilities. Research has shown that when people are in a promotion mode and geared toward goal attainment, their actions are best described as eager, whereas when people are in a prevention mode, vigilance is the best descriptor of behavior. Moreover, if a situation calls for a strategy that contrasts with the type of goal being pursued (e.g., a promotion goal that is pursued by being vigilant), people fail to achieve their goals more oft en than when goal types and behavioral strategies are matched. Recent research suggests that promotion and prevention may not only be suited for certain strategies, but for information processing routes as well. Research by Pham and Avnet (2004) revealed that ideal standards bias people's reactions in terms the emotions evoked by incoming information, whereas ought standards lead to processing a message based on its content. Th at diff erent standards activate diff erent psychological systems (aff ect vs. cognition) has broad implications for behavioral change strategies. Th is fi nding, in addition to providing information such as knowing whether a woman seeks to lose weight because of her dreams of fi tting into a shapely swimsuit or because her partner told her to do so, will help predict whether her diet will be upset by a distressing incident versus new fi ndings indicating that weight is more genetic than people once thought (i.e., emotional vs. cognitive information-processing styles). One type of goal confl ict occurs when people come up against a seemingly unattainable goal. Outside the laboratory, it is oft en diffi cult to know whether one's goals are unattainable or unrealistic. A lack of progress toward the goal may be the fi rst sign, but such signs are hard to read. For example, consider the thousands upon thousand of young men who sacrifi ce years of their lives, plus their best educational opportunities, plus their physical well-being in pursuing the goal of becoming a professional athlete. Th e immense rewards associated with such success make the dream appealing, and the young men can see exemplars who have achieved that level of success on television any time. But far more than 99% of those who pursue the dream will fail, and it may take a very long time (oft en until one has spent 5 years in college, with no degree) to realize that one is never going to succeed at that level. Wrosch et al. (2003) showed that people who disengage from seemingly impossible goals are mentally healthier than those who stay entrapped in the pursuit of this type of goals. In this case, the goal of using one's limited eff ort and time eff ectively confl icts with trying to achieve the impossible, and the healthiest strategy is to drop the frustrating goal. Although little is known about when people consciously decide to abandon a goal (cf. Shah, Bodmann, & Hall, 2005), this line of research has much theoretical and practical importance. Another type of goal confl ict is probably endemic to consumer behavior, because almost all consumers face a variety of tradeoff s in which they want incompatible things. Most fundamentally, perhaps, consumers want to save their money but also to acquire goods and services. And even if they are determined to purchase, there are endless further tradeoff s: higher quality versus lower price; sensible comfort versus fashionable looks; name brand reputation versus more immediate availability; higher safety rating versus better gas mileage; less fi lling or great taste. Rational choice is supposedly the human cognitive tool for making such choices, but recent evidence suggests that requires eff ort and consumes some of the same resources required for self-regulation, as we will explain shortly. MOTIVATION AND COMMITMENT; OR, THE "GUN TO THE HEAD" TEST Having standards does not mean that good self-regulation will necessarily follow. Recall that people may have standards but perceive that their behavior already meets these standards. Others may see that they fall short of standards but not care. People must be motivated to enact a behavioral change. Th e motivation to self-regulate is probably crucial to its success, although it is probably the least studied of the four basic ingredients. How common are irresistible impulses? Some people claim—and some legal institutions condone—that under some circumstances, impulsive actions may not be controllable due to either strong emotional states or other internal breakdowns of will. Self-regulatory researchers generally fi nd these claims dubious. Suppose, for example, that a compulsive gambler was truly unable to resist the temptation to gamble. Taken to an extreme, this would mean that if a gun was held to the head of the person who was about to lay down another bet at the blackjack table, he or she could not help but place that bet. Yet, this rarely (if ever) happens: People, if they really want, are able to avoid giving into all kinds of impulses (Baumeister & Heatherton, 1996). One of the FBI's foremost experts on serial killers observed that although the killers sometimes claimed that their homicidal impulses were irresistible, not one of the thousands of murderers documented by this group had been committed in the presence of a police or security offi cer (Douglas, 1996). Apparently, the irresistible impulses could be resisted if the chances of getting caught right away were high. Considering the truly irresistible impulses is a good way to appreciate the contrast. A person cannot remain standing forever, and sooner or later will sit, lie, or fall down, even if threatened at gunpoint to remain standing or else. People cannot hold their breaths indefi nitely, and even if the willpower is suffi cient to keep them from breathing for a long time, they will pass out and start breathing. Th ey cannot remain awake indefi nitely, and some people die because of falling asleep on sentry duty or while driving. Th ere are of course a few other bodily functions that are likewise truly irresistible, and it is appropriate to refrain from blaming people who break down under such circumstances. In contrast, the spouse who ruins the family's monthly budget by spending an inordinate amount on a new jacket, and who seeks to justify the act by saying "I couldn't resist," is almost certainly speaking merely fi guratively (which is to say lying). For consumer behavior, the important implication is that purchasing impulses are in fact almost always resistible. But consumers may prefer to conceal that fact from themselves and their families. "I had to have it, I couldn't help myself" is much preferred over the more realistic "I deliberately chose to blow a lot of our money on selfi sh gratifi cation for myself."

Th e outcome of the self-control endeavor may be a suffi cient enough prize to encourage controlling oneself. A model of self-regulation from the health domain (Rothman, 2000) describes the desire to initiate a behavioral change as stemming from the positivity of the outcome. Th us, most people believe that smoking cigarettes is bad for them, and many have quit smoking in order to improve their odds of avoiding lung cancer in later life, but others may not value that outcome. Teenagers who disdain old-age health issues as absurdly remote, soldiers in combat zones who doubt their chances of surviving the war, prisoners serving life sentences, and AIDS suff erers, among others, may not fi nd the increased chance of escaping lung cancer in the distant future a suffi cient reason to give up the pleasure of smoking. Motivation may come from perceptions of the diffi culty (or possibility) that the goal can be attained. One model that focuses on outcomes derived from consumption (Bagozzi & Dholakia 1999) places self-effi cacy at center stage, such that people's beliefs about the skills they possess to achieve their goals is crucial to their willingness to self-regulate. Th is model emphasizes selfeffi cacy as key to whether and how the consumer will approach the self-control task. Self-effi cacy is particularly related to the means chosen to reach the goal. Th us, if a person considering a diet thinks, "If I am off ered cake at parties, I am confi dent that I can refuse and instead I eat fruit," he or she is displaying self-effi cacy and its aid in selecting suitable means to attain the larger goal of limiting caloric intake. Research on the overconsumption of food (binge eating) supports the importance of self-beliefs in motivating people to self-regulate—as well as the demotivating eff ects of not believing in oneself. Th is research shows that women who hold high standards for thinness but believe that they are overweight have high binge eating tendencies—but only if they also doubt their ability to reach their goal (Vohs et al., 1999, 2001). Women who believe that they close the gap between their current (perceived) body image and their desired body image do not overeat. Last, motivation may also depend on beliefs about how self-control works. Recent work suggests that laypersons have personal beliefs about how self-control operates (Mukhopadhyay & Johar, 2005). Moreover, personal theories about self-control can help predict variance in goal attainment, presumably because they infl uence commitment to self-regulatory goals and subsequent motivation. MONITORING AND FEEDBACK LOOPS Monitoring involves being aware of the self's behavior or responses and comparing them to a standard. Breakdowns in the monitoring aspect of self-regulation are not as well understood as are breakdowns in the other ingredients, but nevertheless breakdowns in monitoring are a key reason that goals are not met. Monitoring is perhaps more central to understanding consumption than other aspects of goal attainment, which suggests that more work could be done to underscore its value in consumer behavior. Th e study of monitoring is also worth pursuing for practical reasons. Baumeister et al. (1994) proposed that monitoring is the aspect of self-regulation that is most readily susceptible to improvement, and so whenever one desires to improve self-control, improving monitoring generally off ers the most promising opportunity for substantial (and immediate) improvement. Th us, if someone has money problems, it may be diffi cult to increase income or willpower, and revising standards downward (to accept being on the verge of bankruptcy) may be problematic. Nonetheless, keeping close tabs on one's income and expenses, such as by keeping a daily written record of spending, is oft en both viable and eff ective. Likewise, it is no accident that successful dieters count calories and otherwise carefully monitor what they eat, and that the cessation of monitoring oft en undermines dietary efforts.

One reason (and there are many) for the diffi culty of self-control is that eff ective self-control necessitates that people monitor their behavior, but the act of monitoring means a focus on the present time (Vohs & Schmeichel, 2003). Th is "extended-now" state renders people vulnerable to incoming urges and impulses and makes long-term goals seem less pressing. Th is extended-now theory of self-regulation is supported by studies showing that self-regulation changes time perception, such that self-regulators feel that time is moving more slowly as compared to non-regulators (and as compared to veridical durations). Monitoring one's progress, although being an integral part of goal strivings, may, unfortunately, bring about perceptions that time is moving slowly, which in turn reduces self-regulatory eff orts (Vohs & Schmeichel, 2003). Classic work on chronic dieters demonstrates that not only the reliability or strength of the signal is important in monitoring, but also the interpretation of the feedback. Research on dieting versus nondieting1 shoppers shows that dieters buy less when they have not recently eaten than when they have recently eaten, whereas the opposite pattern holds with nondieters (Nisbett & Kanouse, 1969). Why would dieters buy less when they are hungrier? Th e idea is that the bodily signals that one has not eaten in a while is a positive, reinforcing signal that the goal of limiting caloric intake is being met. Th erefore, dieters—who have the goal of restricting caloric intake—buy less food when they get feedback that they are meeting their dieting goals. As another example of how interpretation can undermine monitoring, Gilovich (1983) addressed the seeming paradox that many gamblers continue to gamble and even seem to remain optimistic, even though most lose more than they win, and, in fact, long-term net losses are almost guaranteed by the structure of the gambling system (by which, for example, the casino or indeed the state government must make a net profi t, so it pays out less in winnings than it takes in). Accurate monitoring would have to reveal to gamblers that they had lost more oft en than won. But Gilovich (1990) found that gamblers discounted some losses as "near wins" and so felt encouraged despite losing. Th ey were much less likely to discount their wins as "near losses." By taking credit for all successes and discounting some wins, they were able to transform the objective feedback of overall loss into the subjective impression of effi cacy and confi dence at "continued" success. Monitoring allows people to assess distance to the goal. Th is can be done by looking back at how far one has come or how much more has to be done. A new study suggests that seeing how far one has come may be more eff ective in promoting self-regulation than how much more work is ahead. Nunes and Dreze (in press) gave loyalty cards to customers at a professional car wash. Some customers were given a card that required 10 car wash purchases before one free car wash was earned, whereas others were given a loyalty card that required 8 car wash purchases before the reward. However, those in the 10 car wash condition were given their card with two "free" stamps already affi xed to it, making the amount of eff ort needed to reach the goal equivalent. Perceptions of progress mattered, though—34% of customers fi lled their card and earned a free car wash in the 10 washes-but-2-free condition, whereas only 19% did in the 8 washes condition. Moreover, the goal gradient was steeper for those in the 10-but-2 condition, such that aft er receiving the loyalty card, they came to the car wash more oft en than did the 8 wash condition customers. Believing that one has come a long way apparently increases commitment to the goal, thereby leading to heightened eff orts to reach it. OPERATIONS: USING SELF?REGULATORY STRENGTH TO MOVE ONESELF TO THE GOAL Even if a consumer has clear, unconfl icting, and appropriate standards and monitors his or her behaviors, the goal will not necessarily be met. Without the capacity to move oneself from current to goal state, the best laid plans and all the monitoring in the world will not be good enough. The strength model of self-control has been the most comprehensive model in terms of specifying what allows people to move toward a goal. Self-regulation, from this perspective, is governed by a fi nite supply of energy that is used in all controlled responses and actions (Baumeister & Heatherton, 1996;

Baumeister et al., 1994; Vohs & Baumeister, 2004b). Th e strength model depicts the ability to get oneself to the goal as a function of the amount of self-regulatory resources available when exhibiting the response. Because self-regulatory resources are put toward all acts of self-control, the supply is rather fragile and precious and, according to the model, can diminish to a point where impaired self-control can be observed. Th erefore, laboratory experiments testing the strength model of self-control typically have used a two-task paradigm. Th e fi rst task varies on its self-control demands such that some participants are given a task that is thought to require expending self-regulatory resources, whereas others are given a neutral task that does not require self-regulatory resources. Th e second task, then, is the measure of self-control ability. To test the strength model, the hypothesis put forth is that diff erences in the second task reveal that the experimental condition in the fi rst task was indeed an act of self-control that presumably depleted the self's resources. Indeed, the work of over 30 published experiments (e.g., Baumeister et al., 1998; Muraven et al., 1998; Schmeichel, Vohs, & Baumeister, 2003; Vohs, Baumeister, & Ciarocco, 2005; Vohs & Heatherton, 2000) supports the idea that the "operate" component of selfregulation can be modeled as a stock of energy that becomes temporarily reduced with use, with the consequence being disrupted self-control. Several extensions of the model that are particularly applicable to understanding consumer behavior are discussed hereaft er. Early investigations of the model focused on confi rming basic tenets. Here, researchers took core self-control tasks, such as persisting at a diff erent task, controlling one's emotions or suppressing thoughts and tested whether engaging in these activities left people with less ability to engage in another self-control act. For instance, Baumeister et al. (1998) asked participants to control either emotions to an emotional fi lm, or to watch the fi lm naturally (without instructions). Subsequently, they were given a set of diffi cult anagrams to solve. In line with expectations from the strength model, participants who had to modify their emotions solved fewer anagrams. Notably, both a happy and sad fi lm were used and type of fi lm did not aff ect anagram performance; only being in a condition that required emotional modifi cation mattered. Manipulations of thought suppression complemented these fi ndings. One experiment, which asked participants to suppress thoughts of a white bear (Wegner, Schneider, Carter, & White, 1987) versus complete simple mathematical problems, showed that the former group was less able to control their emotions later when asked to do so (Muraven et al., 1998; Study 3). A host of similar studies confi rmed the basic tenets of the model using a variety of diff erent manipulations and dependent measures. Th erefore, we have concluded that self-regulation relies on a precious, but fi nite, resource that is taxed when self-control is needed. Th e term "regulatory resource depletion" is now used to suggest phenomena when one does not have the strength to exert proper control over one's actions. An important extension of the regulatory resource model indicates that the same resource is used for making choices. A series of studies by Vohs, Baumeister, Twenge, Schmeichel, and Tice (2005/ under review) showed that aft er people make a series of choices, their self-control falters and fails just as it does following prior exertions of self-control (see also Baumeister et al., 1998). In particular, participants in several studies were asked to make a series of binary choices between various consumer items (e.g., would you rather have a red or a blue t-shirt? Would you rather have a vanilla scented candle or an almond scented candle?). Others simply rated the same items on various dimensions, including whether they had used them in the past 6 months. Th ose who made choices were subsequently poorer at self-control on a variety of measures, including holding one's hand in ice water or making oneself consume a healthy but bad-tasting beverage.

Because the same resource appears to be used for both decision making and for self-regulation, Baumeister et al. (1998) introduced the term "ego depletion" to refer to the state of diminished resources. Th e term "ego" was adopted in a deliberate homage to Freud, who was one of the only psychologists to speak (albeit rather vaguely) of the self as an energy system. For consumer psychology, the implication is that two perennially central issues in consumer behavior—namely decision making and self-control—rely on a common resource that becomes depleted when one engages in either activity. Hence either activity can have an adverse eff ect on the other. Making eff ortful decisions is likely to impair subsequent self-control, and, conversely, exertions of self-control may reduce the care and eff ort that people put into their subsequent choices. Examples of both patterns will be covered below. APPLYING THE STRENGTH MODEL TO CONSUMER ISSUES Overeating Eating is one of the most fundamental consumption acts. People must eat to survive, and yet society, dietary, and health reasons prompt many people to regulate their caloric intake at some point in their lives. However, the outlook for people wanting to lose weight and maintain their slimmer size is dim: comprehensive long-term research (Kramer, Jeff ery, Forster, & Snell, 1989) revealed that fewer than 3% of all dieters will manage to keep the weight off , and, by 5 years aft er their weight loss, most will weigh more than they did when they began dieting. Th us, the concept of limiting food intake is a tantalizing topic for self-control theorizing because, unlike other consumption domains such as drinking alcohol, smoking cigarettes, or even having sex, people need to take in calories to live. Consequently, achieving the goal of losing weight by cutting caloric intake cannot be met using the same strategies as could be used to limit alcohol intake, namely refraining from consumption altogether. Th us neither the advantages nor the inherent problems (see above) of zero tolerance self-regulation policies are relevant to eating, and controlled moderation is the only viable strategy for controlling food intake. Stopping oneself from taking in any calories is a route that no one can take without landing in the hospital, which therefore means that people wanting to control their food consumption must use other strategies. Consequently, the intricacies of dieting make it one of the most perplexing and diffi cult regulatory tasks that one may take on. Being exposed to forbidden foods is a situation that many dieters face and if they intend to stick to their diet, they must override their desire to eat the tempting food. Baumeister et al. (1989) recruited a sample of hungry undergraduates (but who were not selected because they were dieters) and created a situation to mimic the forbidden-food situation that dieters oft en face. Participants were seated in front of a tray of chocolate chip cookies that had been freshly baked in the laboratory (with the aroma of warm chocolate waft ing throughout the room for everyone to smell), chocolate candies, and a rather large bowl of radishes. Some participants were told they could eat as many of the cookies and candies as they wanted, whereas participants in the forbidden-food condition were told that their task was to eat the radishes. (Th ere was also a no-food condition.) Aft er 5 minutes of privacy with the foods, participants were given a geometric puzzle to solve, which was unsolvable, although, of course, they did not know this. Persistence in the face of frustration and disappointing failure is one standard measure of self-regulation, because the vexing failures presumably create the desire to quit so as to do something else instead, and, in order to persist, the performer must override this urge to quit. Participants in the forbidden-food condition were less persistent at the puzzle as compared to participants in either of the other two conditions. Being tempted by the chocolates but not being able to indulge presumably taxed the resources of those participants, which therefore impaired their ability to continue on the diffi cult cognitive task.

Another set of studies examined the eff ects of self-regulatory resource depletion in a context in which people have pre-established consumption goals. In these studies, chronic dieters were the main focus, and the hypothesis was that underlying diff erences in long-term goals render people diff erentially aff ected by the same situational self-control demands. Vohs and Heatherton (2000) asked dieters and nondieters to watch a boring video on Bighorn sheep while being seated either next to or far away from a tempting bowl of M&M candies. Th is formed the temptation factor, which was combined with instructions that the candies were available to be eaten ("go ahead, help yourself") or that the candies were needed later in the day, and therefore "please don't touch" them. Aft er watching the boring video for 10 minutes, participants were moved to a diff erent room to "taste and rate" three fl avors of ice cream. Ice cream consumption was the measure of self-control. Given that nondieters do not (by defi nition) control their caloric consumption, they would not have to override the temptation (and hence become depleted) to eat the yummy chocolates. (Th at said, it was not the case that the nondieters consumed many M&Ms—only fi ve nondieters ate the snacks and even they did so minimally.) Hence, nondieters' ice cream intake was predicted to be relatively unaff ected by the two factors of temptation and allowance to eat the snacks. For dieters, however, the urge to eat the chocolates must be acted on. Th erefore, Vohs and Heatherton expected that only dieters would expend regulatory resources in the presence of tempting snacks. However, if an external force prevented them from having to exert self-control to not eat the candies—such as a caution from the experimenter to not partake in the snacks—then their supply of self-regulatory resources would be spared. As a result, the researchers predicted that ice cream consumption would be highest among dieters who sat close to the snacks and were allowed to eat them. Th e predictions were confi rmed. Dieters ate signifi cantly more when they were highly tempted by sitting next to the M&M candies and were told the candies were available to be eaten. Notably, however, dieters ate the least when they were seated far from the chocolates and were told they could indulge in them (which, being dieters, they did not). Th is pattern may represent an inoculation eff ect, which would be an intriguing idea for future depletion research. And as expected, nondieters' ice cream eating was not determined by whether they had sat near or far from the M&Ms nor whether they were allowed to eat the candies. A second study replicated the loss of self-control among dieters aft er having engaged in emotion regulation (Vohs & Heatherton, 2000). In this experiment, dieters watched a sad movie about a woman on her deathbed saying good-bye to her husband, two sons, and mother. Participants were asked either to suppress their emotions or to watch the movie naturally. Ice cream eating again represented self-regulatory ability. As expected, asking these women to engage in emotion regulation, as opposed to being able to watch the same movie but without having to suppress sad feelings, led them to eat more ice cream later. Both groups reported similarly negative feelings aft er the movie, meaning that diff erences in mood did not account for eating diff erences, but having to stifl e those feelings led to a depletion of the resource that later would have helped them control their ice cream consumption. A third study showed that persistence drops aft er dieters have had to overcome the temptation of forbidden foods. In this study, being highly tempted by an array of snack foods led subsequent persistence on an embedded-fi gures task to be impaired, relative to persistence among dieters who watch the same boring fi lm and looked at the same snack foods but who did so from across the room. Th us, regulating the consumption of food determines and is determined by the availability of self-regulatory resources—but only among people for whom caloric regimens were highly important and thus demanded much regulation. Moreover, having to defeat the desire to eat a tempting, but forbidden, food in order to make oneself eat a less appealing, but healthier, food also takes away from the capacity to later bring one's performance in line with standards.

Just as controlling one's eating represents a special kind of self-control problem, so does spending. If one includes the paid consumption of energy and utilities such as water, the typical modern citizen spends money every day. Much spending is fairly inevitable, and other spending is appropriate and judicious. Still, some money is spent impulsively and in ways that the consumer may later regret. Vohs and Faber (2005) turned to the self-regulatory resource model to help explain why people spend money impulsively. Impulsive buying is defi ned purchases that result from an urge that arises spontaneously within the consumer to buy. In impulsive purchasing, the desire to purchase is unrefl ective (Strack, Werth, & Deutsch, in press) and not based on any careful considerations of why the product should be acquired (Rook & Fisher 1995). Vohs and Faber surmised that impulses to buy would arise and be acted upon more oft en when people's self-regulatory capacity is reduced than when it is fully intact. Th e results of empirical work support this idea. Two studies manipulated attentional control demands as a way to alter self-regulatory ability. Participants watched an audioless video of a woman being interviewed that, at the same time, showed irrelevant words appearing at the bottom of the screen every 30 seconds. Some participants were not told anything about the irrelevant words, whereas those in the depletion condition were told not to look at the words and if they found themselves orienting toward the words to revert their eyes back to the interviewee. In one study, participants were then given a scale to measure immediate buying impulses; in another study, participants were shown high-end products (e.g., watches, appliances) and asked to state the price at which they would be willing to purchase the item. Both studies showed an eff ect of self-regulatory resource availability on impulsive spending tendencies: participants who had earlier used their resources to orient their attention away from a distracting stimulus later reported stronger urges to spend impulsively (Study 1) and gave higher willingnessto-pay rates (Study 2), as compared to participants who did not engage in attention control. Feeling a spontaneous urge to buy is, as we saw earlier, the root of impulsive spending, and one way to control that urge is to believe a product is not worth its monetary price (Rook & Fisher, 1995). Th at self-regulatory resource depletion aff ected impulsive spending tendencies both at the level of the impulse and the cognitive strategies to rein in that impulse is noteworthy. Moreover, this research found that actual impulsive spending was aff ected by resource availability. One of these studies asked participants in the resource depletion condition to suppress thoughts of a white bear; the other study asked participants to read aloud a boring text with emotion. Subsequently, participants were given the opportunity to buy in a spontaneous, ad hoc purchasing situation in a mock store. As predicted, participants whose resources had been depleted spent more impulsive than did participants who had not expended their resources. Th is eff ect was found in terms of purchases of bookstore-like products, such as school insignia pens, coff ee mugs, and decks of playing cards (Study 3) as well as grocery store items, such as cookies, pretzels, and potato chips (Study 4). Moreover, the latter two studies incorporated the idea of underlying tendencies toward a certain type of self-control failure, in a similar manner as was done in the work on chronic dieters (Vohs & Heatherton, 2000). In this work, however, generalized tendencies to want to spend money impulsively were measured prior to the experimental manipulation of self-regulatory demands. Similar to the fi ndings on dieters, Vohs and Faber (2005) also found that the eff ect of self-regulatory resource depletion was exacerbated among people who normally feel strong desires to buy impulsively. In contrast to the work on dieters versus nondieters, however, was the fact that even participants who were low in general impulsive spending tendencies showed heightened purchasing behavior when depleted. Th is eff ect is probably due to the idea that nondieters and nonimpulsive spenders differ in that almost everyone needs to control their spending at some level, irrespective of whether buying impulsively is generally a problem, whereas nondieters are presumably not controlling their eating to the same extent. Hence, spontaneous urges to buy something too are aff ected by self-regulatory resources (Vohs & Faber, 2005). Whether from regulating attention, stifl ing thoughts, or modifying one's behavior to appear unemotional, people who had engaged in self-control earlier were more likely to buy impulsively. Perhaps the most intriguing result of this line of research is that decreases in the self's controlled processes strengthen the feeling to buy impulsively. Th eoretically, the strength of the urge and inhibitions on that urge have been considered to be orthogonal, but to detect a change in the potency of the impulse with depletion suggests that empirically the two core components of self-control may be intricately related. Research at the intersection of the urge and the self's regulatory resources (Vohs & Mead, in preparation) presents an exciting new avenue of study. Th us far we have discussed about impulsive consumption in the context of purchasing. Impulses may also aff ect what people consume in another fashion, namely watching movies. Th e core idea behind this research (Novemsky & Baumeister, 2005) was that, at times, choosing a more virtuous option may require overriding an impulse to do something nonvirtuous, and so self-regulation is required for choosing the path of virtue. In one study, Novemsky and Baumeister (2005) off ered students a choice of a movie to watch (for later, not immediate viewing). Th e options contained either intellectually edifying fare and low-brow sleaze. Th ese options were presented either before or aft er an intensive study session, which was assumed to be somewhat depleting. Diff erent levels of depletion were inferred based on study time in the library (i.e. by having students make the choice as they fi rst approached the library to begin the evening's studying, or as they departed aft er several hours of work) or were experimentally manipulated by having participants make a brief series of choices and decisions (e.g., Vohs et al., 2005). Sure enough, when students were fresh and their resources were not depleted from studying, they exhibited a marked preference for the highbrow fi lms. Aft er a study session, however, they shift ed heavily toward the lowbrow fare. Th e implication is that some consumer decisions present a challenge between higher and lower impulses. Self-regulation enables human beings to override the latter sort of impulse in order to pursue the former. But when self-regulatory resources have been depleted, preferences shift toward the less virtuous product.

11

Goal-Directed Consumer Behavior

Goals are internal representations of desirable states that people try to attain and undesirable states that they try to avoid. Goals diff er from other motivational constructs, such as needs and drives, because they tend to be more concrete and domain-specifi c, thus exerting a stronger infl uence on particular consumer behaviors. Although, in the fi nal analysis, high-level goals, such as trying to be independent, converge with terminal values, such as the importance of freedom, goals normally diff er from values because they direct and energize behavior actively, rather than merely providing abstract evaluative criteria for appraising objects, events, or actions. Goals are relevant if an attempt to attain a desirable state can fail, or if consumers need to sacrifi ce something in order to get what they want. Turning off the air conditioner is usually not a goal but an act, but it becomes a goal when it is steaming hot outside and the consumer desires to be environmentally friendly. Following other goal theories, we assume that many of the interesting consumer behaviors are organized around the pursuit of goals, that goals are hierarchically structured from lower to higher levels, that goal-directed behavior is characterized by eff ort expenditure and persistence in the face of temptations and interruptions, and that goals are accessible to conscious awareness, although they need not always be top-of-mind during goal pursuit (Austin & Vancouver, 1996; Emmons, 1996; Locke & Latham, 1990). Before discussing how goal pursuit takes place, we examine goal features and goal structure. First, we discuss several goal features that characterize and distinguish the goals that consumers pursue. Second, since goal-directed behavior usually involves many different goals at varying levels, we describe how goals are organized. Features of Goals Individual goals have several features that give them meaning and account for their infl uence on behavior, and also distinguish them from each other (Austin & Vancouver, 1996; Emmons, 1989; Little, 1983; Winell, 1987). We will briefl y discuss the features of goal content, desirability, importance, and feasibility. Goal content. Goal content refers to what it is that consumers pursue. Several classifi cations of general or domain-specifi c goals or goal categories have been proposed, the only restriction being an author's creativity and drive toward completeness or generality. Winell (1987), for instance, distinguishes goals related to diff erent life domains such as career, family, social/community, leisure, and material/environment. Emmons (1996) lists 12 general categories of goals, including achievement, affi liation/intimacy, power, independence, and self-presentation. Kasser and Ryan (1993, 1996) identify intrinsic (e.g., affi liation and personal growth) and extrinsic (e.g., power, materialism) goal orientations that are refl ected in more specifi c goals. In the most general sense, goals may be approach-oriented (e.g., start an investment program) or avoidance-oriented (e.g., stop smoking).

Goal desirability. Because goals are internal representations of desired states to be attained or undesirable states to be avoided, the desirability of a goal is an important motivational dimension. Although avoidance goals focus on undesirable states, successful pursuit of these goals can be highly desirable, and some goals are more desirable than others. In expectancy-value theories of motivation (Heckhausen, 1977; Kuhl, 1982), value, utility, valence, or incentive are oft en used to capture a goal's desirability. Th e aff ect associated with a goal is an important determinant of goal desirability, and this issue will be discussed in greater detail below. Goal importance. Goal importance is a related but diff erent dimension. Th at is, goals may be highly desirable, such as having the right salad dressing, but not very important in the larger scheme of things. Th e distinction between goal desirability and importance is analogous to the distinction between the valence and strength dimensions of attitudes (Petty & Krosnick, 1995). Goal importance and the closely related notion of commitment are considered to be antecedents of the amount of eff ort expended on goal pursuit and the persistence of goal-directed behavior, and they have been linked to consumer involvement (Celsi & Olson, 1988), defi ned as the personal relevance or importance of a situation or task to a consumer's goals. One way to conceptualize importance is as the discrepancy between the current state of aff airs and a desired state. Th e greater the discrepancy is perceived to be, the more important the goal is expected to be to the person. Commitment to the goal is particularly important when people do not freely choose their goals, but the goals are assigned to them (e.g., in work settings), and when goal pursuit is diffi cult and takes place over extended periods of time (e.g., losing weight or saving money for a new home). Goal feasibility. In general, feasibility is a consumer's perception of control over whether or not a goal can be achieved (see Skinner, 1996). Constructs subsumed under this term include various forms of expectancies, probability of success, confi dence, self-effi cacy, controllability, and ease or diffi culty of goal achievement. Skinner (1996) proposed a useful distinction between agents (the person exerting control), means (pathways through which control is exerted), and ends (outcomes over which control is exerted) of control, and classifi es the various control constructs found in the literature by whether they refer to agent-means, agent-ends, or means-ends relations. Agent-means relations are beliefs held by agents that they can use certain means. Examples of these beliefs are Bandura's (1977) self-effi cacy expectations, Vroom's (1964) expectancies, Heckhausen's (1977) action-outcome expectancies, and Ford's (1992) capability-based personal agency beliefs. Agent-ends relations are beliefs held by agents that they can attain desired and avoid undesired outcomes. Evaluations of the probability of goal success and goal failure, the perceived ease or diffi culty of goal attainment, and confi dence in one's ability to attain a particular goal belong in this category. Skinner also argues that Bandura's later writings on self-effi cacy (Bandura, 1989) place the construct in this group. Finally, meansends relations are beliefs that certain causes (internal vs. external causes, actions vs. attributes of agents, etc.) will lead to desired or undesired outcomes. Rotter's (1966) locus of control, Vroom's (1964) instrumentalities, Bandura's (1989) response-outcome expectations, Heckhausen's (1977) outcome-consequence expectancies, and Ford's (1992) context-based personal agency beliefs are examples that fi t this description. Organization of Goals Goals are organized in semantic networks, with goals and their means as nodes and the relationships between them as linkages. Although goal structures are latent, hypothetical constructs, we can distinguish horizontal and vertical dimensions in them. Th e horizontal dimension in goal structures represents the degree of similarity, relatedness or conceptual overlap between goals, based on goal content. Th us, related goals will tend to be closer together, because they share similar higher-level goals and lower-level means. Th e vertical dimension refl ects the hierarchical organization of goals. Th e idea is that goals are hierarchically organized from lower-level, subordinate, more concrete means to higher-level, superordinate, more abstract ends (Bandura, 1989; Carver & Scheier, 2000; Hacker, 1985; Little, 1989; Locke, 1991; Powers, 1973; Vallacher & Wegner, 1985). Th e vertical location of goals in the hierarchy relative to other goals refl ects their abstractness or specifi cation level. Goal abstractness. Concrete goals are generally more perceptual, observable in nature, referring to specifi c ways in which a desired state can be accomplished. An example would be the goal of eating smaller portions at lunch and dinner as part of a dieting plan. Abstract goals embody high-level motivational concerns that do not provide specifi c guides to behavior but indicate what the individual wants to be. Th e most abstract goals are not restricted to a particular domain and have motivational relevance for many diff erent behaviors. Values are prime examples of abstract goals. Th e consumer behavior literature has explored low-level, domain-specifi c goals for advertising processing and decision-making and high-level goals such as values that guide consumption decisions in an abstract way. In advertising, Pieters and Wedel (2007) distinguish four categories of processing goals that may be active during ad exposure, depending on the goal target (brand vs. ad) and goal content (learning vs. evaluation), based on the work of Keller (1987) and Dweck and Leggett (1988). Th ey point out that most advertising theory is devoted to brand evaluation goals (as in dual process models such as the elaboration likelihood model), which cover a single quadrant of their conceptual model, and they show that once activated each of the goal categories rapidly aff ects advertising processing in systematically diff erent ways. In decision making, Bettman, Luce, and Payne (1998) consider four decision-making goals underlying choice processing: maximizing decision accuracy; minimizing decision eff ort; minimizing negative emotions during decision making; and maximizing the ease of justifi cation of a decision. In attitude research, it is all too frequently assumed that people are motivated to hold accurate attitudes, although more recently other goals have been considered as well, such as the goal to hold attitudes that are congruent with core aspects of the self-concept (defense motivation) or the goal to express attitudes that have desirable interpersonal consequences (impression motivation) (see Chaiken, Wood, & Eagly, 1996). Th ese decision-making goals may govern decisions independently of the specifi c life goals that consumer pursue. Th at is, during goal pursuit consumers need to make decisions between alternative courses of action, which may be infl uenced by various decision-making goals, in order to attain particular, more abstract life goals. However, it is clear that decision-making goals are at a relatively low level of abstraction in the goal hierarchy, particularly if one considers how they have been studied in empirical research (e.g., choosing among three cars described with numerical ratings on two attributes, ride quality, and miles per gallon). In contrast, research on values can be viewed as investigating goals at a very high level of abstraction (Kahle et al., 1986; Kamakura & Novak, 1992). Much work on values has been concerned with investigating the structure of values, and the studies that have tried to relate values to actual behavior have generally shown very modest success. However, it should not be too surprising that goals at the highest level will not predict specifi c consumption behaviors very well, and means-end chain theory (Reynolds & Olson, 2001) was developed to make the linkages between values and consumption behaviors (in the form of preferences for certain product attributes) more explicit. Th ree fundamental goal levels. Th e abstractness or specifi cation level of a goal can be considered as a continuous characteristic, and goal research has applied quantitative measures to assess abstractness in goal structures (Pieters, Baumgartner, & Allen, 1995). Qualitative diff erences in the role and meaning of various levels of goals have been proposed as well.

between goals and behaviors, so-called means-end linkages, which form the fabric of goal structures. We distinguish several such linkages (see Emmons, 1996; Pieters, 1993; Pieters et al., 2001;

Shah, Kruglanski, & Friedman, 2003). First, there can be vertical relations between goals at diff erent levels in the hierarchy. For example, a consumer may want to lose weight in order to look more

attractive, or exercise because of the belief that this is an effi cient means of losing weight. We call

such means-end linkages instrumentalities, because elements at lower levels in the hierarchy serve

as means to achieve elements at higher levels as ends. If a single lower-level goal is connected to a

single higher-level goal, ordinary instrumentality is present. Since consumers can also do diff erent

things simultaneously, each behavior for its own reasons, it is possible that several ordinary instrumentalities co-exist, a form of parallel fi nality. Th is occurs, for instance, when consumers entertain friends while cooking, shop while baby-sitting their neighbors' children, or eat while reading.

Commonly, a given lower-level goal is associated with multiple higher-level goals, or several lowerlevel goals all lead to a single higher-level goal. In the former case we speak of multifi nality, in the
latter case of equifi nality. For example, a consumer who sees physical appearance as instrumental
to both personal confi dence and social acceptance illustrates multifi nality. In contrast, a consumer
who pursues both dieting and exercising in order to lose weight exemplifi es equifi nality. When the
multiple outcomes of an act are dissonant, rather than consonant as in multifi nality, goal confl icts
arise, as discussed later.
Second, there can be horizontal relations between goals at the same level of the hierarchy. For
example, buying a washing machine may involve a sequential process in which information on
various brands and their attributes is collected fi rst, some decision rule is used to make a choice,
and then the chosen brand is actually purchased at some store. Although one could argue that all
three behaviors are instrumental for attaining the purchase goal, the diff erence is that each step
is conditional on the previous step. Furthermore, it is probably more natural to think of the three
behaviors as occupying the same level in the goal hierarchy. One might refer to such relations
as sequential fi nality. Sequential fi nality introduces time and sequences of behavior (scripts and
programs) that need to be executed in some order or combination as an explicit infl uence on goal
pursuit. Goal structures represent consumers' knowledge of how and why to attain specifi c goals
(Shah, Kruglanski, & Friedman, 2003), containing specifi c as well as more generalized knowledge
of goal attainment, such as generalized scripts, which are typically comprised of sequential fi nality
components. Bettman (1979) was one of the fi rst to extensively discuss and use goal hierarchies in

his information processing theory of consumer choice. For example, he considered how lower-level

goals such as buying a washing machine can be broken down into more specifi c subgoals that are

accomplished sequentially over time in pursuit of the overarching goal.

Th e fi ve means-end linkages, shown graphically in Figure 13.2, jointly form the building blocks

of goal structures. In the case of (simple) instrumentality, there is a single means-end linkage without branching. In the case of equifi nality and sequential fi nality, there is a single goal and multiple

means, and, in the case of multifi nality and parallel fi nality, there are multiple goals and one or

more means. Goal structures become activated during goal pursuit, as explained next.

Once a decision has been made to pursue a goal (i.e., a goal intention has been formed), the consumer has to consider the implementation of the chosen goal: possible courses of action have to be planned, actual goal-directed behaviors have to be initiated and maintained, progress has to be monitored and possible adjustments have to be made, obstacles have to be dealt with, and, fi nally, goal achievement has to be evaluated. Almost no research on these issues is available in the consumer behavior literature, and even in psychology literature, relevant research is of fairly recent origin. We will provide a brief overview of this work. Planning. Planning means deliberating what has to be done in order to enact the chosen goal. As observed by Aristotle (1953, p. 58), "we deliberate not about ends but about means ... [people] fi rst set some end before themselves and then consider how and by what means it can be attained. If it appears that it can be attained by several means, they further consider by which it can be attained best and most easily." Planning thus involves thinking about how, where and when to act with the purpose of reaching the goal. Mental simulation about future outcomes and the courses of action to attain them yield plans that encourage goal achievement. Taylor and Pham (1996) distinguish outcome simulations (where only desired results are imagined) from process simulations (during which people imagine the steps involved in achieving a certain outcome) and show that the latter are more likely to lead to goal attainment.

Implementation intentions are expected to promote successful goal pursuit for two reasons. First, they heighten the salience of the critical situation with which goal-directed behavior is
associated. Second, they automate the execution of the relevant behavior when the critical situation
is encountered. A recent fi eld experiment by Kardes, Cronley, and Posavac (2005) in a marketing
context illustrates these benefi ts. All study participants received a free sample of a household liquid
cleaning product to take home. Half of the participants (those in the implementation intention
condition) were asked to indicate the exact dates and times that they intended to use the product
and the specifi c uses they had in mind, whereas the other half (those in the control condition) were
only asked to indicate their intentions to use the product. An unexpected follow-up survey 2 weeks
later revealed that participants used more of the product in a greater variety of diff erent situations
and formed more favorable attitudes and purchase intentions in the implementation intention condition than in the control condition.
Research so far has (a) shown that implementation intentions promote successful goal pursuit;
(b) provided support for the processes assumed to underlie their volitional benefi ts, and (c) identifi ed important moderators of their usefulness (e.g., goal diffi culty, plan detail level). However,
as acknowledged by Gollwitzer, in all of these studies participants were explicitly instructed to
form implementation intentions, and we know little about if and when implementations are formed
under self-generated goals. Furthermore, implementation intentions have usually been studied in
contexts in which the goal was concrete rather than abstract, and we need to know more about
intention formation and implementation in this latter, more realistic case. Moreover, overly specifi c
plans and implementation intentions may backfi re. For example, when a

behavior is identifi ed at a
very low level and a person is focused on the operation (how) of the behavior rather than the attainment of the fi nal goal (why), there may be little room for free choice and fl exibility in the case of
interruptions. In support of this, research (reported in Baumeister et al., 1994) shows that students
who were instructed to formulate global, monthly plans for improving their study skills performed
better and more persistently than students with detailed, daily plans.
Initiation and maintenance of goal-directed behaviors. Goal-directed behavior can be spontaneously triggered by the situational context (either because of previous experiences in which particular instrumental responses have been linked to certain environmental cues or because of previously
formed implementation intentions) or deliberatively initiated by the person. In the latter case, if the
behavior is entirely under volitional control, goal pursuit is unproblematic. However, oft en one
has to wait for an opportune moment to initiate action and maintain goal-directed behavior until
it is completed. It has been proposed that a so-called implemental mindset, in which the focus of
thought is on doing rather than on thinking, may help with this phase of goal pursuit (Gollwitzer,
1996; Gollwitzer et al., 2004). Th at is, aft er people have committed themselves to pursuing a given
goal, they are presumably focused on information that is relevant to goal achievement and will
tune out distracting information. Furthermore, information about the desirability and feasibility
of the chosen goal will be processed in a biased fashion so as to favor continued commitment and
persistent goal pursuit.
Another important contribution to the literature on how people deal with diffi culties in enacting goal intentions is Kuhl's (1984) work on action control. A central aspect of his theory is how
the focal intention can be shielded from competing behavioral tendencies. Th e model assumes that
action control motivation will increase when enactment diffi culties are

encountered, either due to
internal reasons (competing action tendencies) or external reasons (situational features that are
incompatible with the goal intention). A variety of action control processes are specifi ed. First,
selective attention directs processing to information favoring the goal intention, and encoding
control leads to a focus on intention-relevant aspects of the stimulus. Second, emotion control involves regulating one's emotions such that they are conducive to action implementation. Th ird, motivation control deals with biased processing of desirability and feasibility information. Fourth, environmental control means structuring the environment in such as way as to make it supportive of goal enactment. Finally, parsimonious information processing refers to limiting continued deliberation about action alternatives and initiating action execution. Kuhl has also proposed a personality variable called action- vs. state-orientation, which refl ects whether or not a person is generally in an action-oriented mode of control, which favors the implementation of intentions, or a state-oriented mode, which favors refl ection and deliberation. Monitoring of progress. According to control theory (Carver, Lawrence, & Scheier, 1996; Powers, 1973), goal progress is monitored by feedback loops in which the consumer's current situation is compared to a reference standard (i.e., a goal). Th e implications of this comparison depend on the type of feedback loop. In a negative feedback loop, the goal is something to be approached. Th erefore, a perceived discrepancy between the current situation and the goal requires adjustments to the current state. In contrast, in a positive feedback loop, where the goal is something to be avoided, the system is designed to enlarge the discrepancy between the current state and the avoidance goal. Carver and Scheier argue that positive feedback loops are generally unstable and are oft en constrained by negative feedback loops, such that a person trying to avoid an undesirable state eventually gravitates toward a more desirable state. During reasonably complex goal pursuits many diff erent goals at diff erent levels of abstraction have to be monitored. Feedback loops can be specifi ed at various levels of the goal hierarchy. Th e result of the comparison between the current state and a goal can be posited to serve as input to the establishment of a reference value (i.e., a goal) at a lower level of the hierarchy. In this way, an integrated monitoring system for the entire process of goal pursuit can be achieved. Evaluation of goal achievement.

People may hold outcome and process goals (Austin & Vancouver, 1996). With an outcome goal, goal pursuit is terminated when the goal has been reached (e.g., buying a car). With a process goal, goal pursuit is continuous since attaining the goal is not a discrete event and discrepancies are always possible (e.g., avoid making impulse purchases). In the latter case, successful goal pursuit does not lead to the termination of goal striving but attempts to maintain progress.

involves regulating one's emotions such that they are conducive to action implementation. Th ird, motivation control deals with biased processing of desirability and feasibility information. Fourth, environmental control means structuring the environment in such as way as to make it supportive of goal enactment. Finally, parsimonious information processing refers to limiting continued deliberation about action alternatives and initiating action execution. Kuhl has also proposed a personality variable called action- vs. state-orientation, which refl ects whether or not a person is generally in an action-oriented mode of control, which favors the implementation of intentions, or a state-oriented mode, which favors refl ection and deliberation. Monitoring of progress. According to control theory (Carver, Lawrence, & Scheier, 1996; Powers, 1973), goal progress is monitored by feedback loops in which the consumer's current situation is compared to a reference standard (i.e., a goal). Th e implications of this comparison depend on the type of feedback loop. In a negative feedback loop, the goal is something to be approached. Th erefore, a perceived discrepancy between the current situation and the goal requires adjustments to the current state. In contrast, in a positive feedback loop, where the goal is something to be avoided, the system is designed to enlarge the discrepancy between the current state and the avoidance goal. Carver and Scheier argue that positive feedback loops are generally unstable and are oft en constrained by negative feedback loops, such that a person trying to avoid an undesirable state eventually gravitates toward a more desirable state. During reasonably complex goal pursuits many diff erent goals at diff erent levels of abstraction have to be monitored. Feedback loops can be specifi ed at various levels of the goal hierarchy. Th e result of the comparison between the current state and a goal can be posited to serve as input to the establishment of a reference value (i.e., a goal) at a lower level of the hierarchy. In this way, an integrated monitoring system for the entire process of goal pursuit can be achieved. Evaluation of goal achievement. People may hold outcome and process goals (Austin & Vancouver, 1996).

With an outcome goal, goal pursuit is terminated when the goal has been reached (e.g., buying a car). With a process goal, goal pursuit is continuous since attaining the goal is not a discrete event and discrepancies are always possible (e.g., avoid making impulse purchases). In the latter case, successful goal pursuit does not lead to the termination of goal striving but attempts to maintain progress.

Th e most direct way in which aff ect can impact goal setting is when the goal itself is an aff ective experience (i.e., the desired outcome of goal-directed behavior is aff ective in nature or the process of goal pursuit is intrinsically pleasurable): aff ect-as-goal. Pervin's (1989, p. 474) defi nition of a goal, "a mental image or other end point representation associated with aff ect toward which action may be directed," makes this point very well. For example, a person might be guided by values of hedonism and stimulation and generally pursue experiences that are pleasurable and exciting (Schwartz, 1992). Less abstract goals might include spending a fun aft ernoon at an amusement park or watching a romantic comedy in a movie theater. Th ese goals may be called consummatory (as opposed to instrumental), and research has confi rmed that aff ect plays an important role in these types of decisions (e.g., Pham, 1998). Research also indicates that, in situations where aff ective and cognitive considerations are in confl ict (e.g., a chocolate cake may be more aff ectively appealing than a fruit salad, but the cognitive consequences may be less favorable), choices are based on immediate aff ect when processing resourced are limited, at least under certain conditions (Shiv & Fedorikhin, 1999; also see the chapter by Cohen et al., chapter 11, this volume, on the speed of aff ective processing). Oft en, the process of goal pursuit it not pleasurable and even the goal itself is not intrinsically associated with aff ect. Nevertheless, a person may decide to pursue the goal because the act of goal achievement induces aff ect, or goal achievement is instrumental in reaching desired higher-level goals, which may be aff ectively charged. Th e aff ect experienced is not the goal per se, but the aff ective charge of attaining the goal infl uences goal setting, hence aff ect-as-motivation. Expectancyvalue theories of motivation illustrate this perspective in a general sense, although they usually do not deal with aff ect directly. Goal choice in these models depends on the multiplicative combination of incentive (value) and likelihood of occurrence (expectancy or instrumentality). Although the incentive component may include aff ective experiences, any kind of outcome or consequence associated with the goal can have incentive value. For example, Heckhausen (1977) argues that selfevaluations such as feelings of pride and shame may serve as incentives for behavior. Several attempts have been made to explicitly incorporate (anticipated) aff ect into expectancyvalue models of behavior (see van der Pligt et al., 1998). Th e basic idea is that conventional models (e.g., the theories of reasoned action and planned behavior) only study evaluative responses based on beliefs associated with the behavior, but that people may also have anticipated aff ective reactions to the behavior or process (e.g., they may enjoy eating junk food) as well as anticipated postbehavioral aff ective responses (e.g., they may anticipate feeling bad aft er having eaten a lot of junk food). Th us, anticipated aff ect enters the goal setting stage in a way similar to mental simulation (Taylor & Pham, 1996). In an illustrative study, Richard, van der Pligt, and de Vries (1996) assessed evaluations, aff ective reactions, and anticipated postbehavioral aff ective responses for four behaviors (eating junk food, using soft drugs, drinking alcohol, and studying hard) using the same semantic diff erential scales (pleasant-unpleasant, nice-awful, good-bad). Th ey found that while evaluations and aff ective reactions toward the behavior were not empirically distinct, anticipated postbehavioral aff ective responses diff ered from both evaluations and aff ective reactions and had a unique infl uence on behavioral expectations, controlling for attitudes, subjective norms, and perceived behavioral control. Richard, van der Pligt, and de Vries (1995) obtained a similar fi nding for a more specifi c measure of anticipated postbehavioral negative emotions (worry, regret, and tension) in the context of behavioral expectations about HIV preventive behaviors. Th ese fi ndings illustrate the function of aff ect-as-motivation in goal setting. A similar but more explicitly goal-based model was proposed by Baumgartner, Pieters, and Bagozzi (forthcoming). Th ey draw a distinction between two types of future-oriented emotions, anticipatory emotions and anticipated emotions (see also Loewenstein et al., 2001; Loewenstein & Lerner, 2003). Anticipatory emotions are emotions that are currently experienced due to the prospect of a desired or undesired future event. Th e prototypes of these emotions are anticipatory excitement or hope in the case of positive future events and anticipatory worry or fear in the case of negative future events. Anticipated emotions, on the other hand, are based on imagining that certain desired or undesired events have already happened (possibly because of what one has or has not done) and then experiencing actual or imaginary emotions in anticipation of these simulated events. Th ere are several important diff erences between these two types of emotions. First, anticipatory emotions are currently experienced, veridical aff ective responses to possible future events that have positive or negative implications for the self, whereas anticipated emotions are based on pre-factual thinking about a future positive or negative event. Th ey could be real emotional experiences, but may also function like aff ective forecasts (Gilbert et al., 1998). Second, anticipatory emotions are a subset of the complete range of discrete emotions that people can experience, namely, those related to the possible occurrence of future desired or undesired outcomes (i.e., hope and fear). Furthermore, the experienced emotion is generally either a positive or negative emotion, depending on the valence of the future event (unless the event is emotionally ambiguous). In contrast, any discrete emotion that can be experienced may be anticipated in advance, based on a mental simulation of future outcomes, and the anticipation of positive and negative future events can lead to the simultaneous experience of both positive and negative aff ective states. Th ird, since anticipatory emotions are current aff ective responses to the prospect of future events that have positive or negative consequences, uncertainty about what is going to happen constitutes part of the meaning of the emotion and is inseparable from the emotion (e.g., anticipatory hope in the case of desired events and anticipatory worry in the case of undesired events). In contrast, the likelihood of the focal event happening is a mental event distinct from anticipated emotions related to the event. In a study dealing with the millennium transition (i.e., the so-called Y2K problem), Baumgartner et al. showed that positively and negatively valenced anticipatory and anticipated emotions were empirically distinct and that people who were fearful and experienced positive and negative anticipated emotions more intensely were more likely to form behavioral intentions aimed at averting possible negative consequences of the millennium change. Although goal intentions were not directly assessed in the study, intentions for a wide variety of behaviors were collected so that the measure is interpretable as the intensity of a person's goal to avoid or limit the expected problems caused by the millennium problem. Th is demonstrates how anticipatory and anticipated emotions can infl uence goal intentions, expressing the aff ect-as-motivation function. In Baumgartner et al.'s study, anticipated emotions were assessed as people's aff ective experiences to simulated goal .

success and goal failure. However, more generally one might investigate how aff ect associated with the outcomes or consequences of the focal goal infl uences the desirability of the focal goal. A related literature in decision making has focused on the emotions of regret and, to a lesser extent, disappointment (Zeelenberg et al., 2000). In an early study, Simonson (1992) showed that when consumers were reminded that they might later regret a bad decision, they were more likely to choose a higher-priced, brand-name product, presumably because this was expected to shield them from possible future regret. More recently, Mellers and her associates (e.g., Mellers & McGraw, 2001) developed a comprehensive framework for considering the eff ects of anticipated emotions on choice called subjective expected pleasure theory (see Heyman & Mellers, chapter 27, this volume). Infl uence of Exogenous Aff ect on Goal Setting Exogenous moods and emotions, which originate outside current goal pursuit, can have both direct and indirect eff ects on goal setting. With regard to direct eff ects, it has been known for quite some time that incidental positive mood (induced by a small gift , for example) tends to increase the likelihood of pro-social behaviors (see Cohen et al., chapter 11, this volume). More recently, researchers have become interested in the eff ects of specifi c exogenous moods and emotions on behavior and goal pursuit. As a case in point, Raghunatham and Pham (1999) contrasted the eff ects of sadness and anxiety. Th ey argue that since sadness is associated with appraisals of loss, sad individuals will be motivated to replace their loss with something else that is rewarding, leading to an implicit goal of reward acquisition. In contrast, fear is associated with appraisals of uncertainty and lack of control, which may prompt a goal of uncertainty reduction. Consistent with expectations, sad individuals had a greater preference for high-risk/high-reward options, whereas the opposite was true for anxious individuals. Exogenous aff ect can also infl uence goal-directed behavior indirectly by impacting judgments of the desirability and feasibility of goals. A well-established fi nding in the mood literature is that moods tend to bias evaluations in mood-congruent directions (see Cohen et al., chapter 11, this volume). Th is suggests that a goal, or the outcomes and consequences associated with the goal, may be evaluated more positively when a person is in a good mood and more negatively when the person is in a bad mood. Exogenous mood can also infl uence estimates of the likelihood that particular events will occur, thus aff ecting feasibility. For example, Johnson and Tversky (1983) found that people who read happy newspaper articles provided more optimistic risk judgments than people who read sad articles. Recent research has qualifi ed and extended these fi ndings by arguing that judgments may be sensitive to the particular exogenous aff ect experienced. For example, Lerner and Keltner (2000, 2001) proposed the so-called appraisal-tendency hypothesis, according to which the appraisal dimensions that caused an emotion also infl uence people's evaluation of objects and events that are encountered while they experience the emotion in question. Lerner and Keltner apply their model to fear and anger, and reason that since fear is characterized by uncertainty and situational control, it should lead to higher risk perceptions, whereas anger should lead to lower risk perceptions since it is characterized by certainty and personal control. Th e authors fi nd support for these predictions not only for dispositional fear and anger (measured with personality variables) but also experimentally manipulated exogenous sources of fear and anger. Such fi ndings refl ect what we call the aff ect-as-fi lter function in goal setting , where the perception of incoming information is biased toward the currently experienced aff ect and its appraisal dimensions.

success and goal failure. However, more generally one might investigate how aff ect associated with

the outcomes or consequences of the focal goal infl uences the desirability of the focal goal.

A related literature in decision making has focused on the emotions of regret and, to a lesser

extent, disappointment (Zeelenberg et al., 2000). In an early study, Simonson (1992) showed

that when consumers were reminded that they might later regret a bad decision, they were more

likely to choose a higher-priced, brand-name product, presumably because this was expected to

shield them from possible future regret. More recently, Mellers and her associates (e.g., Mellers &

McGraw, 2001) developed a comprehensive framework for considering the eff ects of anticipated

emotions on choice called subjective expected pleasure theory (see Heyman & Mellers, chapter 27,

this volume).

Exogenous moods and emotions, which originate outside current goal pursuit, can have both direct and indirect eff ects on goal setting. With regard to direct eff ects, it has been known for quite some time that incidental positive mood (induced by a small gift , for example) tends to increase the likelihood of pro-social behaviors (see Cohen et al., chapter 11, this volume). More recently, researchers have become interested in the eff ects of specifi c exogenous moods and emotions on behavior and goal pursuit. As a case in point, Raghunatham and Pham (1999) contrasted the eff ects of sadness and anxiety. Th ey argue that since sadness is associated with appraisals of loss, sad individuals will be motivated to replace their loss with something else that is rewarding, leading to an implicit goal of reward acquisition. In contrast, fear is associated with appraisals of uncertainty and lack of control, which may prompt a goal of uncertainty reduction. Consistent with expectations, sad individuals had a greater preference for high-risk/high-reward options, whereas the opposite was true for anxious individuals. Exogenous aff ect can also infl uence goal-directed behavior indirectly by impacting judgments of the desirability and feasibility of goals. A well-established fi nding in the mood literature is that moods tend to bias evaluations in mood-congruent directions (see Cohen et al., chapter 11, this volume). Th is suggests that a goal, or the outcomes and consequences associated with the goal, may be evaluated more positively when a person is in a good mood and more negatively when the person is in a bad mood. Exogenous mood can also infl uence estimates of the likelihood that particular events will occur, thus aff ecting feasibility. For example, Johnson and Tversky (1983) found that people who read happy newspaper articles provided more optimistic risk judgments than people who read sad articles. Recent research has qualifi ed and extended these fi ndings by arguing that judgments may be sensitive to the particular exogenous aff ect experienced. For example, Lerner and Keltner (2000, 2001) proposed the so-called appraisal-tendency hypothesis, according to which the appraisal dimensions that caused an emotion also infl uence people's evaluation of objects and events that are encountered while they experience the emotion in question. Lerner and Keltner apply their model to fear and anger, and reason that since fear is characterized by uncertainty and situational control, it should lead to higher risk perceptions, whereas anger should lead to lower risk perceptions since it is characterized by certainty and personal control. Th e authors fi nd support for these predictions not only for dispositional fear and anger (measured with personality variables) but also experimentally manipulated exogenous sources of fear and anger. Such fi ndings refl ect what we call the aff ect-as-fi lter function in goal setting, where the perception of incoming information is biased toward the currently experienced aff ect and its appraisal dimensions.

So far we have examined how aff ect infl uences goal setting. However, the goals that people set may have aff ective implications (i.e., externalities) that are independent of the specifi c outcomes of goal pursuit. We call these infl uences hedonic spillover (see Table 13.1). We distinguish two types of spillover here. First, there is evidence that certain goal orientations (i.e., individual diff erences in how goals are represented mentally) have characteristic eff ects on subjective well-being such as life satisfaction and the frequency with which positive and negative aff ective states are experienced. Second, goal content seems to have important ramifi cations for well-being. Specifi cally, extrinsic goals such as those related to fi nancial success and materialism have generally been linked with lower well-being. Th e fi rst goal orientation is abstractness or level of goal specifi cation. Th is goal dimension refers to whether people tend to frame their goals in concrete or abstract ways. For the present purposes, it suffi ces that there appear to be reliable individual diff erences in the extent to which people identify their goals and behaviors in superordinate or subordinate terms (i.e., "level of personal agency" in action identifi cation theory). For example, high-level agents may identify the act of eating as getting nutrition, whereas low-level agents might think of it as chewing and swallowing. Emmons (1992) investigated the relationship between level of goal specifi cation and psychological and physical well-being. He asked three diff erent sets of participants to generate 15 personal strivings (i.e., goals that they were typically trying to attain) and had coders rate a person's strivings as either relatively concrete, specifi c and more behavioral in nature, or as abstract, refl ective, and involving greater self-scrutiny. Emmons also collected reports of daily moods, ratings of life satisfaction, and other measures of psychological well-being (e.g., depression, anxiety), as well as various indices of physical well-being (e.g., health center visits). Interestingly, high-level strivings tended to be associated with certain indicators of lower psychological well-being but fewer symptoms of physical illness. Emmons (1992) argues that it is more diffi cult to attain and monitor progress toward abstract goals, which leads to negative aff ect for high-level strivers. On the other hand, low-level strivers may be more prone to repress stressful experiences and as a consequence suff er physical illnesses. Psychological and physical well-being have also been linked to another goal orientation, namely, whether people frame their goals as approach or avoidance goals. Approach goals are desired states that one wants to attain (e.g., spending time with others), whereas avoidance goals are aversive states that one wants to avoid (e.g., being lonely). Emmons and Kaiser (1996) coded the personal strivings elicited from four sets of respondents into approach and avoidance strivings and then correlated the proportion of avoidance strivings (which ranged from 9 to 15% overall) with measures of psychological and physical well-being (similar to those used in Emmons, 1992). People with a relatively high proportion of avoidance strivings tended to experience less positive aff ect, lower life satisfaction, and more anxiety. In addition, they reported more symptoms of physical illness. One reason for these diff erences might be that, compared to avoidance strivings, approach goals were rated as more desirable and important, success was seen as more likely, and goal pursuit was based more on intrinsic reasons. A third goal orientation is goal confl ict, which we introduced earlier. In Emmons' work on personal strivings, ambivalence (approach-avoidance confl ict) is assessed as the degree of unhappiness one would feel about succeeding at the striving, whereas goal incompatibility is measured as the extent to which success at one striving has helpful or harmful eff ects on another striving (averaged across all possible pairs of strivings). Both ambivalence and incompatibility have been associated with lower psychological well-being and various physical symptoms, including more frequent health center visits (Emmons & King, 1988).

Th e fi nal goal orientation is goal diff erentiation. Emmons and King (1989) defi ne diff erentiation

as the degree to which diff erent goals (i.e., personal strivings in their study) are independent rather

than interdependent. For example, one operationalization of this construct is the rated dissimilarity between a person's strivings. Emmons and King argue that striving diff erentiation should be

associated with greater aff ective reactivity, and in two studies they fi nd support for this hypothesis

for both a measure of aff ective intensity (i.e., the intensity of experiencing positive and negative

moods over a period of time) and aff ective variability.

Th e second approach to studying the relationship between goals and subjective well-being is

based on the notion that well-being is not only a function of structural characteristics of goals,

such as their level of diff erentiation, but also the content of goals. Of particular importance to

consumer behavior is the fi nding that extrinsic goals such as fi nancial success, social recognition,

and appearance can have a detrimental eff ect on well-being (although the direction of causality

is not always clear from the existing studies, the fi ndings are usually interpreted in this way). For

example, Kasser and Ryan (1993, 1996) established that people who assigned greater importance to

aspirations such as self-acceptance (concern with growth, autonomy, and self-regard), affi liation,

community feeling, and physical fi tness, and thought they could attain these goals in the future,

rated more highly on a variety of indices of well-being (including diary measures of experienced

positive aff ect and depression and anxiety), whereas people who endorsed values relating to fi nancial success, appearance and social recognition had lower well-being scores.

Th ere is generally good support for a negative eff ect of materialism on well-being, but there also

seem to be important boundary conditions. Burroughs and Rindfl eisch (2002) propose that materialism will lead to stress and lower well-being when it confl icts with collective-oriented values. In

two studies (a large-scale survey with a representative sample of American adults and an experiment with students) they fi nd support for this notion for two of the three collective-oriented values

studied, namely, religious and family values, although not for community values. Th e foregoing

results show mostly negative aff ective implications of particular goals and goal setting situations,

and more research about potential positive implications would be welcome.